CONTEMPORARY LAW SERIES

KAREN GROSS

Failure and Forgiveness

Rebalancing the Bankruptcy System

Yale University Press   New Haven and London

Set in Sabon type by à la page, New Haven, Connecticut.
Printed in the United States of America by Edwards Brothers, Inc., Ann Arbor, Michigan.

Library of Congress Cataloging-in-Publication Data
Gross, Karen, 1952–
   Failure and forgiveness : rebalancing the bankruptcy system /
  Karen Gross.
      p. cm. — (Contemporary law series)
    Includes bibliographical references and index.
    ISBN 0-300-06820-4 (alk. paper)
    1. Bankruptcy—United States. I. Title. II. Series.
KF1526.G76 1997
346.73'078—dc20
[347.30678]   96-9870

A catalogue record for this book is available from the British Library.

The paper in this book meets the guidelines for permanence and durability of the Committee on Production Guidelines for Book Longevity of the Council on Library Resources.

10 9 8 7 6 5 4 3 2 1

To Stephen and Zack
The two very special people in my life

CONTENTS

ACKNOWLEDGMENTS

In writing this book, I have been influenced by family, friends, colleagues, and students who took time out of their busy schedules to support this project in important ways. A number of people listened to my ideas and enriched my thinking with their comments and critiques. Special thanks to Robert M. Lawless, Lynn M. LoPucki, and William Whitford. A group of truly dedicated friends and family read (and reread) and commented on various parts and versions of the manuscript, and I am deeply appreciative. In particular, I wish to thank Rena and Walter Abelmann, Kathryn Heidt, Quintin Johnstone, Deryck Palmer, Michael Perlin, J. P. Rosensweig, and Laura Stein. Many students at New York Law School assisted me in my thinking and in preparing select materials in the book; I am especially grateful for the efforts of Matthew Barr and Matthew Couloute, Jr. I am deeply indebted to Enid Braun, a truly gifted teacher, who taught me how to draw and helped me understand how to see. The research and technical aspects of this project also required considerable help, and I wish to thank Dorothea Coleman, Nicole Fisher, Elaine Costa Imp, and Joseph Molinari for their excellent, prompt, and cheerful assistance. I also want to thank Ed Flynn of the Administrative Office of the United States Courts and Jeffrey B. Baker, President of Poorman-Douglas Corporation, for their assistance with data on bankruptcy. I am most appreciative of the encouragement that I have received from Harry Wellington, Dean of New York Law School, and John Covell of Yale University Press. They both supported this project from the beginning and understand what this book means to me. I am also grateful to my manuscript editor at Yale University Press, Jenya Weinreb, who, while retaining my voice and style, provided me with countless careful and thoughtful suggestions for improving the manuscript. Finally, a project of this magnitude could not have been accomplished without the support of my husband, Stephen H. Cooper, and my son, Zack Cooper. The underlying premises of this book—fairness and decency—were evident in how my family treated me over the several years it took to complete this project and reflect how we have worked together through life's exigencies.

FAILURE AND FORGIVENESS

Just when Alice thought the little white rabbit had disappeared, he suddenly stood next to her and said, "Now, we go to Rankbustland." Alice had no particular desire to go there, never having heard of it, so she asked, "Where is Rankbustland?" The little white rabbit said, "It is everywhere and nowhere."
  —*Edwin Otterbourg, Esq.*, Alice in Rankbustland
  (a satire of the bankruptcy system in the 1930s)

A dry and discouraging topic: that is how bankruptcy has been characterized by one of its leading historians[1]—and I suspect this perception is shared by many others, lawyers and nonlawyers alike. In this book, I refute this view and provide a more compelling counterdescription and understanding of the bankruptcy process.

The U.S. bankruptcy system is really a docudrama about the hopes and frailties of people. It is the stage on which American society acts out its choices concerning how to treat those who have failed in a credit-based economy. It is the arena in which we, as a society, are forced to consider the prices—expressed in both economic and noneconomic terms—that we want to exact and are willing to pay for the individual and business failures that express themselves in monetary terms. It is about individuals' responsibilities to one another and to society and about society's responsibilities to individuals. No topic could be more vibrant and—in this business, economic, and political climate—more timely.

This book is both descriptive and prescriptive. It describes existing U.S. bankruptcy laws and assesses what is happening in practice.

The bankruptcy system has encountered marked criticism. Indeed, critiquing existing bankruptcy law has become quite fashionable.[2] For some politicians, commentators, and scholars, it seems to have become an end in itself.[3]

Articulating what is wrong with the current bankruptcy system presupposes that the critics can identify just what it is that law-makers are trying to accomplish—and ought to be accomplishing—through the bankruptcy system. Despite the zeal and stridency of the bankruptcy system's critics, many of them have not confronted, and some have not even recognized, this prescriptive challenge, namely, addressing what bankruptcy law *ought* to be in contemporary American society.[4] And where prescriptive efforts have been made, they have focused only on limited aspects of the bankruptcy law, have been confined to scholarly legal journals, have employed a language that is virtually impenetrable to those who are not bankruptcy experts, or some combination of all three.[5] The result has been effectively to exclude from informed participation in the bankruptcy debate most people who, while not necessarily direct participants in the bankruptcy process, are inevitably affected by its operation.

In this book, I respond to the prescriptive challenge. First, I provide a justification for the fresh start for individual and business debtors, based on notions of forgiveness and rehabilitation. Second, I proffer a new perspective on how to treat the many types of creditors that bankruptcy affects, and explain why, based on a theory of equality, some creditors are more deserving of repayment than others. Third, I recognize and justify the role of community in the bankruptcy process. When the perspective of communities is taken into account, the competing interests that bankruptcy must balance are at once expanded and complicated.

In providing these three prescriptive responses, I challenge many explanations of the current bankruptcy process. This book upsets long-established beliefs about which debtors should obtain bankruptcy's benefits and why. In it, I refute the concept that all creditors of a like kind should be treated similarly. I suggest that parties and concerns that previously had no place at the bankruptcy table should be included. My approach thus moves away from reigning philosophical trends supporting individualism in favor of less well accepted theories of social welfare and, as such, challenges the underpinnings of American bankruptcy laws.[6]

I recognize that because I question existing beliefs about bankruptcy and the philosophical theories that underlie those beliefs, the burden is on me to justify why we need to depart from what is. It is not easy to uproot well-established notions, particularly when the effort addresses fundamental notions about how individuals, businesses, and society should operate. My goal is not to make all readers adopt my approach to the bankruptcy system. Indeed, acceptance (or rejection) is not an all-or-nothing proposition. I am less concerned about total acceptance than I am about expanding the debate. It is my hope that this book will stimulate new voices and raise the decibel level of the existing voices so that, perhaps for the first time, a real and productive broad-based debate can take place about what is and what should be happening in the world of bankruptcy.

I also recognize the disjuncture between the prescriptive and the practical. Even if my prescriptive offerings provide new and useful explanations of what bankruptcy law ought to be, that does not mean they either can or should be implemented. Some of my explanations and proposed solutions can be viewed as impractical based on logistical and political realities. Some changes can be brought about only at a price, and we as a society need to assess on whom the price should be levied and whether it is a price they (or we) are willing to pay. But concerns about implementation do not mean that the underlying theoretical explanations are wrong. Nor do they indicate that the proposals will never become realities. I know that my solutions cannot be completely implemented today. But if people begin to think differently about bankruptcy issues, if they pause where they did not pause before, if they argue one case differently or decide a dispute on different grounds, then I am satisfied that progress has been made.

This book has not been written for lawyers, law professors, and judges alone. I believe that the policies underlying U.S. bankruptcy laws, and their implications, can be understood and appreciated by a much wider audience. Indeed, the implications of the American bankruptcy system are far too important to be left for consideration by those trained in the law. I hope this book will interest a wide spectrum of readers—educators, economists, historians, anthropologists, sociologists, psychologists, businesspeople, philosophers, and social workers as well as lawyers, law professors, and judges—who can begin to think collectively and in an informed way about the myriad of issues raised by a system that affects millions of individuals and businesses both in the United States and abroad each year.

Dissecting the innards of bankruptcy on both practical and theoretical levels is not immediately appealing to most people. Many people see bankruptcy policy as Dickensian: something dark and dank and immensely complicated. In contrast, most people are uninhibited about expressing their feelings, whether based on experience or perception, about the existing bankruptcy system. When nonlawyers speak about the bankruptcy system, their commentary frequently takes the form of questions that reveal an underlying sense that something about bankruptcy is just not right. "Why should someone who runs up twenty-five thousand dollars of credit card charges be allowed to 'get out' for ten cents on the dollar?" "Why do banks and finance companies lend to those they knew, or should have known, could not repay their debts?" "Why should an entrepreneur whose corporation has defaulted on more than $1 million in loans be allowed to proceed with a new business venture?" "How can a manufacturer whose products have injured thousands of people be relieved of the obligation to compensate them fully for those injuries?" "Why should an employer be allowed to break its union contracts just because it finds those agreements burdensome?" And "why should creditors of a troubled company be able to simply shut it down, leaving the employees with no source of income and a community in chaos?" One commentator summed up these perceptions ably by comparing bankruptcy to a roach motel: companies check in and they don't check out.[7]

I suspect that many people, including some in the legal academic community, reach their conclusions about the bankruptcy system based on understandable but faulty and often unarticulated assumptions. This situation will persist if these premises are not identified and clarified. First, people establish their view of bankruptcy based on extrapolations from a narrow range of particulars without realizing that the chosen particulars are not representative of the whole. They may, for example, cite the failure of the Eastern Air Lines bankruptcy case as a reason why all corporate bankruptcy is unworkable. Or they may assume that all individual debtors are well known based on the cases of John Connelly, Bowie Kuhn, Kim Basinger, Denton Cooley, Wayne Newton, and Peter Kalikow. Second, people assume that the unfairness they observe is a product of bankruptcy law itself without realizing the vast interrelationships between bankruptcy and such other bodies of federal and state law as tort law, environmental law, and property law.[8] Third, people assume that bankruptcy is intended to protect only select debtors and creditors, and this dual-pillared approach narrows considerably their perspective on the goals of our bankruptcy system and the consequences that flow from them. This approach, for example, eliminates the need to think about bankruptcy's impact on public, as distinguished from private, welfare. Fourth, people confuse defects in the means to accomplish a chosen goal with defects in the goal itself and hence are overly eager to discard the goal. So, an overcrowded docket that makes court hearings difficult to arrange in a timely manner does not indicate that people's rights are eradicated by the bankruptcy law itself. Finally, people focus on the system's failures rather than its successes and thus are discouraged by what they see. Confirmation of approximately 20% of business reorganizations could, and indeed should, be seen as evidence of the system's success, for without the bankruptcy process these businesses might have faded into oblivion.[9]

Even given these assumptions, the questions about unfairness remain important because they tell us something about bankruptcy. They tell us that, at its core, the bankruptcy system has to do with some basic questions about how Americans want to function as a credit society. It is for this reason that people will have many different visions of what any bankruptcy system can and should accomplish.

Two fundamental assumptions underlie this book and the prescriptive challenges it offers. First, for better or worse, Americans live in a credit economy. If people obtained goods and services only in exchange for cash or with comparable equivalents, as in traditional systems of barter, there would be no debt and, therefore, no need for a bankruptcy system. In a communist regime, with only state-owned businesses and no market economy, there would also be little need for a bankruptcy system.[10] The U.S. credit economy is complex, with credit being extended in many obvious ways by private lenders and in less obvious ways by the government. Although others may want to reconsider the benefits of a credit economy and the ways credit (both secured and unsecured) has been extended in American society today, in this book I accept as a premise that the United States has, and will continue to have, a credit-based economy.[11] I assume that both secured and unsecured credit will persist. We may want to return to a simpler time—when private and government lending was not the lifeblood of the economy or when collateralized loans were nonexistent—but I suspect we are past that point.

Second, I have a positive view of human nature and a firm belief in the inherent goodwill of human beings. I operate from the premise that individuals can be, and most frequently are, motivated by a concern for the well-being of others and a desire to act in ways that are decent and benefit society. This positive view of human nature is clearly not universally shared.[12] Some argue that I am inappropriately optimistic or even dead wrong about human nature, as people are inherently aggressive, greedy, vicious, self-interested, and unconcerned.[13] Many view cooperation and self-restraint as learned behaviors that are necessary for survival in society but are easily forgotten or disregarded. I agree that not every person behaves in ways we want. Human beings are immensely complex and can express a wide range of behaviors—including aggressive self-centeredness. Hard though it may be to prove, however, I remain convinced that, at their core, human beings not only should but do care very much about making the world a better place, both for themselves and for others.

The importance of this conceptualization of human nature to the world of bankruptcy may not be obvious at first. But it profoundly affects how people think about bankruptcy issues. How society treats both individual and corporate debtors depends in part on what we believe motivates and underlies their financial failure. Our beliefs about human nature influence how we want creditors to be treated and explain why some creditors are more deserving than others. These beliefs affect the role of community and justify the redistributive effects that consideration of community imposes on other interests.

A contradiction seems to exist between my positive perception of human nature and the role and function of corporations and their directors within the bankruptcy system. Although most debtors are individuals, corporations (as both debtors and creditors) are significant participants in the bankruptcy process. Clearly, the corporate entity does not itself think or feel; it thinks and feels through those who run and own it. So at one level, corporations, through the individuals who run them, can behave in ways that reveal something positive about human nature.[14] Moreover, although directors of financially solvent entities are charged as fiduciaries under state corporate law with maximizing corporate profits for the benefit of shareholders, altruism is not necessarily unprofitable or incompatible with this goal. Some scholars feel that corporations do have at least some social responsibilities,[15] and insolvent corporations may owe a duty to a community of interests that extends well beyond shareholders.[16] Accordingly, a positive view of human nature can affect our expectations of both individuals and businesses.

This book begins with a discussion of how to think about bankruptcy issues from a policy perspective and proceeds to examine
what we should strive to accomplish within the world of bankruptcy from the co-existing perspectives of debtors, creditors, and
communities. The book concludes with a synthesis of my recommendations for change within the bankruptcy system, in which I
identify the important distinctions and parallels between what is,
what ought to be, and what realistically can be.

PART I

Setting the Stage

CHAPTER ONE

How to Think about Bankruptcy

Hypothetical scenarios, based on an amalgamation of real cases that raise issues about bankruptcy, provide a useful way to begin thinking about the bankruptcy process. I shall invoke two scenarios, one involving a corporation and the other an individual, in various permutations throughout the book as a way of making theoretical issues concrete.

The first hypothetical scenario concerns Seat Co., a family business formed in 1954 that manufactures seat belts for domestic automobiles. The company has a factory in Blytheville, Arkansas, that employs five hundred workers and has seventy-five retired workers for whom it pays medical expenses and maintains a pension. Seat Co. is the largest employer in the community. The factory workers, who are unionized, entered into a three-year collective bargaining agreement under which they are to be paid eighteen dollars per hour. Seat Co. has borrowed money from banks primarily for acquisition of new equipment needed for plant modernization, which is secured in part by the company's machinery and equipment. The company also owes unsecured obligations, including those to the trade creditors that have sold Seat Co. the component parts needed to manufacture seat belts. With the decline in the U.S. automobile market and the growing importation of foreign cars, Seat Co. has insufficient business to generate the cash necessary to pay its workers (past and present), banks, and unsecured creditors.

The second hypothetical scenario is that of Jason Smythe, a twenty-five-year-old car mechanic who earns twenty-five thousand dollars annually by working at a local service station. He is unmarried and lives in a small apartment three miles from his parents' home in Raymond, Maine. One year ago, while driving to work, Jason unintentionally struck a pedestrian who consequently became a paraplegic. The pedestrian brought suit and received a judgment against Smythe that exceeded his insurance coverage by $2 million. Smythe owes various credit card companies five thousand dollars for consumer goods. He is also indebted to a technical school where he took an auto mechanics course. He cannot satisfy all these obligations.

What relief is and should be available to Seat Co. and Smythe under either state or federal law or both? And, as a corollary, what are the consequences on all affected parties of whatever relief is granted to Seat Co. and Smythe? Asking these questions is a way of determining what Americans, as a society, are trying to accomplish through a bankruptcy system.

Many readers may already have a sense of how they believe Seat Co. and Smythe should be treated, either within the parameters of the existing U.S. bankruptcy system or under some other hypothetical system of their choosing. These answers are important, but having answers does not explain how they were divined. So, let us first think about how to answer these questions.

Just Not Enough Money or Collateral to Go Around

Both Seat Co. and Smythe confront the same problem. They lack sufficient current assets to repay all their obligations. Seat Co. cannot pay its workers, banks, and unsecured creditors while maintaining pension and health payments for its retirees. Smythe cannot pay the injured pedestrian, his credit card companies, and the trade school simultaneously. Of the unpaid obligations of Seat Co. and Smythe, some portion is a direct result of a credit economy. In a noncredit economy, the banks would not have advanced money with insufficient collateral and the unsecured creditors would not have supplied product or consumer goods without equivalent compensation. Other aspects of these two examples of financial difficulty are not a product of improvident credit. Seat Co.'s inability to provide ongoing health care and a pension for retirees is caused primarily by escalating costs and a longer-living group of retirees. The tort victim in Smythe's case was an involuntary extender of credit entitled to recover based on a judicial remedy.

So, what should happen to Seat Co. and Smythe? Outside of bankruptcy, under the existing system of state law, when a debtor cannot satisfy a contractual commitment, a breach exists. And the law provides unsecured or undersecured creditors a remedy for this breach, which usually takes the form of damages—a monetary assessment of the value of the failed commitment. If Smythe, for example, owes a vendor of car parts five hundred dollars and fails to repay this amount when due, the vendor can sue Smythe in a state court and get a judgment in that amount. Then the vendor can try to collect on that judgment under applicable state law. And assuming Smythe has either available assets or garnishable income, that judgment will be satisfied. A simple breach-of-contract action would be followed by standardized collection procedures.[1] Similarly, if Smythe injures his neighbor's property by intentionally cutting down the neighbor's hedges, the neighbor can sue Jason under tort law principles, and a state court can award monetary damages. Again, assuming Smythe has assets or future income, the tort judgment will be satisfied.[2] For the corporate entity, Seat Co., the issues would be similarly resolved under state law. Under either contract or tort law, a creditor would sue, obtain a judgment, and proceed to recover in whatever way possible, including from future income, if necessary.

In the hypothetical scenarios, however, these traditional state law remedies will not work. Neither debtor currently has enough money or assets to satisfy all the outstanding commitments that have been or will be breached. Several creditors could get judgments, but there would be no way to repay all creditors in full. Smythe could pay the trade school the money it is owed, for example, but then he could not pay the credit card companies or the tort victim. Similarly, Seat Co. could fund its pension for the benefit of past and existing employees, but the trade creditors and the banks would then not be

paid. Even if Smythe or Seat Co.'s creditors were permitted to attach
an unlimited amount of future income, the amount of debt that
could be satisfied over the foreseeable future is small in comparison
to the total obligations.[3] Even secured creditors will be stymied if
the value of the collateral in which they took an interest is less than
the amount they are owed. Although the secured lenders can foreclose on the collateral and recover some of what they are owed,
these creditors too will be left without full repayment. What this
means is that the standard state law collection remedies are inadequate to handle the multiple breaches.

Some other body of law—whether created at the state or at the
federal level—is needed to resolve the problem of multiple breaches
or breaches for which there is no remedy. At the federal level, the
body of law designed to solve the problem of breach is termed
"bankruptcy."[4] The bankruptcy system is intended to provide the
ultimate remedy and is invoked when other remedies, particularly
those under state law, prove inadequate.

How should a bankruptcy law treat Seat Co. and Smythe? A
distinction can be made between how the bankruptcy law currently answers this question (a descriptive approach) and how a
bankruptcy system ought to address this question (a prescriptive
approach). Chapters 2 and 3 address how the current law answers
the question. This chapter contains the beginning speculations on
how to determine how the bankruptcy law ought to answer the
question.

Thinking about What Bankruptcy Law Ought to Be

Suppose that our society had no extant bankruptcy law
and was thinking about creating one. This is obviously a hypothetical exercise. Congress is not suddenly going to abandon—nor
should it—all of the current bankruptcy system (although some
academics have called for the repeal of the business reorganization chapter of the bankruptcy law, while another scholar has suggested repealing the liquidation chapter).[5] This exercise is designed

to allow readers to wrestle, as emerging nations currently are doing, with the panoply of choices that go into creating a bankruptcy system.[6]

The starting point is identifying what the goals of such a system would be. Without a sense of what the bankruptcy system ought to accomplish, it is difficult to figure out where to go and how to get there. The current vogue is to determine "ends" by starting with a general overreaching philosophical or political theory, a meta-theory, and then to apply that theory to a concrete context. This approach can be characterized as proceeding from the outside in.[7] It is also possible to proceed in the opposite direction, from the inside out.[8] This requires looking directly at the concrete context, in this case the bankruptcy system, and then considering what we want to accomplish based on an understanding of the participants in the process and the problems they encounter on a day-to-day basis. This is not to say that general philosophical issues are irrelevant; indeed, they ultimately are very important. But they are best discussed later, once focus is placed on the real questions involving a real system that affects real people.[9]

In viewing bankruptcy from the inside out, the question of perspectives is omnipresent. From what or whose perspective should the analysis proceed? Answering this question requires assessing bankruptcy's impact. If that impact is broad, then the perspectives must be broad enough to take all those affected into account. Otherwise, the process proceeds unidimensionally and resembles the telling of history only from the perspective of kings, princes, and wealthy lords.[10]

Contemplate a bankruptcy system purely from the perspective of such debtors as Seat Co. and Smythe. Viewed from this perspective alone, the bankruptcy process is immensely complex because debtors have different goals. For Smythe, the ideal solution might be a legal system that provided complete financial and emotional relief from all obligations and a return to where he would have been if these problems had never existed. Future income—whether business or personal—would be his alone to enjoy, and prior debt problems would not impede his future. His debts would be completely forgiven, with no repercussions.

But a debtor could respond very differently to financial distress. Perhaps the officers and directors of Seat Co. would be concerned about their failures, the harm they caused to others, and the future implications of nonpayment. Failure of a family-owned business could produce shame and embarrassment. In these situations, debtors might be less concerned about absolution and more concerned about finding some methods of redressing their past behavior, repaying at least some creditors and salvaging their pride.

Regardless of their approach, debtors want and need to fashion some solution to their financial dilemma. At times that solution will be consonant with and at other times in conflict with the needs and interests of creditors. So a bankruptcy system fashioned solely from the perspective of debtors would be cause for concern. Whether Seat Co. and Smythe should be relieved of some or all their obligations requires looking beyond these two specific parties and considering what consequences flow from giving these (or any other) debtors relief of the particular sort they may want.

Should Seat Co., for example, be able to break its collective bargaining agreement, which would deprive 575 workers of the benefits for which they bargained? If the company is able to cease making payments to retirees for health and pension benefits, many individuals would no longer be able to obtain health care. If Smythe is allowed to leave the injured pedestrian penniless, he returns to live his life while the victim cannot be restored to hers. If Smythe's obligations to the credit card companies are excused, he receives the benefits of what he purchased without having to pay. Finally, if Smythe is relieved of his obligations for tuition even though he benefits daily from what he learned, his school will have fewer funds to distribute to other needy students.

If, in contrast, the system were focused on creditors, most debtors would be required to do whatever is necessary to ensure that creditors are repaid as fully as possible in the shortest time. Seat Co. would be forced to shut down its factory in Blytheville, even though many individuals would become unemployed. The bank would sell all the machinery and equipment in which it has a security interest, even though that would effectively preclude Seat Co. from continuing to operate its business. Smythe would move in with his parents to avoid having to pay rent and would take a second job to generate additional income. He would also sell all his worldly possessions for the benefit of his creditors. These approaches are draconian, and almost punitive. They make debtors pay for their nonpayment, both literally and figuratively. In a sizable number of situations, these approaches conflict with what debtors seek.

But like the debtor-focused perspective, the creditor-focused perspective is not monolithic. Some creditors may think in longer terms than others. Seat Co.'s major vendors may be concerned less with immediate payment than with preserving an ongoing business with a key customer. These creditors do not need repayment now for their own survival. If the creditors happen to be the debtor's employees and they fear downsizing, they may be bitter and eager to exact a pound of flesh. Or employees may want the debtor's business to continue, as their livelihood is inextricably linked to the debtor's prospects for success. Indeed, their interests and those of the debtor may be more consonant than interests of two diverse creditors such as a retiree and a lending bank. Hence, creditor-focused solutions are as multifaceted as debtor-focused ones.

Both perspectives, however, fail to distinguish the possible disjuncture between how each of the parties wants to be treated and how society wants them to be treated. They also fail to address fully the consequences of the suggested solutions. Seat Co.'s owners could be left with nothing even though they had been in business for well over a quarter of a century. Smythe's tort victim could make him work in perpetuity even though she would recover only a fraction of what she is owed. The credit companies would be repaid even if they made no effort to determine Smythe's suitability for credit and failed to monitor his ongoing ability to pay. As the examples of Seat Co. and Smythe demonstrate, the viewpoints of debtors and creditors are at once intertwined and frequently competing.

Figure 1. Is this a duck, a rabbit, or a duckrabbit?

Whatever decisions are made with respect to one perspective affect the other—in sometimes positive and sometimes negative ways.

To assist in recognizing that dual perspectives exist simultaneously, consider figure 1.[11] Some people see a rabbit; others see a duck. At some level, both viewpoints are correct. Looking at the drawing from left to right, one sees the image of a rabbit. Looking at the drawing from right to left, one sees the image of a duck. But to see only the duck or the rabbit—a single perspective—is to see less than the whole.

In artistic terms, this drawing presents "rival-form ambiguity."[12] Once one can see both forms, the duck and the rabbit, it is hard to know exactly which image one is seeing at any given moment. The images collide, and complexity sets in. More important, once one has seen both pictures, one can no longer go back to seeing just one.

The problem of debtor and creditor perspectives in bankruptcy is also one of rival-form ambiguity. If one sees the perspective of only the debtor or the creditor, one is observing less than the full picture. If one is unaware that another image exists, the image one sees appears complete. But more than one image exists. Development of a complete bankruptcy system requires that we consider the perspectives of both debtors and creditors—the duck and the rabbit, and the many different kinds of ducks and rabbits that exist. And, as in the image, the ducks and rabbits co-exist yet are separate.

If one squints a bit when looking at the drawing, it is possible to see the images of the duck and the rabbit simultaneously. Although one can still identify both the duck and the rabbit as distinct images, what emerges is a "duckrabbit." The duckrabbit, the creation of the intertwined and competing images, is an unfamiliar image created out of two familiar but distinct images. And discovering this image is somewhat disquieting because the single drawing becomes all at once three images: a duck, a rabbit, and a duckrabbit.

This approach as applied to bankruptcy suggests that while creation of a bankruptcy system requires consideration of the frequently rival perspectives of debtors and creditors, the essence of bankruptcy is what is created by the merger of the debtor and creditor images into a complex single yet ambiguous image created by rival imagery—namely, the legal and conceptual equivalent of the duckrabbit.

Adding the Perspective of Community

In the bankruptcy context, dual perspectives are insufficient. There is yet another perspective to consider: the interests of community. *Community* is not a self-defining term and therefore requires some elaboration. Although in some respects it can overlap with the interests of either debtors or creditors or both, it brings a markedly different perspective to the bankruptcy table. Given the American philosophical orientation toward individualism, accepting the importance of community represents something of a radical shift in orientation.[13]

Bankruptcy touches on many communities, and these communities simultaneously co-exist, much like concentric and interlocking circles. If every community that had any relationship to a bankruptcy case were given voice, the potential interests could be attenuated.[14] The particular communities that the bankruptcy system should recognize are those with a substantial nexus to the debtor (see chapters 12 and 13 in this book). This group would then include the communities in which the debtor lives, works, and conducts business. But explicitly recognizing even a limited range of communities that are not creditors and have no defined stake under current bankruptcy law is a largely new concept in bankruptcy.

Suppose Seat Co. were to shut down its factory in Blytheville, Arkansas. Many people would thus lose their jobs. Other businesses in Blytheville would experience a ripple effect, and some of them might need to shut down. Blytheville's tax base would diminish. The owner of Seat Co., who may have guaranteed the corporate obligations, could also experience financial trouble. If Seat Co. were to relocate aspects of its business to another location, say Salt Lake City, Utah, another community would be affected. At first blush, it looks as though one city's loss (Blytheville's) is just another city's gain (Salt Lake's). That would be true if people and business locations were fungible, which they are not (except perhaps as mathematical equations). In a bankruptcy context, the greatest attention should be paid to the debtor's community for, as the host community, it has the greatest nexus with the debtor. Continuity of the host community is not assessed in a vacuum, however, and Blytheville's loss would need to be weighed against Salt Lake's gain.

Suppose Seat Co., in manufacturing its product, polluted the environment.[15] Suppose further that the cost of cleanup for the existing hazard is prohibitive and that pollution control devices for prospective use are equally expensive. Seat Co. simply cannot afford either. When the company fails to correct the environmental hazard, the government will shut the business down. Because Seat Co. is financially unable to pay the cleanup costs, the government will be forced to step in to both perform and pay for the cleanup. The government's action stops the existing and ongoing hazard to Blytheville's citizens, another community.

Action in response to community concerns in a bankruptcy case have both narrow and broad implications. When the pollution is eradicated through governmental intervention, Seat Co. will have to close its doors, with all the concomitant consequences on a range of local communities. If the pollution does not doom Blytheville, the loss of its major business will. This scenario reveals the tension between the need to save businesses and the need to maintain a safe environment. Whatever bankruptcy system is created necessarily sets policy on both the narrow question of a particular company's survival and the broader question of what we want to happen to companies in jeopardy in a credit-based society.

In the context of an individual, the concept of community seems less obvious. In this case, the community includes the debtor's family, friends, and co-workers. Suppose Smythe is married with two small children. His financial failure affects his family—that is, his ability to provide for them today and in the future. Family members are the often unnamed, noncreditor parties touched by financial failure. Smythe's friends and neighbors, some of whom may also be creditors, are part of another community. Broader community interests are implicated because of the consequences of requiring Smythe to work all his life to repay the accident victim. Smythe would never be able to better himself economically. Perhaps this would be so emotionally debilitating that Smythe would stop working altogether and then require some social welfare benefit. This line of questioning makes us confront how we, as a society, want to treat individual failure and whether we are willing to tether a debtor to obligations for the benefit of the creditor to the detriment of not only himself but his family and his community.

If notions of community are included in a consideration of bankruptcy, a *dual* rival-form ambiguity does not completely describe the situation. We need yet a third image—not another duck or rabbit but a pond. To an image that moves in two dimensions (left to right and right to left), this new perspective of "pond" would add a third dimension. With this new multiple rival-form ambiguity, whether one sees a duck, a rabbit, or a pond would depend on one's perspective. All three images exist simultaneously.

But the essence of the system is what is created by the combination of the three images—the duck, rabbit, *and* pond. This entirely new and unfamiliar creation could be called a duckrabbitpond. The

choice of the pond (rather than another animal) as the image analogous to community evidences the realization that ducks and rabbits live in a context, whether ponds, fields, or woods.[16] The absence
of a context would literally destroy the animals' ability to live. A
world with no pond would be an artificial construct. Moreover,
unlike ducks and rabbits, which die or move on, a pond endures,
suggesting that notions of community are enduring and hence worthy of considerable attention.

It is fair to ask whether we really need this third perspective.
Some people may reason that if our understanding of the rival-form
perspectives of the debtor and creditor are sufficiently nuanced,
then the interests of community can be subsumed within existing
categories. Although in some situations this may be true, in other
situations community interests do not have voice as either creditors
or debtors. What motivates and justifies inclusion of community is
different from what motivates and justifies the interests of debtors
and creditors. The community-focused perspective presents different economic choices and makes us address directly the extent that
we as a society are willing to pay for the outcomes we desire. As
such, it needs to stand as a separate force with which to be reckoned.

We are not used to viewing a bankruptcy case through a broad
lens, and it is hard to see the duckrabbitpond. One of the reasons
for this difficulty has to do with bankruptcy having been in the
province of lawyers and judges for so long. Lawyers tend, indeed
are required, to view problems from the perspective of their respective clients. Clients, by their very nature, come to the lawyer with a
distinct and narrow perspective. Thus, a lawyer for a debtor may be
hard-pressed, given the exigencies of day-to-day law practice, to
consider the social (community) implications of bankruptcy, particularly if this consideration would undermine the result the particular debtor wants and needs. Smythe's lawyer, for example, may not
approve of Smythe's discharging the tort judgment and may feel
great sympathy for the tort victim. But if the lawyer is retained to
represent Smythe and the law permits the discharge, the personal

ethics of the lawyer become secondary to his obligations to his client. Similarly, a lawyer retained by Seat Co.'s lending bank has to try to foreclose on the company's machinery and equipment to protect his client's interest even though he is personally concerned about the workers' well-being. Legal practice, then, discourages the very types of perspective enhancement that seeing the duckrabbit-pond requires.[17] This is reminiscent of the anecdote about the law student who commented in class to the professor that the result in a case wasn't fair. The law professor responded, "If it's justice you are looking for, you should have gone to divinity school."[18]

Nonlawyers are also unaccustomed to employing a broad-based perspective in thinking about bankruptcy. Part of the reason for the traditionally narrow approach to bankruptcy is that many people do not view bankruptcy as raising serious social issues. It does not involve life and death. It does not seem as morally poignant as issues of abortion, rape, capital punishment, equal protection, affirmative action, religious freedom, and sexual harassment. Even Supreme Court justices view bankruptcy as unimportant and unalluring.[19] They, too, want to address the issues they think are important, such as constitutional and criminal law.

This view occurs because most people assume that bankruptcy is all about money. It is easy to see why. A debtor has made commitments to a wide range of individuals and businesses and now cannot fulfill them. This failure manifests itself in economic terms. But we have to think about money—and the lack of ability to repay it—as symbolic of much larger issues. Bankruptcy involves failures that manifest themselves in economic terms but that are not purely economic failures. Money is the stand-in for larger failures—failures of particular industries, or failures in the health care system, the social welfare system, the tort system, the commercial and personal lending system, and the educational system. Bankruptcy addresses the failures within families, such as death or divorce, and the failures caused by nature, such as hurricanes, floods, and tornadoes. Looked at as society's mechanism for addressing these many failures, bankruptcy becomes a receptacle for some of society's most weighty problems. It cannot be dismissed as insignificant.

Bankruptcy is like a three-legged stool, once the third leg—the interests of community—becomes visible. Recognizing multiple perspectives is just the first step, though. We now need to begin thinking from these three complex and interconnected perspectives. A multi-perspectival approach pulls us away from neat categories and easy answers. It avoids generalizations that do not work and yet acknowledges the necessity of some level of generality. It forces us to look at issues in all their complexity. Before reconceptualizing the bankruptcy system in light of these perspectives, it is useful to understand both how the current bankruptcy law is structured and what is currently happening within the bankruptcy system—to the extent that that can be determined.

CHAPTER TWO

Understanding the Bankruptcy Code

The Bankruptcy Reform Act, a federal law passed in 1978 and amended various times since then (including as recently as 1996), is the locus of the current U.S. bankruptcy laws. Known as the Code, the new law was passed in response to the perceived and real sense that its predecessor, the Bankruptcy Act of 1898, had become outmoded and unresponsive to the needs of both debtors and creditors. The Code substantially revised the Act, and views vary as to the adequacy of the Code, depending on whether the critic adopts a debtor- or creditor-centered perspective. As originally enacted, the Code favored the interests of debtors over those of creditors. This pro-debtor stance has been curtailed by the more recent amendments to the Code.[1] Yet discontent continues on all sides, and at almost any given moment legislation is pending to amend the Code further.[2] The growing criticism of the Code has led to increased attention focused on not only its content but also its effects.

To explain what the Code provides for debtors and creditors, the discussion can be divided into two pieces: first, what type of relief is available to debtors, and then, who can partake of that relief. Because this chapter is intended to provide an overview of bankruptcy, many subtleties have, by necessity, been omitted.

The Liquidation Option

Debtors, the official term used for any persons or entities that seek relief under the bankruptcy laws, have two basic options under the Code: they can liquidate or reorganize. In a liquidation

(Chapter 7 of the Code), all the debtor's nonexempt assets (a concept that will be explained shortly) are sold and the proceeds used to repay creditors. The liquidation process, including all sales, is overseen by an appointed trustee. Once the liquidation is complete, debtors are relieved of any further liability on the vast majority of their obligations, even if creditors have not been repaid in full.

For individual debtors, the release from liability is termed a discharge. The discharge is necessary because a liquidation does not mean that the individual debtor literally liquidates and physically dies. Therefore, some legal mechanism is necessary for ensuring that creditors do not seek to collect from these individuals in the future. Nonindividual debtors, such as corporations and partnerships, do not receive a discharge in Chapter 7. By liquidating, they are going out of business. Because the business entity will not exist prospectively and is literally dying, it does not need the prospective legal protection of a formal discharge. The ability to obtain relief from the unpaid portion of one's liabilities, whether or not this ability is called a discharge, is a significant aspect of debtor protection.

Because debtors usually have insufficient assets to repay all creditors, creditors commonly receive less than one hundred cents of every dollar they are owed. This is often termed being paid in bankruptcy dollars. Suppose Seat Co., a corporate debtor in Chapter 7, has $1 million in easily salable assets and $4 million in valid creditor claims. For simplicity's sake, assume that all creditors are of like kind and that there are no expenses entitled to be paid ahead of others (such as costs of sale and trustee fees). In this situation, the trustee would liquidate the $1 million of assets by selling them at the best available price. The monies generated from the sale ($1 million) would be used to pay creditors. Because the assets yielded one-fourth the amount of total debt, creditors would receive twenty-five cents on every dollar owed. Thus, a creditor owed $1,000 would receive a distribution of $250. The remaining unpaid portion of the debtor's obligation to the creditor ($750) would be unrecoverable from Seat Co. as it would no longer be in business. The sting of the loss to the creditor is diminished somewhat by its ability to take a bad debt deduction under federal tax law, assuming it has income against which to offset the loss.

To explain the lack of a discharge for corporate debtors, a non-bankruptcy-law doctrine needs to be introduced. Under existing corporate law, officers, directors, and owners (known as equity holders or shareholders) of a corporation have no personal liability for a corporation's debts. This doctrine, termed limited liability, enables individuals to participate in running a business without personal financial exposure.[3] Because of this, when a corporation is liquidated, individuals within the corporation are generally not responsible for repaying the outstanding portion of a corporation's debts unless the individuals have guaranteed the corporate debt. If they have provided a guarantee, they become personally liable. In addition, in several other situations, by either statute or common law, individuals in management positions can incur personal liability.[4] Limited liability, then, permits the owners, officers, and directors of a liquidated business to enter into another business venture unencumbered by past mistakes.

There are several important limitations on Chapter 7 relief for individual debtors. Conduct of some individual debtors is considered so egregious that the debtor is denied the benefits of the bankruptcy law. Examples of such conduct include fraud, destruction of financial documents, and perjury. Also, individual debtors who have liquidated within the past six years cannot do so again. There are also certain specific types of debts, as distinguished from debtors, that cannot be discharged. This category of obligations is deemed so significant to particular creditors or society that the law will not give debtors a reprieve. These debtors can get a general discharge, but the specifically identified debts survive the bankruptcy filing. Examples of nondischargeable obligations are debts for alimony, maintenance, and child support, injuries caused by drunk driving, willful and malicious injury, restitution orders, back taxes, and student loans.

These limitations on discharge are like bankruptcy's gatekeepers; they permit the "good" individual debtors or at least the good debts to be discharged, and they keep the "bad" debtors or bad debts from partaking of the system's benefits. But these limitations are not foisted on corporate debtors. Just as there is no need for formal discharge for corporations, there is no need to limit their release of obligations. The limitations exist because individual debtors will generate future income through their labor, and this income can be used to repay the nondischarged debts. In contrast, liquidated corporate debtors have no future income and thus no prospect of future repayment. For nonindividual debtors, then, all debts, even those incurred through fraud, are eliminated.

The dichotomy between the treatment of individuals and that of corporations is troubling. A corporation may cease to exist, but its officers, directors, and shareholders do not die with the business. Similarly, under partnership law, the partnership may cease to exist, but the individual (or corporate) partners remain in existence. Under current bankruptcy law, the individuals within a corporation can proceed in the future, with limited exceptions, unrestrained by their corporation's debt. Suppose Seat Co. incurred its bank debt through fraud. If the corporation conducted itself with the proper formalities (for example, if there was no commingling of the assets of the corporation and its owner), nothing precludes Seat Co.'s owner from establishing a new business under a different name, unencumbered by the business' prior fraud and free of old debt. This leads to perceptions of unfairness.

The disparate treatment of corporate entities and individuals is justified by accepting the artificial distinction between the two. A corporation is considered a discrete legal entity. It is founded on a fiction because a corporation is certainly owned by individuals, or by other entities that are in turn owned by individuals (the shareholders), and it is run by individuals who serve as officers and directors. In a sense, a corporation is a hollow shell; it does not exist apart from its owners and managers. The fiction continues to be observed because it enables individuals to invest in and run businesses, usually without personal exposure. This promotes increased investment in corporate America because the extent of the risk, particularly for shareholders, is curtailed. It is worth recognizing, however, that partnerships are something of a hybrid entity (depending on the nature of the partnership), and partners are not necessarily released in their individual capacity.

Outside the area of bankruptcy, efforts have been made to circumscribe the scope of limited liability.[5] But within the bankruptcy context, the exceptions crafted to ensure that individual debtors do not discharge selected debts have not been engrafted onto corporate insiders. The corporation is discharged, and the individuals within the business entity emerge free of debt as well.

The Reorganization Option

In addition to liquidation, the other option available to debtors is reorganization. For both individuals and nonindividuals, a reorganization allows debtors to keep their existing assets. In exchange, they have to pay creditors at least as much as those creditors would receive in a Chapter 7 liquidation. Even in a reorganization case, creditors are not necessarily repaid in full. If creditors are not fully repaid, then the concept of discharge comes into play again. This time, because a reorganization entails survival, not death, discharge is relevant for both individual and nonindividual debtors, and assuming that certain preconditions are met, both individuals and nonindividuals can obtain a discharge.

The most common reorganization chapter for individuals, including sole proprietors, is Chapter 13. Individuals with regular income (generated from any source), secured debts below $750,000, and unsecured debts below $250,000 are eligible for Chapter 13 relief. In a procedure that is designed to be relatively easy to accomplish and that is overseen by a standing trustee, debtors repay their creditors over a three- to five-year period by developing a repayment schedule, or "plan of reorganization." Under the plan, the debtors allocate the portion of their income that is not reasonably necessary to support themselves and their family ("disposable income") to creditor repayments. Unlike a Chapter 7 case, future income is encumbered in a Chapter 13 case. Creditors have no opportunity to vote on the debtor's plan, although they can object to its approval (or "confirmation") on the basis that it does not fulfill the explicit requirements of the Code.

Chapter 13 is particularly appealing for several reasons. The scope of the discharge is greater than that available in Chapter 7, although the generosity of the Chapter 13 discharge has been chiseled away over the years.[6] A Chapter 13 debtor, for example, can discharge debts incurred while acting in a fiduciary capacity or debts obtained through fraud, but not debts for alimony, maintenance, or child support. Chapter 13 also offers homeowners some unique benefits. Under this chapter, a debtor can cure arrearages on home mortgages and, in limited circumstances, can reduce the amount of the secured claim of the mortgagee.[7]

Certain aspects of Chapter 13 are troubling, however. Seat Co. would not be eligible for a Chapter 13 because it is not an individual. Thus it cannot partake in the speedy reorganization process. Smythe is an individual, and he does have regular income—he is employed full time. But Chapter 13 requires that a debtor's unsecured debts fall below $250,000. Because Smythe has a judgment against him in excess of this ceiling ($2 million above his insurance cap), he is not eligible for a Chapter 13. Assume for a moment that Smythe sought bankruptcy relief right after the injured pedestrian commenced her lawsuit but before any judgment could be entered. In this instance, Smythe would qualify for Chapter 13 relief because his liquidated debts at the time of filing fell below the ceiling and he had less than $250,000 in other unsecured debts (credit cards and student loans). Now suppose that Seat Co.'s owner guaranteed the company's bank debt and hence had a large contingent claim. Suppose this individual filed for bankruptcy relief before the bank tried to realize on its guarantee. Because this claim was contingent, it would not be included for purposes of determining the debt limits, and hence the owner would be eligible for Chapter 13 while Smythe, in the original scenario, would not.

Although the threshold amount of debt an eligible Chapter 13 debtor can hold was increased in 1994, the calculation of the debt limits remains problematic. The determination of who can seek relief under Chapter 13 is unjustifiably arbitrary. One possible solution—which is employed in Chapter 12, the reorganization chapter added in 1986 to assist family farmers—is to create a ceiling based on an aggregate of secured and unsecured debts. Debtors would be eligible for Chapter 13 if, for example, their debts fell below $1 million. (Under current law, the debt limit in a Chapter 13 case totals $1 million, but secured and unsecured debt is not aggregated.) Aggregating saves the cost of ascertaining which debts fall into which categories.

Chapter 11 is another reorganization chapter. It is available to businesses (corporations, partnerships, and select trusts), although individuals are also eligible for relief under this chapter.[8] Both Seat Co. and Smythe would thus be eligible for Chapter 11 relief. Chapter 11 enables a debtor to repay creditors over an extended period. It is the Code chapter most commonly addressed by the media and criticized rather resoundingly by commentators. Many well-known companies have partaken of Chapter 11's benefits: Dow Corning, Olympia & York, Continental Airlines, Alexander's, Child World, Macy's, Texaco, TWA, Revco, Federated, Orion Pictures, and Pan Am are just a few. These are the companies involved in "mega" Chapter 11 cases, defined as those cases involving entities with more than $100 million in assets. It is also the chapter used by such less well known companies as Auto Parts Center in Illinois, which had liabilities of $4,409; Desert Restaurant in California, with liabilities of $824,789; and the Pet Store in Texas, with liabilities of $72,300.

One of the most significant features of a Chapter 11 case, which distinguishes this chapter from most other chapters of the Code, is that a debtor's management is entitled to remain in place and continue to run the business. Except for situations involving fraud or misconduct, a trustee or examiner is not appointed. The Chapter 11 debtor is termed a debtor-in-possession, or DIP (more than one joke has been made about the appropriateness of the acronym). Many people are startled by the notion that the Code permits the very folks who got the debtor into financial trouble to lead the charge to get it out of trouble. There are several reasons for allowing management to remain in control. First, a debtor's existing management knows a great deal about the business. The debtor remains under the watchful eye of the court, creditors, and the United States Trustee, which is the arm of the Justice Department charged with overseeing the administrative aspects of the bankruptcy process. Keeping existing management in place is efficient, as it would take time and money to educate someone else about the debtor's business. Although numerous critics have charged that Chapter 11 serves only to keep existing management entrenched to the detriment of creditors, managers of large financially troubled companies are frequently replaced just before or during a large case.[9] Bringing in new management is generally well received by creditors because it demonstrates a visible effort to right a sinking ship.

A Chapter 11 case has other significant features. Unless the debtor has elected to be treated as a small business, the debtor has a 120-day exclusive period within which to file a plan of reorganization. That time period can be extended, and frequently is. After expiration of this period, unlike a Chapter 13 case, any party in interest (usually one or more creditors) can propose its own plan. Although this option exists, it is exercised only rarely, most frequently in the context of the mega Chapter 11 cases. Unlike Chapter 13 cases, in Chapter 11 cases, reorganization plans are not limited by time. Debtors can repay creditors over extended periods, often well beyond the three- to five-year period contemplated by Chapter 13. Also, unlike in a Chapter 13 case, creditors (except in a small business case) are entitled to form one and sometimes more committees designed to monitor the Chapter 11. Moreover, creditors vote on a Chapter 11 plan. A Chapter 11 is generally more complex, cumbersome, and costly than a Chapter 13, owing in no small part to the increased number of creditors and the increased role that they can play in the reorganization process, the absence of any cap on the size of the debts, and the participation of a wide array of professionals (attorneys, accountants, and investment bankers) in the reorganization effort.[10]

The most striking feature of Chapter 11 is termed the absolute priority rule. Under this rule, creditors and equity holders are classified, and each higher-ranking class must be paid in full before any lower-ranking class of creditors or equity holders can be paid, unless the higher class agrees to be paid less. The absolute priority rule means, stated simply, that existing equity holders, which generally rank lower than creditors, can have their interest wiped out if junior creditors are not repaid in full. There is considerable debate over whether the absolute priority rule can be modified by the contribution of new capital.[11] Absent such an exception, the debtor's principals cannot dedicate new monies to the faltering business and retain their equity share unless creditors are repaid in full. The Bankruptcy Code also requires that at least one class of impaired creditors (those not being paid in full) affirmatively vote to accept the plan.

Suppose that Seat Co. wanted to reorganize by repaying all its trade creditors twenty-five cents on the dollar. Suppose also that Seat Co.'s owners wanted to retain their ownership of this family business. According to the absolute priority rule, unless these unsecured creditors agreed to this limited payout, the owners would not be able to retain their equity interest because no junior class (in this case, equity holders) could be paid unless the senior class (here, the trade creditors) had already been paid in full.

The scenario becomes more complex if the owners offer to pay new monies into the estate, say two hundred thousand dollars, in exchange for retaining their equity interest. If this is permitted, the owners will retain their equity even though more senior creditors are not paid in full. Stated in bankruptcy parlance, the question is whether the giving of new value (here two hundred thousand dollars) is or should be an exception to the absolute priority rule and whether the amount contributed is sufficient. Considerable uncertainty remains about both these issues. What is clear, however, is that if the owners of Seat Co. offer to work for the reorganized company on a go-forward basis in exchange for retaining an equity position instead of offering two hundred thousand dollars in new money, this will not be sufficient under current law to satisfy the new value exception to the absolute priority rule.[12]

Lawyers involved in Chapter 11 cases obviously care whether the new value exception to the absolute priority rule exists because this affects how a plan of reorganization is crafted. Ambiguity on this fundamental issue also leads to possible litigation and cost. But, for our purposes, the more critical question is whether such an exception should exist and, if so, why sweat equity (working), as opposed to green money (cash), is not good enough to satisfy the test.

Two other reorganization chapters and several special reorganization provisions are available only to a limited category of debtors. Chapter 9 is for municipal reorganizations. Orange County, California, for example, sought relief under Chapter 9 in December 1994.[13] Several years earlier, the Town of Bridgeport, Connecticut, sought relief (ultimately unsuccessfully) under this chapter.[14] Chapter 12 is for the reorganization of family farmers, whether individuals or corporations, and is patterned after Chapter 13. This chapter, which expires by its own terms in 1998, is intended to give special help to those in the depressed farming industry and has been used since 1992 by only a limited number of debtors. Finally, special reorganization provisions exist for railroads, small businesses, and single-asset real estate cases. The last two categories were made part of the bankruptcy law in 1994, and early data suggest that these provisions are being used, although their level of use over the long haul is unknown. The railroad reorganization subchapter, once used with some frequency, now lies largely dormant.

Debtor Eligibility

Most debtors have a choice between liquidating and reorganizing, and many complex reasons dictate why a debtor would choose one over the other.[15] A business that believes it has a viable future will want to reorganize, as reorganization will enable it to remain in existence. Chapter 11 allows this debtor to obtain relief from obligations that are draining its resources and limiting its ability to borrow prospectively. In contrast, suppose three doctors formed a partnership but, because of disagreements over money and working styles, now want to go their separate ways. For this partnership, Chapter 7 is the best option because the partners have no interest in continuing the enterprise. The individual debtor with significant obligations and few assets to preserve may want to liquidate, particularly if most obligations can be discharged. The individual debtor with significant assets and high future income may want to use Chapter 13, which permits debtors to retain possession of their assets. Chapter choice could also be affected by personal and perhaps idiosyncratic reasons. A debtor may believe that less stigma is involved in filing a Chapter 13 case than in filing a Chapter 7. A debtor may simply want to find the quickest solution and hence choose to liquidate under Chapter 7. Perhaps in some instances a reorganization case is filed to buy time when liquidation is inevitable. Or a Chapter 13 could be filed simply to avoid foreclosure. In addition to these endogenous factors, there are exogenous reasons for why a debtor might choose one chapter over another.[16] Evidence suggests that local legal culture and lawyers' counseling affect a debtor's choice of bankruptcy relief. Some judicial forums, for example, are more receptive to reorganization cases, while other locales favor liquidations.

Moreover, not all debtors are eligible for all chapters (table 1). Individuals and corporations that are not farmers cannot use Chapter 12. Individuals without regular income or with debts above the prescribed statutory limits cannot use Chapter 13. The regular income requirement is intended to ensure that Chapter 13 debtors have the wherewithal to fund a reorganization plan. If too much is owed, creditors are better protected in Chapter 11, with its increased procedural mechanisms, such as creditors' committees, creditor voting, and added disclosure. A limited group of debtors has no choice between liquidation and reorganization. Railroads cannot liquidate under Chapter 7. Banks and insurance companies cannot liquidate under Chapter 7 or reorganize under Chapter 11. Stockbrokers and commodity brokers are prohibited from reorganizing under Chapters 11 or 13.

The rationales for these limitations are varied. Requiring railroads to reorganize ensures that transportation will continue throughout the United States, as a liquidation could deprive segments of the country of rail service. Because the liquidation or restructuring of banks and insurance companies is governed by nonbankruptcy state and federal law, there is little need for a bankruptcy system to intervene.[17] Finally, the reorganization of stockbrokers and commodity brokers is disallowed for fear that these individuals will restructure their business with the money that others entrusted to them.

These explanations do not stand up well under scrutiny. Although the protections for railroads may have made sense in the early twentieth century, other forms of transportation (airplanes, trucks, and ships) are now as crucial as trains, and perhaps even more so. Yet the law provides protection only for railroads. Similarly, we rightly may be concerned about stockbrokers and commodity brokers restructuring with other people's money, but many financially troubled companies do the same thing, although the money is frequently obtained through direct loans as opposed to misappropriation.

One final group of debtors has, until recently, been denied access to the bankruptcy system: debtors who are too poor to pay the bankruptcy filing fee, which is $160 in Chapters 7 and 13. Although other types of lawsuits can be commenced *in forma pauperis,* the term for the legal mechanism for waiving filing fees, no such possibility exists in bankruptcy except for those individual debtors filing Chapter 7 cases in a six-district pilot program (in effect until 1997).[18] Although the Code permits debtors to pay the filing fee in installments, debtors who cannot pay at all (other than those in the pilot districts) are not eligible for a discharge. One can be too poor to go broke.

Table 1. Bankruptcy Code Chapters Available to Debtors

Category of debtor	Chapter 7	Chapter 9	Chapter 11	Chapter 12	Chapter 13
Individuals (other than stockbrokers and commodity brokers)	Yes	No	Yes	Yes (if family farmer)	Yes (if regular income and debts are within pre-scribed limits)
Business entities (other than railroads and selected banks and insurance companies)	Yes	No	Yes	Yes (if farmer)	No
Stockbrokers and commodity brokers	Yes	No	No	No	No
Railroads	No	No	Yes	No	No
Municipalities	No	Yes	No	No	No

The Supreme Court has defended this position on the theory that there is no right to file for bankruptcy relief. Bankruptcy is a privilege that can be granted or denied by Congress. Moreover, the Supreme Court and others have suggested that if a debtor cannot afford this low filing fee, bankruptcy relief would not be of much use.[19] Others are concerned that if the filing fee requirement is lifted, there will be a flood of new bankruptcy filings, particularly from prisoners, which will stress the already overburdened system. In light of these perceived fears, the number of bankruptcy filings is artificially limited, and this result has been justified on both a pragmatic and a constitutional basis.

What is most striking to those not expert in bankruptcy law is that, with the exception of municipalities, a debtor need not be insolvent to seek bankruptcy relief. People can be debtors even if they are capable of repaying their creditors. Most debtors are "balance sheet insolvent," which means that their liabilities exceed their assets. But some debtors are "equitably insolvent": they cannot meet their current obligations. They are "cash poor." Assume, for example, that a debtor owns a home free and clear of any mortgage. The home is valued at $100,000. The debtor owes $30,000 to credit card companies, educational institutions, doctors, and utilities. The debtor, who was employed as an engineer, has just lost her job and cannot now make the minimum monthly payments on all her obligations after paying for such basic living expenses as food, clothing, transportation, insurance, and medical bills. Assume that the debtor has no nonexempt assets and that the state homestead exemption permits the debtor to retain only $10,000 of the equity in her primary residence. On a balance sheet basis, this debtor is solvent: her nonexempt assets are worth $90,000 and her obligations total $30,000. But the debtor cannot pay her obligations because she does not have sufficient cash flow on a day-to-day basis to both stay in her home and repay creditors. She is equitably insolvent. In contrast, if the debtor owed her creditors $120,000 and had nonexempt assets of only $90,000, she would be balance sheet insolvent; her liabilities would exceed her assets.

Husbands and wives can file for bankruptcy jointly. This makes sense when they have joint obligations. Moreover, a joint filing eliminates one filing fee, which is often significant ($130 plus a $30 administrative charge for a Chapter 13 case). Although some people pooh-pooh the savings of $160 as insubstantial, I am reminded of Justice Marshall's dissent in *Kras v. United States,* the decision that denied in forma pauperis filings. He chided the majority when they scoffed at the debtor's inability to pay $1.28 a week for the filing fee. Justice Marshall stated, "It may be easy for some people to think that weekly savings of less than $2 are not a burden. But no one who has had close contact with those poor people can fail to understand how close to the margin of survival many of them are."[20]

Although more than 99% of filings are voluntary,[21] creditors are still able to put certain debtors into bankruptcy involuntarily. The law, however, places key restrictions on this ability. If a debtor has more than twelve creditors, for example, at least three creditors with claims aggregating more than ten thousand dollars have to seek an involuntary filing jointly. Some of a partnership's general partners can also file an involuntary petition against the partnership. In contrast, individual debtors can never be forced to reorganize in a Chapter 13, and family farmers cannot be forced into any Code chapter. Not-for-profit organizations also cannot be forced into bankruptcy. The Code even has a special provision for damages to be assessed against a creditor and paid to the debtor if a bankruptcy case is commenced involuntarily in bad faith.

The limitations on involuntary cases are justified according to several theories. Because Chapter 13 requires the individual debtor to allocate future income to repay creditors, the spirit, if not the letter, of the Thirteenth Amendment (the antislavery amendment to the Bill of Rights) could be implicated if a debtor is forced to work to pay debts involuntarily.[22] Moreover, individuals may not work as hard at repayment if they must work by force rather than by choice. The Code protects farmers in part because of the cyclical nature of the farming business, the extraordinarily strong farming lobby, and the historical import of farming to the American economy. But even though involuntary filings constitute a small percentage of the total filings, the threat that a creditor will force a debtor into bankruptcy is a potent one and encourages debtors and their creditors to attempt to resolve their differences if at all possible.

Simply because debtors are eligible for relief under the Code does not mean that these debtors can accomplish their desired goals. The Code is structured to provide easy access to relief, but access is not synonymous with results. Other Bankruptcy Code sections may limit the availability of the desired relief. Return to the Seat Co. and Smythe examples for a moment. Seat Co. is eligible for relief under Chapter 11; it is not a stockbroker or commodity broker. But that eligibility does not mean that Seat Co. will necessarily be able to terminate unilaterally its collective bargaining agreement or its obligations to retirees. This is because the Code adds special protections for employees and retirees. Similarly, Smythe may be able to file for relief under Chapter 7, but that does not mean he will obtain a discharge. The court could find that he cannot proceed in Chapter 7 because it would be an abuse of the Code. Moreover, Smythe may not obtain a discharge of his credit card debts in Chapter 7 if he lied on the credit card applications. He will not be able to discharge the personal injury judgment if it is demonstrated that the injury was the result of drunk driving or a willful and malicious act. What happens during a bankruptcy case is thus of central concern.

CHAPTER THREE

Getting Down to Basics

This chapter will guide readers through the unfamiliar and complex bankruptcy process (figure 2). Like the preceding chapter, it is intended to be descriptive, although the prescriptive creeps in from time to time.

The Automatic Stay

When a bankruptcy case is filed, most collection efforts against the debtor immediately cease. This debtor protection takes effect automatically and is technically termed the automatic stay.[1] The scope of the stay is intended to be broad. Creditors cannot sue the debtor to collect what is owed them, and all harassment of a debtor must stop. Creditors cannot write or call the debtor demanding payment. Secured creditors cannot foreclose on their collateral, debt collectors cannot repossess the debtor's property through either self-help mechanisms or judicial proceedings, and wages cannot be garnisheed. The whole world of state and federal debt collection basically comes to a rip-roaring halt.

The automatic stay has several functions. First, it gives the debtors an opportunity to regroup, think about their financial problems, and contemplate options for resolving the difficulties. Most debtors have experienced significant pressure both internally and from creditors before bankruptcy, and the stay is a welcome breather. It is similar to the "time out" taken in sports—a time to regroup and settle down. Second, the stay, although touted as the primary debtor protection of the bankruptcy laws, also benefits creditors because it prohibits one creditor from rushing to collect from the

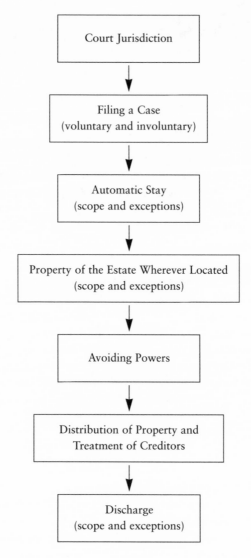

Figure 2. An overview of the bankruptcy process

debtor ahead of all the others. Contrary to a race, where the fastest is the best, the bankruptcy system equalizes creditors and forces them to look to a collective remedy (bankruptcy) as opposed to an individual solution (first come, first served). The stay, then, permits the liquidation or reorganization to proceed in an orderly fashion.

A limited but growing number of creditors' activities do not fall within the scope of the stay. The government, for example, can proceed with a criminal case against a debtor. The government can also mandate that the debtor comply with certain financial criteria established by a federal agency. The government can order the debtor to stop polluting. A former spouse can commence or continue actions to establish a right to receive alimony, maintenance, child support, and other similar payments. Collection of these spousal payments can even proceed in certain situations. Some lawsuits can also proceed if the debtor is not a necessary party.

The stay, though automatic, is not permanent. Under certain circumstances, it can be terminated or modified during a bankruptcy case, and it evaporates at the end of a case or once a plan is confirmed. As one might assume, many creditors try to have the stay lifted during a case so they can continue their collection efforts. Debtors, in contrast, are anxious to keep the stay in place for as long as possible and to have it remain effective against as many creditors as possible. The desire to give debtors a breathing space and the need to protect the legitimate interests of particular creditors are in constant tension.

The battles surrounding the stay can best be seen by returning to the example of Seat Co. As soon as Seat Co. files bankruptcy, all of its creditors—secured and unsecured—are forbidden from pursuing any action to collect what is owed them. For creditors who did not know that bankruptcy was imminent, this comes as quite an unwelcome surprise, particularly if they had already commenced a legal action to try to collect.

Suppose Seat Co.'s secured creditor banks want to collect what is owed them. They can try to do so by enforcing their liens on all the debtor's machinery. To accomplish this during a bankruptcy case, these banks will need to ask the court to vacate the automatic stay. If Seat Co.'s banks are permitted to foreclose on this equipment, the company's reorganization effort will fail because it will not have the equipment to make the seat belts. This failure could hurt all the other creditors, particularly the unsecured creditors and employees. But if the equipment is deteriorating in value and is uninsured, the secured creditor banks run the risk that their collateral will not be available to repay them.

Seat Co. can try to fight the lifting of the stay by demonstrating that the collateral is not decreasing in value, insurance is being maintained, and the machinery is essential to the reorganization effort.[2] Alternatively, Seat Co. could provide its secured lender banks with interim payments or liens on other assets that are not encumbered (such as realty, inventory, or receivables). The court will generally keep the stay in place if it is confident that the bank creditors' collateral is protected. The Code even stipulates that if the court errs in making this assessment and the banks are harmed, the banks' claims are lifted to a higher priority when payments are ultimately made.[3]

Property of the Estate and Exemptions

Among the major activities that transpire during a bankruptcy case is the determination of what assets the debtor has available for creditors—assets that are either to be sold in a Chapter 7 liquidation case or used as the basis for a plan of reorganization in Chapter 11, 12, or 13. When a case is filed, all the debtor's existing assets become part of the bankruptcy estate and are referred to as "property of the estate," as opposed to "property of the debtor."[4] Most debtors have some property, which can take a wide range of forms. Household goods, antiques, machinery, computers, tables, and chairs are all examples of tangible personal property. Homes, land parcels, office buildings, and factories are examples of real (as distinguished from personal) property. Other, less obvious types of property that individual and corporate debtors own include leases, contract rights, accounts receivable, goodwill, trademarks, and copyrights. Although these assets are invisible, they have significant economic value. In addition, there is also property in which a debtor has an interest but that is not now in the debtor's possession.[5] A lender could be holding certain property as collateral, for example, or property could be co-owned with several parties and held by an owner other than the debtor. Finally, there is property that will yield benefits in the future. Numerous items fall into this category, such as royalties from a book or a product that has been developed but not yet sold. For individual debtors who file a case under Chapter 7 as opposed to Chapter 11 (in some jurisdictions), 12, or 13, future income is not property of the estate and is retained by the debtor.[6]

The greater the value of the property of the estate, the greater the potential distribution to creditors. The reorganizing debtor, too, may want to maximize the currently available property because the more property the debtor has, the less he or she will need to rely on future income to satisfy creditors. To assist the debtor and creditors in maximizing this pool of assets, the bankruptcy law permits the debtor to recover property, regardless of who is holding it and where it is being held.[7] Suppose, for example, that the property (a car or a piece of land) is in Kansas but the debtor resides and files a bankruptcy case in Alabama. The bankruptcy laws permit the Alabama bankruptcy court to exercise control over the property in Kansas. Stated in terms of state and federal law, the federal bankruptcy law takes precedence over the State of Kansas' possessory interest in the property.

Although most property is included in the estate, not all of it is available for distribution to creditors. For individual debtors, both federal and state law permit the retention of certain property as "exempt," that is, free from the grasp of creditors.[8] Common examples of exempt property are one's home (or a portion of one's interest in it), one's car (sometimes up to a specific dollar amount), tools of the trade (for example, medical instruments for a doctor; law books for an attorney; hammers, drills, and saws for a carpenter; or art supplies for an artist), clothes, jewelry, household furniture, and medical devices (such as hearing aids and wheelchairs). Some exemption systems list categories of items that are exempt (cars, books, tools of the trade), other systems focus on the value of items (personalty up to five thousand dollars in value), and yet other systems provide a combination of the two (for example, one can retain one's car up to twelve hundred dollars in value).

What property a state or federal government allows a debtor to retain is based on a societal value judgment that the selected items are so important to an individual's survival or well-being in the present and future that they are beyond the reach of creditors. But not all these judgments are necessarily sound. Debtors are allowed to exempt all or part of their home, for example, in part to foster home ownership but also because society respects the home as an important, private sanctuary. Also, family stability and household continuity are considered important by-products of permitting continued use of the family dwelling. But this protection is not extended to rental property. So, in reality, the domicile is protected for a limited range of debtors—private homeowners. The bankruptcy system specifically protects cars and stereos but not artwork. This suggests that American society favors transportation by car as opposed to bus, subway, or train, and that music is more important than the visual arts.

We could learn something significant about social history by looking at the changing nature of exemptions over the past two hundred years. Exemption laws once extended to farm animals, bales of wheat and hay, and cords of wood when these items were essential to personal and economic survival. Apparently, in the United States of the late twentieth century, cars, private home ownership, and clothes are of utmost significance.

The extent of a debtor's exempt property differs dramatically from state to state. The Bankruptcy Code also contains specific debtor exemptions, the dollar value of which were increased by the 1994 Amendments. Some federal exemptions enumerated in the Code are more and some are less generous than what a particular state may offer. The Code stipulates that states can force their citizenry to use only state exemption law and nonbankruptcy federal exemptions. Almost three-quarters of the states have elected to apply their own exemption laws rather than those embodied in the Code. Thus individual debtors unfortunately receive disparate treatment depending on where they reside. As a natural consequence, some creditors receive a greater distribution than other creditors that are owed similar amounts by a similar debtor in a different state.

Consider the following example. The states of Florida and New York have chosen to apply their respective exemption laws within an individual bankruptcy case.[9] Assume that the hypothetical debtor Smythe lived in a house in Florida valued at $1,000,000. Suppose Smythe had purchased the home with money he inherited from a wealthy relative and hence had no mortgage on the property. Under Florida law, Smythe would be entitled to retain his entire homestead as exempt. In a Chapter 7 case, Smythe's creditors would not be able to reach an asset (the home) valued at $1,000,000. If, in contrast, Smythe lived in New York and filed a Chapter 7 case there, he would be entitled to retain an interest in his home only to the extent of $10,000. The other $990,000 in equity in Smythe's home ($1,000,000 in value minus the homestead exemption of $10,000) would be available to repay creditors. Smythe, in this situation, would have two basic options: he could either sell his home, in return for which he would receive $10,000 from the proceeds as his homestead exemption, or he could retain the home by coming up with $990,000 (the equity minus the value of the homestead exemption) in cash to pay the trustee, an unlikely scenario at best.

Now assume that Smythe lived in Michigan, a state that has not elected to use its own exemption laws to the exclusion of federal bankruptcy exemptions.[10] Under this scenario, Smythe himself (through his attorney) could elect either the federal homestead exemption of $15,000 or his own state's homestead exemption of $3,500. Smythe would likely choose the federal bankruptcy exemptions as they have more generous homestead protection, if the other property he seeks to exempt is also treated more beneficially under federal bankruptcy law.

As these three examples demonstrate, debtors and their respective creditors experience different outcomes under the bankruptcy law depending on whether a state or federal exemption is in place and on which particular state system is operative. The resulting disparities create unjustifiable results for several reasons. To begin with, the scope of the debtor's fresh start and the creditors' recovery hinges on something as arbitrary as where a debtor happens to reside. If a federal policy favoring debtor relief exists, then that relief should be uniformly available. Moreover, if there is a nexus between the amount that creditors can recover through bankruptcy and the amount of credit extended to individuals, creditors would grant credit more easily to those individuals living in Michigan than to those in Florida. In a nation of credit, this distinction does not make sense. Notice that this is not a problem of bankruptcy law; it is a problem of the intersection of federal and state law.

Nonuniformity encourages prebankruptcy planning for a limited group of debtors who are geographically mobile. These individuals move to states specifically to partake of their more advantageous exemptions, which has led some commentators to refer to such states as Florida as a "debtor's haven."[11] This practice resembles forum shopping, in which litigants choose where to file because of the judicial temperament in a selected region.[12] But most debtors cannot simply pick up and move the moment they perceive financial difficulties on the horizon. For debtors with jobs, working spouses, children in schools, or other obligations to family and friends, skipping off to Florida is neither feasible nor desirable.

The focus on overgenerous exemptions has caused two problems. First, it has created a public perception that all debtors are manipulating the system to partake of its benefits, and second, it treats the issue of exemptions as one of bankruptcy law. But disparities, to the extent that they exist, are not caused by the bankruptcy law per se; they are caused by the state law that is retained in the Code. If the federal bankruptcy exemption system were the only existing system, then the problems would cease. To achieve that result, state exemption law would need to become subordinate to federal bankruptcy law.

One myth related to exemptions can now be dismissed. When the frequency of bankruptcy filings rose following the passage of the Code, many people assumed that this increase was related to generous exemptions. Many of the studies looking at the relationship between filing rates and exemptions, however, reveal no direct correlation between the rate of filings and the generosity of the exemptions.[13] States with low exemptions do not necessarily have low filing rates, and states with enormous filing rates do not necessarily have exceedingly generous exemptions.

The absence of exemptions for nonindividual debtors (such as corporations, partnerships, and trusts) is also worthy of attention. Since existing laws view nonindividual debtors as inanimate legal entities, there is less concern about their future well-being—particularly in the context of liquidation. Because individuals who liquidate remain in existence whereas nonindividuals who liquidate cease to exist, the need to preserve the future by enabling the debtor to retain select property is reserved for individuals. But the dividing line between individuals and businesses is not nearly as clear as might be expected. An individual's debt could result from a failed business. If a small business fails, for example, its owner or manager may be personally responsible for some of the debts. Although the corporation will not have exemptions, the corporate filing may trigger the filing of the corporation's principal, who in turn will seek bankruptcy relief and partake of the available exemptions.

The Avoiding Powers

The pool of available assets is usually not sufficient to repay creditors in full. One way of increasing that pool is through what are termed the trustee's avoiding powers. These powers enable a debtor in select situations to recover monies and property that have passed into the hands of creditors. The three common avoiding powers are the ability of the debtor (or trustee) to avoid preferential payments, recover fraudulent transfers, and eliminate certain liens.[14] The import of these powers cannot be underestimated.

Preferences

Of the trustee's powers, preferences are the easiest to explain. The Bankruptcy Code provides that any payments the debtor makes to creditors within ninety days before bankruptcy, subject to certain significant exceptions, have to be returned for the benefit of all creditors. Suppose that Seat Co. had only ten creditors and owed each of them one thousand dollars, making its liabilities ten thousand dollars. (Real life can be imitated by using unrounded numbers of varying amounts and, in the larger cases, adding several zeros to the selected numbers.) Suppose further that Seat Co. had assets in the bankruptcy estate totaling only one thousand dollars after payment of all administrative and priority expenses. Given these facts, when the property of the estate was distributed, each creditor would get one hundred dollars (one thousand dollars divided by ten creditors). That is, each creditor would get ten cents on the dollar (the creditors would thus receive bankruptcy dollars—less than a hundred cents on the dollar). In this scenario, creditors would share ratably in the pool of available assets but would not be paid in full.

Now assume that Seat Co. is very friendly with one of the ten creditors. Suppose that just before bankruptcy, Seat Co. decided to repay this one creditor the thousand dollars it was owed. If this payment were permitted to stand once a bankruptcy had been filed, the other nine creditors would not receive any money, as all the available assets (one thousand dollars) would have been distributed before bankruptcy to repay one creditor. If one creditor is repaid first, thereby depriving all other creditors of any recovery, every creditor will struggle to be the first in line to recover.

Preference law acts to equalize creditors by making the one creditor who was paid (in full, in the previous example) disgorge the money received. So, in the Seat Co. scenario, the creditor would have to repay the estate one thousand dollars, and this money would become property of the estate, available for distribution to all creditors, not only the select one. The disgorging creditor would go back to being a general unsecured creditor like all the others and would share in the pool of available assets. Preference law thus assists the overall body of creditors by increasing the pool of available assets for distribution through elimination of unequal prebankruptcy payouts. To complicate matters further, if a creditor actually controls the debtor or, for example, happens to be the debtor's brother-in-law, the preference period becomes one year rather than ninety days.

Even within preference law, some creditors are preferred over others. For example, payments made in the ordinary course of business are preferential, but they cannot be avoided. This encourages debtors to continue operating their day-to-day businesses. Payments to fully secured creditors are not treated as preferences because these creditors are not getting more than they are entitled to receive (the value of the collateral). Creditors who extend new credit to a debtor in an amount equal to what they were paid within ninety days of the bankruptcy filing also get to keep the payment received.

Preference law is arbitrary in that it considers only payments made within the ninety days before bankruptcy. Suppose the friendly creditor in the Seat Co. example was repaid on the ninety-first day before bankruptcy as opposed to the eighty-ninth day. In this situation, absent being an insider, this creditor could keep the thousand dollars he or she received, to the detriment of the other nine creditors. Setting a limit is always a problem. Some creditor will always be just shy of the line. Although the difficulty and arbitrariness of drawing such lines does not mean we shouldn't have lines (they do save costs), in some instances we may need a way of circumventing the absoluteness of the line to promote a result more consistent with what lawmakers are trying to accomplish through bankruptcy policy.

The timing of preferences also enables debtors to do some creative prebankruptcy planning. A corporate debtor could decide to repay those creditors it will need prospectively more than three months in advance of a bankruptcy filing while stalling other, less useful creditors. This issue is similar to that raised in the context of exemptions. Is an individual who decides to convert nonexempt assets into exempt assets by moving to Florida any better or worse than the debtor who repays only selected creditors before the ninety-day period? One obvious difference is that in the exemption situation the debtor directly benefits, whereas in the preference exam- ple the debtor benefits only indirectly by retaining its friendship with selected creditors. Also, the ability to manipulate is housed in different bodies of law: the manipulation of exemptions is based on state law, whereas preference law is housed in the federal Bankruptcy Code. But in both situations at least some creditors are damaged in the sense that the size of their distributions is diminished.

Fraudulent Transfers

Under another of the avoiding powers, based on either federal or state law, a debtor (or trustee) can avoid actual and constructive fraudulent transfers made by the debtor. Suppose that immediately before filing bankruptcy, Smythe sells all his assets (his car, tools, clothes, jewelry, stereo, tape deck, and guitar) to his best friend for one dollar with the implicit understanding that after all the dust has settled the friend will return the property unused and unharmed. Suppose the property, after taking account of exemptions, was valued at five thousand dollars. With this transfer, Smythe has effectively removed his property from the reach of all creditors. On the date of the bankruptcy filing, he has no legal or equitable title to these goods; they belong to his best friend. Ostensibly, Smythe's creditors are unaware of or unable to find his property. The bankruptcy law requires the trustee to reverse this type of transfer, whereupon the property would come back into the estate. And the best friend would then be a creditor of Smythe's in the amount of one dollar. Depending on proof of Smythe's intent in making the transfer, Smythe could discover that not only is the transaction nullified but that he is denied a discharge for committing actual fraud on his creditors. This observation goes to the heart of the distinction between preferences and fraudulent transfers. Preferences are not bad in and of themselves; the federal bankruptcy law makes them bad. By contrast, fraudulent transfers are, in and of themselves, evidence of improper conduct. Under state law, with or without a bankruptcy, fraudulent transfers are deemed improper, and the federal bankruptcy law incorporates both state law concerning fraudulent transfers and its own provisions governing improper conveyances.

Not all fraudulent transfers are nearly as obvious as the example, and many do not involve malicious intent. Indeed, successful efforts have been made to apply fraudulent transfer law to such sophisticated corporate transactions as leveraged buyouts. A simpler transaction demonstrates the point. Suppose that Seat Co. sold several major assets to a creditor in exchange for that creditor's releasing the company of its obligations. In this situation, the company was not intending to defraud all its other creditors. But assume that Seat Co. owed this creditor sixty thousand dollars and instead gave the creditor machines with a value of one hundred thousand dollars. (Assume for these purposes that this valuation is correct, although in the real world, determinations of value often play a central role in a bankruptcy case.) Through the transfer of the machines, Seat Co. has effectively deprived its other creditors of forty thousand dollars, that is, the value of the equipment over and above the amount owed to the single creditor who received the transfer. This example thus illustrates constructive, as opposed to actual, fraud on creditors.

The avoiding powers entitle the debtor or trustee to recover the amount in excess of the sixty thousand dollars that the creditor was owed, namely, forty thousand dollars. This can be accomplished in a variety of ways. The creditor can repay the estate forty thousand dollars or it can return the equipment (valued at one hundred thousand dollars) and obtain a lien on the returned equipment to the extent of sixty thousand dollars. The creditor that received the equipment in satisfaction of its debt obviously will not be pleased with this result, as it considered the deal done. Indeed, if this transfer took place within ninety days before bankruptcy, the sixty thousand dollars would constitute a preferential transfer and the creditor would have to return it as well.

Hypothetical Lien Creditors

Finally, the debtor (or trustee) can act as a secured creditor or judgment lien creditor as of the bankruptcy filing date. This ability is specifically dubbed the trustee's strong arm powers. Through application of the strong arm power, any unperfected secured creditor will be subordinated to the rights of the debtor. Suppose, for example, that Seat Co. wants to borrow five hundred thousand dollars from a bank several years before the bankruptcy. The bank tells Seat Co. that it will lend the money only if it can take a security interest in the company's present and future inventory. In order to have a first-priority security interest in inventory under state law, the bank has to file financing statements with the secretary of state; assume that the bank fails to file the requisite documents. Upon the filing of Seat Co.'s bankruptcy, the bank asserts that it is entitled to all of the company's inventory. At this juncture the debtor, standing in the shoes of the trustee, will use the strong arm power. Seat Co. will assert that because the bank failed to perfect its interest in the inventory (by failing to file the necessary documents with the secretary of state), the bank is now only an unsecured creditor. Hence, it has no rights to the inventory, which will remain property of the estate. The inventory will be available for distribution to all unsecured creditors (which would include the bank).

All the avoiding powers reveal an effort to equalize the distribution among creditors. It is for this reason that their operation is of particular interest to those who are concerned about the rights of creditors. These powers are an effective mechanism for increasing the size of the pool of assets. And, arguably, it is overall more efficient to force some creditors to disgorge than to let individual creditors race to the courthouse. This reasoning assumes that had creditors thought about all this beforehand and acted as rational economic maximizers, they would have wanted distributions to be equalized. A given creditor may have to disgorge monies in one case, but in subsequent cases that same creditor will benefit from other creditors' having to disgorge. Additionally, creditors can plan their behavior (how much to lend, and when and on what basis to be repaid) based on their knowledge of the avoiding powers.

Distributing the Property

Once there is an estate, the debtor's determination to liquidate or reorganize becomes relevant. If the debtor is liquidating, a trustee is appointed, and that trustee sells the debtor's assets and distributes the available proceeds to creditors on a pro rata basis.[15] The Code states that a limited group of creditors are entitled to be paid ahead of others. The types of debts that become a priority include administrative expenses (lawyers' fees belong in this category), unpaid employee wages and benefits earned within ninety days before bankruptcy up to a prescribed cap of four thousand dollars, consumer deposits up to a prescribed ceiling of eighteen hundred dollars, and certain state and federal tax liabilities. After priority claims, unsecured creditors are paid, and thereafter, if anything is left over, the remaining sum is remitted back to the debtor.

After payment of priority expenses, frequently nothing is left over for the unsecured, nonpriority creditors. In this situation, bankruptcy is, in essence, a mechanism for cleansing the debtor of unpaid prebankruptcy obligations.[16] Indeed, after discharge, creditors are prohibited from pursuing the debtors for past obligations, and the government and private employers are prohibited from discriminating against individual debtors solely because relief was sought under the bankruptcy laws. In a sense, the discharge and antidiscrimination provisions are like a permanent injunction in that they bar future efforts by creditors and others to diminish the relief a debtor receives through bankruptcy.

For the debtor who is reorganizing, the goal is to structure a plan, which is like a contractual agreement in many ways, one being that it requires approval.[17] The plan must satisfy the Bankruptcy Code's standards of confirmation, which differ in some respects for individual and corporate debtors. All plans of reorganization must be proposed in good faith and must pay creditors at least as much as they would receive in a liquidation case. Like a liquidation case, priority expenses, including the costs of administration, are paid ahead of other classes of claims.

An important feature of all reorganization cases is that a plan binds creditors, even those who do not like what the plan provides or did not vote in favor of it. There are limits on how a debtor can treat creditors, some of which are prescribed by the Bankruptcy Code and others of which derive from constitutional law protections.[18] But many creditors and outsiders trying to understand the bankruptcy process are shocked to learn that creditors' rights can be changed in bankruptcy without their consent. Equally surprising is the extent of those changes. Thus although a plan is a contract in some respects, it is not a situation in which the parties are free to bargain unconstrained; each party's bargaining is orchestrated by what the Bankruptcy Code permits and prohibits.

Suppose that one of Seat Co.'s banks lent it five hundred thousand dollars. Assume that the bank held a valid and perfected security interest in the debtor's present and future inventory of finished seat belts, which could not be upset by the trustee standing in the shoes of a hypothetical lien creditor. Suppose that Seat Co. obtains a huge order in April to supply its belts to Ford Motor Co. in exchange for payment sixty days after shipment. In May, Seat Co. ships three hundred thousand dollars' worth of inventory to Ford. Seat Co.'s remaining inventory totals two hundred thousand dollars in value. Suppose that on May 15, Seat Co. defaults on its loan to the bank. At that point, the bank is owed five hundred thousand dollars, but the company's existing inventory is valued at only two hundred thousand dollars (assuming that no work in progress of any value exists).

Outside a bankruptcy, the bank would move to recover the on-hand inventory and would sell it and retain the proceeds (to which its security interest also attaches).[19] Because of the remaining shortfall of three hundred thousand dollars, the bank would try to get the debtor to grant it an interest in other valuable collateral, and it would continue to collect monies from all future inventory that was produced. That is, the bank would be able to become proactive and take concrete steps to collect.

A bankruptcy filing changes all that.[20] Four major differences can be observed immediately. First, on the date of filing, the bank is deemed secured only to the extent of the value of the collateral then in existence (and any proceeds therefrom), namely, two hundred thousand dollars. Therefore, the bank has a secured claim of two hundred thousand dollars and an unsecured claim of three hundred thousand dollars against Seat Co. This aspect of the treatment of a secured creditor is not all that shocking. Under state law outside of bankruptcy, a secured creditor is secured only to the extent of the value of collateral. The bank's interest in the future inventory, however, is cut off by the filing; the bank's interest is limited to the inventory (and its proceeds) in existence on the date of filing.

Second, the bank is precluded by the automatic stay from recovering the two hundred thousand dollars in inventory now in the debtor's hands. The Code protects a debtor from being dismantled piecemeal by its creditors; as long as that inventory is not decreasing in value, the bank cannot touch it. If the debtor sells the inventory, the bank does retain an interest in the proceeds generated by the sale but cannot necessarily recover the proceeds.

Third, the bank is precluded from trying to obtain additional collateral from the debtor to make up for the shortfall in inventory. The stay stops the bank from trying to capture additional property of the debtor on the theory that such property now belongs to the estate generally and must be used to protect *all* creditors, not just the bank's undersecured claim.

Finally, the bank, if it had some of the debtor's inventory, could not proceed to dispose of this inventory through a foreclosure sale. Again, absent debtor consent, the automatic stay precludes the bank from exercising its remedial options under state law. Instead, it permits the debtor to dispose of the collateral as long as the bank retains its lien in the proceeds.

The consequences of these changes are dramatic. Because funds are frequently insufficient to pay all unsecured creditors in full, the bank will find itself paid in bankruptcy dollars on the portion of its claim that is unsecured (three hundred thousand dollars). The bank cannot try to improve its position as it could under state law; the bank's undersecured portion of the claim is treated like the unsecured claim of every other unsecured creditor.

As if these four differences were not enough, the bank creditor is not entitled to an immediate cash-out of the secured portion of its claim.[21] Bankruptcy law does not require that the secured portion of the claim (two hundred thousand dollars) be paid in cash on confirmation of the plan. Instead, Seat Co. can stretch out payments to the bank as long as the present value of the bank's claim equals two hundred thousand dollars. In other words, Seat Co. has to pay the bank a sum equal to what the bank would be paid if it were paid immediately.

Consider this concrete example. Assume that current market interest rates are 10% per annum. If Seat Co. so chose, it could pay the creditor bank $220,000 one year after confirmation, namely, the principal of $200,000 plus 10% simple interest ($20,000) for the use (time value) of the money. Alternatively, Seat Co. could choose to pay the bank the $200,000 it owes in four equal installments of $50,000 over the next four years, plus interest equal to what the principal sum would have earned had it been paid immediately on confirmation (again, time value of money). Assuming simple interest (for the sake of simplifying the calculations) at a noncompounding rate of 10% per annum, the required payments would be

$70,000 at the end of year one ($50,000 in principal and $20,000 in interest), $65,000 at the end of year two ($50,000 in principal and $15,000 in interest on the then-unpaid principal of $150,000), $60,000 at the end of year three ($50,000 in principal and $10,000 in interest), and $ 55,000 at the end of year four ($50,000 in principal and $5,000 in interest). It is the debtor, Seat Co.—not the bank— that selects the payment option, although the arrangements are commonly negotiated to curtail litigation. These options may trouble creditors, but the courts have been clear in stating that the options do not change the value of what the secured creditor is getting (in a monetary sense). What is changed is *when* the creditor will be paid. Forcing a stretched-out payment onto a secured creditor against its will has not-so-politely been termed "cramdown."

The previous two chapters have provided an overview of how the Code treats debtors and creditors. In broad strokes, these chapters speak to how the bankruptcy system is designed to operate. But to probe these provisions more fully, we need to look at what is actually happening within the bankruptcy system. A statute does not address who chooses to seek bankruptcy relief and how successful that relief is. It does not speak to the consequences of filing on creditors and communities. In order to examine these reality-based issues, we need to look at empirical data of the Bankruptcy Code in action.

CHAPTER FOUR

Empiricism and Bankruptcy

Many people outside the bankruptcy field may assume that a great deal is known about debtors and creditors: exactly how many debtors seek bankruptcy relief, why they choose to file for bankruptcy, what they experience during the bankruptcy process, and the condition in which they emerge from bankruptcy—both economically and psychodynamically. Similarly, people probably assume that we know who debtors' creditors are, how many creditors and equity holders are affected by bankruptcies, and the extent of bankruptcy's impact on them. People may believe that we have a good sense of the nature and extent of bankruptcy's impact on debtors, creditors, and their respective communities. Unfortunately, nothing could be farther from the truth.[1]

The Absence of Data

Despite a growing number of thoughtful studies on the bankruptcy system,[2] a great deal of information has not been gathered. The complex U.S. bankruptcy system has been formulated based on limited empirical data. Ultimately, we may want to formulate a bankruptcy system based on perceptions—idealized or not—of the bankruptcy world and its participants. But before doing so, we should be able to distinguish what actually exists from what we hypothesize reality to be.

There are several obvious and many less obvious reasons for the lack of adequate empirical data about bankruptcy. First, bankruptcy has traditionally been viewed as a topic solely within the legal domain. And within the law, it has not been regarded (until the

advent of the mega cases) as an area of prominence, as are constitutional law, criminal law, and even basic commercial law. Only
since the 1970s have big law firms in major cities become involved
in bankruptcy matters.[3] Additionally, until the 1980s, few scholars
had dedicated much time and attention to bankruptcy issues, and
the field has only in the past fifteen years generated a sizable body
of scholarship that moves beyond a description of what the law currently is.[4] Moreover, empirical research of any kind is costly, time-
consuming, and difficult, and its importance in all legal fields has
been undervalued by legal scholars. This has caused law professors
to shy even farther away from collection of empirical data and
instead to focus on theoretical models for addressing legal problems, including bankruptcy.[5] This outside-in approach may not
yield as fruitful or complete an analysis as one that starts from the
inside and works out to a broader theoretical framework.

Other reasons, peculiar to bankruptcy, also account for the reluc-
tance to do empirical research. The bankruptcy system is remarkably complex, involving a wide range of individuals and entities. The
number of bankruptcy filings in the United States—more than
920,000 in 1995 alone—creates an enormous data base, and the number of separate legal disputes within any single bankruptcy case can
be vast (including, for example, stay litigation, claims resolution,
and recovery of preferences). Assuming that one has the ability to
cope with the morass of information, there is no easy, cost-effective
way to access the data. To do a nationwide hard-data study of every
case, a researcher would have to obtain information from courthouses
around the country. In the 1990s, many courts have introduced, and
others are instituting, telephonic links to data in case files, enabling
a researcher (or lawyers) to call courthouses and obtain information.[6] But even though researchers might not have to travel to each
courthouse, the costs of any nationwide study would be enormous.
And even if scholars had access to all the case files in all the courts,
these filed documents would tell only part of the bankruptcy story.

The court papers primarily reveal the aspects of bankruptcy that
are addressed by the courts. They do not show what happens outside

the courthouse—the negotiations that failed or succeeded, the sense of success or failure a debtor and creditor experience, or the impact of a debtor's bankruptcy on those whose names do not appear in the bankruptcy files. The data do not necessarily explain what led a debtor into bankruptcy or a creditor to lend. The data also do not follow a debtor and the creditors after filing and thus do not assess the long-term success or failure of the chosen approach. Finally, the data do not wrestle with bankruptcy's impact on communities. The data are thus limited in terms of both the time period covered and the nature of the information collected.

Further, the story told in the court papers is not always accurate. This is not because the debtors or creditors are falsifying records. Rather, a great deal of uncertainty accompanies bankruptcy issues. The dollar amounts of assets or liabilities, for example, often reflect only a debtor or creditor's best "guesstimate," and the guesstimate is often refined as a case progresses. Therefore, information found in early documents in a case may later be contradicted in a different context with no cross-referencing to assist a researcher. Moreover, the debtor and creditors are often required to value specific property, and this valuation is, in and of itself, an inexact science. The method of valuation can differ depending on why the valuation is needed, and a valuation in one context is not necessarily binding in another. Further, the value of property can change from the beginning of a case to the end.[7]

Risks of Limited Data

These problems account for why much of the existing bankruptcy data are based on small-scale empirical studies of select groups within the bankruptcy system, often within select geographical regions. One well-publicized (and often-criticized) study of Chapter 11, for example, addressed only the cases of publicly traded companies.[8] Another study investigated confirmation and consummation of Chapter 11 cases in one region of a large, arguably unrepresentative state.[9] Another major study focused on individual debtors in only three, albeit diverse, states.[10] Yet another study expressed a theory of corporate bankruptcy based on data from three mega cases in Chapter 11, even though these three cases were not representative of all mega cases, let alone all reorganization cases.[11] Another detailed study involved a single mega-case filing.[12] And finally, one study looked at costs of small-business cases filed in one city.[13] These examples illustrate the growing number of important but limited studies of the bankruptcy system. They could be defined as micro data studies, which, like their counterparts in economics, focus on a narrow range of items rather than assessing the whole.

These micro studies are valuable. They provide some insights into the real world of bankruptcy as seen by those participating in the system. But, like a little knowledge, a little data can be a dangerous thing. Limited data can cause people to make incorrect inferences. A study can always be tailored to demonstrate what someone wants to prove. And even the most carefully crafted studies are not truly objective.[14] Decisions concerning what is chosen to be studied, how a study is constructed, and how it is interpreted are made based on value judgments that can affect what is and—often more important—what is not derived from data.

Another risk of limited data is particular to bankruptcy. The practice of gathering data on a limited category of debtors or creditors in representative geographic regions and then extrapolating to national norms involves the assumption that the chosen regions reflect the nation. Frequently, they do not. Although Article I, Section 8, of the U.S. Constitution requires a uniform system of bankruptcy law, the law operates differently in different parts of the country. The words of the bankruptcy statute itself are uniform across the country, but the function of those words, what they mean in practice, is subject to considerable variation. Some of this difference is a result of differing judicial temperaments, local legal cultures, and diverse client-lawyer counseling strategies. It is also partly due to the odd interplay between state laws and the federal bankruptcy law. In various contexts, the federal bankruptcy law relies on state law to determine the underlying rights of debtors and creditors. Therefore, uniformity exists in the sense that the federal law consistently requires reference to state law. But because state laws differ so dramatically, uniformity does not exist in consequence.[15]

How a creditor perfects a security interest, for example, varies from state to state. Because the Bankruptcy Code looks to state law to determine issues of perfection, identically situated creditors operating in different states can be treated differently from one another. One creditor could end up with a perfected interest (and hence a priority), while another creditor could be deprived of its perfected status. Indeed, judges within a single state can interpret the rules of perfection differently. The *federal* law is uniform: perfection is governed uniformly by state law. What is not uniform is the way a creditor is treated under state laws. So a study on the effects of a bankruptcy filing on creditors in one state could produce dramatically different results from a similar study conducted in another state, and these differences would hinge on both inter- and intrastate disparities.

The difficulties created by disparate state laws governing perfection have not gone completely unnoticed. In 1994, Congress amended Section 552(b) of the bankruptcy law to deal more uniformly with the treatment of rents and fees from hotel property. Prior to this legislative change (which regrettably is fraught with its own ambiguities), hotel revenues were not considered rents under some state laws, and even if they were considered rents, they could not be perfected before bankruptcy. Under the new legislation, unless a court orders otherwise, rents and hotel revenues provided for in a security agreement can be treated as perfected even though state perfection requirements are not satisfied.[16] But this single legislative fix does not solve the broader problem.

The problems of limited data collection are evidenced by the following nonbankruptcy example. Suppose we wanted to find out whether being left-handed affected longevity.[17] Assume that in 1992 we counted the number of left- and right-handed children in the third grade in Mineola, New York. Then suppose that in the same year we counted the number of left- and right-handed people in Mineola over the age of seventy-five. Suppose that the percentage of people over the age of seventy-five who were left-handed was significantly smaller than the percentage of children in the third grade who were left-handed. Would it be accurate to conclude that, nationwide, left-handed people die sooner than right-handed people?

Clearly, this conclusion is unwarranted based on the limited data presented. First of all, is Mineola, New York, representative of the entire United States? Second, was the third grade in Mineola representative of all grade-school-age children in Mineola? Did this third-grade group have the same number of students as other grades? Was the group balanced in terms of age, race, gender, and ethnicity? Were the percentages of left-handed and right-handed children consistent with national norms? Finally, are there other possible explanations for the limited number of left- and right-handed people in Mineola over the age of seventy-five? What if Mineola had very few senior citizens? This would mean that the two groups studied could not be compared easily. Perhaps the ratio of left- to right-handed people born over the past century has not remained constant. Or perhaps the social norm of seventy-five years ago that encompassed changing left-handed individuals into right-handed individuals accounts for the small number of left-handed individuals among senior citizens generally. The data simply do not prove what was sought. This does not make the conclusion wrong; it may be that left-handed people die sooner. But this conclusion has not been proved by the data.

The risks of relying on limited data are also evident in an example drawn from the context of bankruptcy. Based on certain empirical work (known as the Purdue Study, issued in 1981) that was challenged at the time and that has been challenged on many occasions since, Congress enacted a provision of the Bankruptcy Code, known as Section 707(b), in 1984 to curtail individual debtor abuse of the bankruptcy system. Stated simply, this section provides that the case of a consumer debtor can be dismissed if the case represents a substantial abuse of the bankruptcy system. Yet evidence suggests that this provision has not functioned as many, particularly those in the consumer credit industry, had hoped and anticipated.[18] First, the section has not been frequently used. Second, not only has individual debtor relief not declined, but it has significantly increased since the passage of Section 707(b). Finally, there is no judicial consensus as to what "substantial abuse" means, and hence the section has not yielded uniform results. Given these consequences, some members of Congress have tried to add even more teeth to this section. And therein lies the risk.

Establishing that filing rates have increased does not imply that debtor abuse exists or that Section 707(b) has failed to eradicate abuse, any more than showing that proportionately fewer elderly citizens in Mineola are left-handed demonstrates that left-handedness is correlated with early death. There may be multiple reasons why Section 707(b) has not produced the results many anticipated. Judges may not have had the time or interest to implement the section. Or the perceived debtor abuse simply may not exist, at least not in the contemplated proportions. Alternatively, whether abuse actually exists may depend on one's perspective. What is viewed as an abuse from the creditor's standpoint may not be viewed as abusive from the debtor's standpoint. Finally, other data suggest that the cause of rising bankruptcy rates and increased defaults is not debtor abuse, an endogenous factor, but an elusive combination of exogenous factors, including creditor behavior.[19] The cure for debtor abuse—in the form of either Section 707(b) as it now exists or a strengthened version—thus lacks utility. Further amendment will not produce better results from the creditors' perspective if the underlying data are incorrect or if the reason for high filing rates is unrelated to debtor conduct.

Understanding the Extant Data

In spite of the difficulties of bankruptcy data collection, the effort to amass this information should not stop. Looking at the existing information raises questions that, but for the data, would not have come to anyone's attention. Among the most difficult data to assess are those that appear the most simplistic, namely, the data about the number of filings within the bankruptcy system. This information, together with related data, form what could be termed macro bankruptcy data. It is the most basic information about what is happening in the world of bankruptcy. But uncovering what is happening in bankruptcy is anything but basic.

The Administrative Office of the United States Courts (AO) collects the largest amount of macro data on the bankruptcy system. These data are derived primarily from a cover sheet that accompanies the bankruptcy petition when it is filed in the clerk's office of each court. Although the AO is obtaining an ever increasing amount of data, its efforts, as freely admitted, are far from perfect or complete.

The AO chooses to collect only select information. This choice, understandably, is keyed to its own purposes. The AO is charged with collecting information for all U.S. federal courts in order to develop more efficient court systems. Concern has been expressed as to whether the AO gathers all the data needed for its own goals; clearly, it does not collect data on other issues that may be of interest to scholars and others outside the court system. The AO does not supply information on, for example, the gender, race, ethnicity, or age of debtors. Data about the nature of the creditors are lacking. The AO could, but does not, determine how much the creditors are owed, and it does not analyze the composition of the overall body of creditors in terms of their size of business, legal status, and nature. Similar information about equity holders and debenture holders is also lacking. No one keeps track of how much money is ultimately distributed to creditors or equity holders. The effect one bankruptcy filing has on other local businesses or individuals is also unknown. Some people may be discouraged to realize that more is known about the mating habits of fruit flies and moths than about those involved in the bankruptcy system.[20]

What could be learned if more data existed? With data on the gender, race, ethnicity, and age of individual debtors, we could determine if any of these factors affected filing rates. These data would interest not just lawyers but sociologists, historians, educators, and anthropologists. Suppose, and this is purely speculation, that women of color were using the bankruptcy system significantly less frequently, nationally and even regionally, than any other group of individuals—whether white men, white women, or men of color. This finding would make researchers wonder what caused the hypothesized differences in filing rates. Are women of color denied access to bankruptcy relief because they cannot pay the bankruptcy filing fee or the requisite fees for legal representation? Is the bankruptcy system failing to offer them the type of relief they actually need? Are they less aware of the benefits bankruptcy can offer? Are women of color finding other, either more or less beneficial, ways of resolving their financial problems? Are they able to obtain credit in the first instance? Are they experiencing fewer financial problems?

Both current and retrospective macro data relating to gender, race, age, or ethnicity would also be important for ascertaining trends related to filing rates. With the growing extension of credit to women and the increasing feminization of poverty, for example, have women's filing rates showed dramatic increases over the past thirty years? If they have not, are women obtaining financial relief, and if so, where and how? If the rates have gone up, can ways be developed to help women out of the cycle of poverty of which they have become a part? Suppose the age of individual debtors has increased. If many elderly individuals are accessing the system, then American society should reassess what a fresh start means for them and what is needed to preserve their security in old age. Relying on their future earning capacity as a basis for relief in bankruptcy is problematic at best.

At present we cannot answer even a basic question about whether race, gender, ethnicity, or age affects filing rates. To gather this sort of data on a current basis would not be particularly difficult. The cover sheet that every debtor fills out in conjunction with filing a bankruptcy petition could request this information. The information could then, with some incremental labor and computing costs, be put into the computer data base of material collected about debtors' filings. The government may be concerned that obtaining this type of data will violate debtors' privacy, although the worry could be alleviated by allowing the debtor to choose whether to divulge the information. Even if some individuals chose not to participate (which would skew the data), at least the beginnings of an important data base could be assembled.

Some signs indicate that this type of work is under way. The Office of the United States Trustee has begun nationwide data collection, and Teresa Sullivan, Elizabeth Warren, and Jay Westbrook have expanded their 1982–83 study to include more detailed information regarding gender, race, ethnicity, and age of individual debtors from a broader spectrum of states.[21] Other empirical studies by individuals and by such organizations as the American Bankruptcy Institute are in progress.

Even with these inroads, serious problems accompany the retrieval of past and current data. I have found that identifying a debtor's gender by examining a case file is possible in most cases, though far from easy. But race, ethnicity, and age are much harder to identify, as a petitioner's name alone does not supply this information.

Two of my collaborators and I, funded by the National Conference of Bankruptcy Judges Educational Endowment Fund, set out to find the first women to seek bankruptcy relief under the United States' early bankruptcy laws, which were in existence for a total of five years, from 1800 to 1803 and from 1841 to 1843. To find these women debtors, we had to travel to the regional archives around the country that housed bankruptcy files from the nineteenth century. For some regions, we consulted docket books that listed the names of all debtors. Then we identified and retrieved the files of those who appeared to have women's names. For other regions, where there were no dockets, we looked at every case file to identify a woman's name. In total, we reviewed more than twenty-seven thousand cases and identified forty-nine women who sought federal bankruptcy relief—in and of itself a significant historical finding. We cannot be sure, however, that we found all the women debtors. Some case files during this period were either missing or destroyed, and some women's names were difficult to identify. Further, women debtors who did not file under their own names but were a part of their husbands' bankruptcy cases were not identified. And the information in the bankruptcy files that we reviewed was sometimes sketchy. Although we could determine gender, we were frequently unable, without additional research, to determine a debtor's age, marital status, race, and ethnicity. So what we found is the floor: at least forty-nine women sought federal bankruptcy relief before the mid-nineteenth century.[22]

An extraordinary amount of information could be gathered from a comprehensive study of aspects of the current bankruptcy system. Congress, for example, has called for a study of the pilot in forma pauperis program and a report on the costs and benefits of the program. Although the legislation does not define what costs and benefits should be evaluated, an expansive interpretation of these terms could yield important data on the individuals who use the bankruptcy system:

- The demographics of the debtors filing in forma pauperis (IFP Debtors), including their race, gender, ethnicity, national origin, age, marital status, number of dependents (children, infirm individuals, or elderly people), and occupation
- The demographics of the creditors of IFP Debtors, including information on when the debts were incurred, the amounts unpaid, the nature of the obligations, the debtors' payment

history, monitoring activities conducted by the creditors, and creditor collection efforts under applicable state law

- The amount of property IFP Debtors have, including an assessment of whether the property is exempt under federal or state law
- Descriptive information, obtained in interviews with IFP Debtors, determining what gave rise to their financial difficulty, including information on their family, medical, and employment history
- A follow-up assessment of what happened to the IFP Debtors during and after entry into the bankruptcy system
- An evaluation of the type and quality of the legal representation the IFP Debtors received during the bankruptcy case
- Information from interviews with bankruptcy judges, trustees, and U.S. Trustees determining how the cases of IFP Debtors progress in comparison to individual debtor cases not filed in forma pauperis

Obtaining this kind of data from in forma pauperis debtors since the inception of the pilot program would be useful on several fronts. It would allow an evaluation of the pilot program based on a better understanding of the debtors and creditors who partook of its benefits. It would provide a "before, during, and after" snapshot. It would enable people to see the context in which in forma pauperis would be operating. And perhaps once we as a society know who our poorest debtors are and what their needs are, we can work to make their lives, within and outside the bankruptcy system, better. Perhaps an understanding of what led debtors into bankruptcy can enable the development of programs to curtail bankruptcy filings in the first instance. Perhaps an understanding of the behavior of creditors will signal ways the extension, monitoring, and repayment of credit can be improved.[23]

As for the AO data, the omissions are not their only troubling aspect. First, cases are classified as business or nonbusiness, and these classifications are problematic, as the AO admits. How to determine a business filing is by no means clear, and the criteria supplied to local clerks' offices are not uniformly applied. It is easy to see that the filing of a publicly traded company falls into the category of business. But personal bankruptcy cases are not so easily classified. An individual debtor could have incurred business-related debt that shows up on the list of creditors as credit card debt. Suppose our hypothetical Smythe's credit card debts are for mechanic's tools that Smythe purchased for repairing cars at home. Suppose he injured the pedestrian while driving his car to the location of a stranded vehicle. He then has business-related debts that appear to be personal, and his filing could erroneously be characterized as personal.

Additionally, not all the data the AO collects is readily ascertainable by the public, and the available data are not published in a single location. Further, the type of data the AO collects (such as the number of filings by chapter and region) homogenizes the bankruptcy system. Looking only at the number of cases fails to reveal the marked diversity among debtors in terms of the amounts they owe, the nature of their obligations, and the reasons for their nonpayment. Lumped together under personal filings could be a nonmarried individual with children, a nonworking wife and a working husband filing jointly, a wealthy doctor, a former bank officer, and a single individual like Jason Smythe. Business debtors could include a small family-owned business, a medium-sized retailer, a large real estate development partnership, an airline, a health maintenance organization, and a local manufacturing business like Seat Co. All these difficulties notwithstanding, the AO data constitute the biggest existing data base on bankruptcy cases and hence are a useful starting place.

If empirical data (whether from the AO or elsewhere) are so problematic, one might ask why even bother with them. If the data currently collected are not complete and can, in some instances, be downright misleading, perhaps we should just continue as we have done, formulating policy based on what seems right from a theoretical perspective. Problems in capturing and interpreting bankruptcy data, however, do not mean that existing data are worthless and that the task of collecting data is impossible. We can, within limits, gather different kinds of data that will better inform our decision making about bankruptcy. We can look at information that will enable us to see more than numbers. We can collect data that will help us see what is actually happening to the people within the system. We can ask new questions and investigate more complexities. In the interim, life in the world of bankruptcy does not stop. So we can still move ahead in our thinking about bankruptcy, using the limited material that currently is available, including data from the AO. We proceed, though, armed with cautionary flags.

CHAPTER FIVE

What Is Transpiring in the Bankruptcy System?

The most commonly cited bankruptcy statistic involves the number of cases filed. Newspaper headlines broadcast these statistics, whether the filings are up or down: "Personal Bankruptcies Increased 21.5 Percent in 1991," "Bankruptcy Filings Set Record," "U.S. Bankruptcy Filings Hit Peak," "Business Bankruptcy Filings Keeping Courts Busy," "Business Failures Hit Record Levels," "California Leads Nation In Bankruptcy Filings," "Fewer Business Bankruptcies," "Bankruptcy Party Crashes, Filings Fall 14%," "Hard Times Hit Bankruptcy Law." Indeed, the numbers are impressive.[1] More than 8.9 million cases have been filed since the Code went into operation. For the calendar year 1991, there were 943,987 bankruptcy filings; the filings for 1992 were 971,517. Between 1984 and 1992, filings increased by more than 179% (figure 3).

Behind these numbers lies a wealth of other information that can inform an analysis of what is happening in the bankruptcy system. Consider the following questions: How many debtors and creditors are actually involved in the bankruptcy system? Did all the debtors go into bankruptcy voluntarily, or was there a significant number of involuntary filings? As a percentage of the population, have filings increased? On a per household or per business basis, have filings increased evenly nationwide? Have the increases and decreases in filings been uniform around the country? Have the increases and decreases happened in all types of cases, whether personal or business? Are the increases and decreases the same for Chapters 7, 9, 11, 12, and 13? Do the increases and decreases occur uniformly

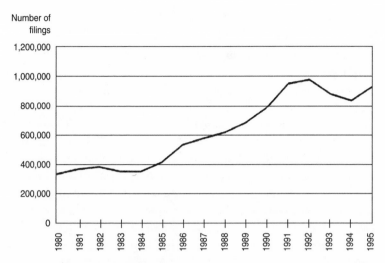

Figure 3. Bankruptcy filings, 1980–95

throughout the year? How well is the bankruptcy system handling the huge volume of filings? This is, at one level, a purely administrative issue, one of whether the existing structure to oversee bankruptcy administration is overtaxed. What is the caseload for judges, and does it vary across the country? How much time do bankruptcy judges spend on their cases? Do certain types of cases require more time than others? How are the claims of creditors processed? At another level, the volume of cases raises questions about other kinds of costs—for example, the costs to creditors to recover what they are owed, the costs of waiting for distributions, and the costs of obtaining legal representation. And then there are bankruptcy's less quantifiable costs: the cost of more than a million bankruptcy filings for individuals, families, businesses, communities, and society.

What Do the Numbers Mean?

Even though we do not yet have answers to many of these questions, the available information does give us a starting point, however shaky, for considering how to think about bankruptcy data. Begin with the filing figures. The number of filings in a single year does not reveal anything about the rate of bankruptcy filings, and understanding rates is what enables people to observe upward and downward trends. Between 1989 and 1990, the rate of filing of bankruptcy cases increased by more than 15%. Between 1990 and 1991, the rate of filings increased by more than 20.5%. This shows dramatic, almost frightening growth, not just in absolute numbers but in percentages. It also suggests a trend: upward filing rates. The number of filings in 1992 was then the largest in American history. But the most significant factor regarding the 1992 filings is not that they set this record. What is more important is that the rate of increase from 1991 to 1992 was 2.9%, the smallest gain in eight years. Indeed, in some regions of the country filings actually decreased in late 1991 and into 1992. Total filings in 1993 reveal a decrease of 9.9% over 1992, although filings actually increased in a few regions of the country. In 1994, although total filings were again down, what is significant is that the rate of decrease was slower—less than 5%. For 1995, filings were up, as was the rate of increase (over 10%). The trend over recent years is clear: the overall number of filings went up until the end of 1992 and beginning of 1993. Filings for 1994 reveal a decline from the 1993 figures. Figures for 1995 were up (see figure 3). Early projections for the mid- to late 1990s suggest that filings are on the increase again, and filings will reach 1 million per year for 1996.

Number of Filings versus Number of Debtors

The number of petitions filed is an incomplete statistic in that it does not correlate perfectly with the number of actual individuals and businesses that have sought bankruptcy relief. A single petition, for example, could involve more than one debtor. According to the methodology of the AO, a joint filing between a husband and a wife counts as one petition. But it actually involves two debtors. Therefore, the number of filings is underinclusive as it relates to joint filings. The AO keeps data on the number of joint filings annually, and for 1991 this number was 333,558. This would increase the number of debtors filing in 1991 by 333,558, meaning that more than 1.27 million debtors were involved that year in the bankruptcy process. Similarly, in 1992, approximately 35% of filings were joint. Moreover, it is likely, because joint filings are available only to spouses, that some other petitions of individual debtors involve the debts of a lover or a family member. Only one bankruptcy petition would be filed, but one or more of the debtors would not officially appear on any court papers and hence would not be counted. No data are available to determine how common this situation is.

Conversely, multiple petitions could be filed for what is, in fact, one person or entity. One debtor can file separate petitions under several names (Jason Smythe, Jason Smythe Auto Repairs, Jason Smythe d/b/a Smythe's Repairs) and receive separate case numbers for each petition. Additionally, petitions could be filed for several or many corporations, all of which are distinct legal entities but which function as one entity in the business world. Within the bankruptcy system, many of these cases will be administratively consolidated, that is, dealt with as a single unit for administrative convenience. Yet the AO counts each entity separately. Also, debtors may file for relief more than once in a single year due to a dismissal of an earlier filing (such debtors are typically termed repeat filers), and the AO would thus count them twice. The numbers relating to overinclusiveness do not fall into categories of data officially maintained by the AO. But an informal study conducted by Ernst & Young for the AO on Chapter 11 cases revealed that 16.7% of the cases with confirmed plans were substantively consolidated. Consolidation was more likely in the Southern District of New York, where some of the largest cases are filed.[2] Indeed, Ernst & Young found that the higher the assets, debts, and proposed payment amounts, the greater the likelihood of consolidation.

Because the number of corporate filings is significantly less than the number of individual filings, it is fair to assume that the net increase because of joint filings (the problem of underinclusiveness) will far outweigh the decrease caused by multiple corporate filings and repeat filers (the problem of overinclusiveness). Taking into account estimates of the possible additions (more than 330,000) and deletions (less than 100,000), we can speculate that the number of individuals and businesses that were debtors in 1991 exceeded 1.17 million. The figures for 1992 would be slightly higher, and those for 1993 and 1994, somewhat lower. The AO data on the number of filings thus provides only a rough estimate of the number of debtors who sought bankruptcy relief in a given year.

Counting Creditors

The estimate of the actual number of debtors annually only begins to describe the dimensions of the bankruptcy system. If one considers the number of creditors, equity holders, employees, retirees, families, and communities that are affected by bankruptcy, the numbers grow exponentially. But there is no easy way of tallying the total. At a basic level, the number of creditors can be obtained by counting those involved in each case and then adding them up. Notice, though, that the actual number of creditors is different from the identity of the creditors. Some creditors are likely to appear in more than one bankruptcy case. A credit card company such as American Express, for example, has lent to a large number of individuals who file for bankruptcy. Similarly, a large national bank, such as Citibank or Chase Manhattan Bank, could have lent to a number of companies that are in bankruptcy. Suppliers in an industry hit by the recession could also find that more than one of their customers is in bankruptcy. In the retailing industry, both Macy's and Alexander's sought Chapter 11 relief within months of each other. Creditors involved in both cases included dress designers, cosmetic suppliers, and shoe designers, to name but a few. So the total number of creditors in all bankruptcy cases is much greater than the actual number of individual creditors.

Further, what constitutes a creditor for bankruptcy purposes is an exquisitely complex question. Certain categories of creditors are clear: entities that extended credit to a debtor on a secured or unsecured basis, such as trade creditors, banks, utilities, and leasing companies. Suppose, however, that the debtor had provided extended service contracts beyond the manufacturer's warranty period on products sold to hundreds of thousands of consumers. Such audio and appliance stores as Crazy Eddie, Newmark & Lewis, and Nobody Beats the Wiz are examples of entities that could have operated in this manner. When such debtors go into bankruptcy, the hundreds of holders of the service contracts are creditors. Suppose a debtor airline that ceases operations had a frequent flyer program; the thousands of holders of unused mileage benefits are creditors of that airline. Suppose the debtor had manufactured a product that could produce extensive personal injury. Those individuals injured at the time the manufacturer went into bankruptcy would unquestionably be creditors. But injuries commonly do not manifest themselves immediately. Moreover, some individuals, though exposed, might never experience ill effects. Whether these potentially-to-be-injured individuals are creditors is an issue raised by cases involving such entities as Johns-Manville, A. H. Robins, Dow Corning, and Piper Aircraft.

Several pieces of statistical information may supply a preliminary sense of the number of creditors involved in individual debtor cases. One source estimates that, on average, 13 claims are filed in each Chapter 7 and Chapter 13 case.[3] Another group of scholars found that among 1,529 individual debtor cases, 23,426 creditors could be identified. Without adjustments upward or downward for duplicative, missing, or erroneous creditors, this works out to about 15 creditors per individual case.[4] If one accepts for a moment that nonbusiness filings totaled 872,438 in 1991 (this number is inflated because some individual cases actually involve business debt) and multiplies that number by 13 creditors per case (a conservative number), one finds that more than 11.3 million creditors were involved in bankruptcy cases in 1991. As described, this number would have to be reduced by repeat or erroneous claims, which could be substantial in number. Still, the number of creditors is enormous. In a

speech in 1992, United States Supreme Court Justice William Rehnquist estimated that between 15 million and 20 million Americans
were either debtors or creditors in consumer cases.[5]

As for business cases, the debtors can range from small businesses
that employ only family members to large national and multina-
tional conglomerates with thousands of workers and hundreds of
locations. Although no organized data base exists for determining
the number of creditors in business cases, bankruptcy specialists
agree that this number, particularly in the mega cases, is enormous.
Poorman-Douglas Corporation, a claims-processing agent retained
in some large cases around the country, has estimated the number
of claims in these cases it handled:[6]

Company Name	Number of Creditors
Best Products	15,300
Braniff	47,200
Greyhound Lines	55,000
Orion Pictures	24,000
Total	141,500

Although these numbers must be viewed with caution, the figures
are startlingly large.

In cases involving mass torts, such as those of A. H. Robins (the
Dalkon Shield), Johns-Manville (asbestosis), and Dow Corning (sil-
icone implants), the number of existing and future claimants could
reach the tens of thousands.[7] In the Johns-Manville case, it was estimated that there were more than 110,000 possible future claimants.
Although mega Chapter 11 cases by no means constitute the bulk of
all filings (indeed, Chapter 11 cases constitute less than 3% of all
cases, and mega Chapter 11 cases make up less than 1% of all Chapter 11 cases),[8] these numbers do indicate the magnitude of the impact
of bankruptcy.

Extrapolating from existing studies, assume that on average, non-
mega business cases nationwide have 50 creditors per case, exclusive
of employees and retirees. Thus, conservatively, more than 2.6 million creditors are involved in these business cases annually. If one as-

sumes that 50 large- to mega-sized cases are filed annually (cases with assets exceeding $100 million ranged from 40 in 1993 to 70 in 1994) with 30,000 creditors per case, then more than 1.5 million creditors are involved in these cases. Adding the estimates of creditors in mega and nonmega cases, one can estimate that more than 4 million creditors are associated with the business cases filed annually.

Counting Workers, Retirees, and Beyond

Most business bankruptcy cases affect employees and retirees. Some employees will be creditors because they have not been paid their back or current wages. Others may be creditors because they have not been reimbursed for expense account items already incurred. Other employees will have contractual relationships with the debtor, including those for health care and pension benefits. If unfulfilled, these obligations will give rise to claims. Retirees will also have claims against the debtor if it fails to honor guarantees of pension and medical benefits. The number of employees and retirees affected by bankruptcy filings in the United States is not counted, but several figures provide insight into the dimensions of this group of individuals. The following table shows the number of employees in some of the largest bankruptcies filed over the past several years:

Company Name	Number of Employees
Restaurant Enterprises Group	36,750
Carter Hawley Hale Stores	36,000
Hills Department Stores	29,600
Farley	28,900
Best Products	24,900
Pan Am	24,600
Total	180,750

This is a significant number, and only six companies have been listed.

All these estimates of the numbers of creditors, employees, and retirees do not account for all the people and businesses affected by the bankruptcy system. Companies that are publicly traded have equity holders, and there is frequently more than one class of equity holders. The mechanics and cost of giving notice just to equity holders of the publicly traded companies that file annually (which number between approximately 40 and 125) must be recognized. And there are debt instruments that are frequently publicly traded and held by a wide range of individuals and institutions. Other cases involve limited partnership interests. These interests are held by hundreds of thousands of individuals and institutions. Approximately three hundred thousand notices, for example, were sent early in the Chapter 11 case of Integrated Resources to owners of record of limited partnership interests.[9]

Even if we could identify all these participants, the estimates of the number of people affected by bankruptcy are still low because some of these people will not appear in any of the bankruptcy documents filed with the court. Consider the nonfiling families and neighbors of debtors. Consider the businesses that are affected if another major business ceases to exist. Consider the families of the creditors and the creditors of the creditors who may be influenced by nonpayment. Consider the impact on the local community and its resources if a factory shuts down or retiree medical benefits are not paid. These are the people who experience bankruptcy's ripple effects. A study has been contemplated to try to assess how wide and far the ripple goes, and in the interim certain preliminary observations can be made by returning to the Seat Co. and Smythe scenarios.

Seat Co. has five hundred employees and seventy-five retirees. We have to consider bankruptcy's impact on each of these individuals and their families. Assume that Seat Co. has one hundred trade and bank creditors. If Seat Co. ceases to exist, the luncheonette that serviced the factory workers will fold, and this will affect another whole group of individuals and businesses. The dry cleaning service that washed employee uniforms will collapse, again affecting yet another group of individuals and businesses that do not appear in the bankruptcy files (until they themselves become debtors). And finally, the owners of Seat Co., a family business, will be affected.

Similarly, the pedestrian whom Smythe injured may have a family that she can no longer support financially. The trade school may be unable to continue to exist if enough students fail to repay loans. Certainly other students who need loans may not get them. Smythe's parents no doubt feel the effects of his financial downfall, although their names are nowhere in the papers filed with the bankruptcy court.

Indeed, at some level, the question of how many people are affected by the bankruptcy process is unanswerable. The number of cases filed annually is truly just the beginning.

The Lack of National Uniformity

The number of annual bankruptcy filings does not reveal another aspect of bankruptcy: the increases in filings are not uniform nationally. Between 1990 and 1991, overall filings increased by 20.5%. But in certain states, this percentage was considerably higher. In 1991 filings increased by more than 40% in six states: New Hampshire, Rhode Island, New Jersey, Maryland, Massachusetts, and Connecticut. One state, Alaska, had fewer filings in 1991 than in 1990. Similarly, whereas filings increased nationally by only 2.9% between 1991 and 1992, six states had increases of more than 14%: Delaware, Hawaii, Connecticut, Massachusetts, California, and Maryland. Notice the overlap of three states from the previous year's list.

Another way to look at filing rates is by geographic region. Between 1987 and 1991, for example, filings increased nationwide by 64%. In the Southwest of the United States (Fifth and Tenth Circuits), the increase for this period was 18%. In the Midwest (Sixth and Seventh Circuits), the increase was 57%. In the Northeast (First and Second Circuits), the increase was 203%.

Although these data tell us about increased filings overall in a state and region, they do not reveal whether that increase is evenly divided statewide or falls only within certain districts within a state. They also do not explain the reasons for the increase. One way of getting a better understanding of the increase is to look at a breakdown of cases by chapter (figure 4). Even though Chapter 11 cases

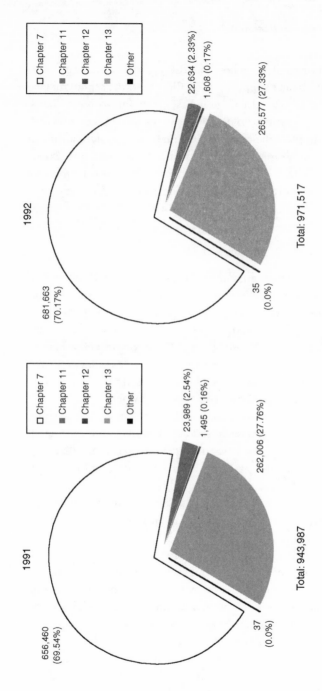

Figure 4. A breakdown of bankruptcy cases by chapter

receive the greatest public attention, their numbers are not great as a percentage of total filings. In 1991, Chapter 11 cases constituted approximately 2.5% of all filings.[10] Chapter 7 cases constituted the greatest number of filings, followed by Chapter 13. When viewed as a percentage of business cases only, Chapter 11 cases rise to 29% of the total.[11]

The increases in the number of cases between 1990 and 1991 are quite similar for each chapter: Chapter 7 cases increased by 21% while Chapter 13 cases increased by 20%; Chapter 11 cases increased by 15%. Between 1991 and 1992, however, the figures are different. The number of Chapter 7 and Chapter 13 cases increased, but the number of Chapter 11 cases decreased. This trend continued in 1993. These figures, however, mask several important issues. We need to consider whether these increases were in the business or nonbusiness cases (recognizing the problem with the distinction) and, once we know this, whether the increases can be correlated to the type of case filed (Chapter 7, 11, 12, or 13). We also need to look at patterns which reveal that certain locations have a greater number of certain types of cases than other locations. Finally, we need to evaluate the dollar values involved in filed cases.

The AO, in addition to categorizing cases on the basis of chapter type, divides all cases into two categories: business and nonbusiness. Even taking into consideration the general consensus that the statistics kept by the AO underestimate the number of business filings, nonbusiness filings greatly outnumber business filings. The AO's figures reveal that the ratio of business to nonbusiness filings over the past years has decreased. In 1984, for example, business cases totaled 18.4% of all filings. In 1988 business filings totaled 10.4% of all filings, and in 1991 business filings totaled 7.6% of all filings. In 1992, business filings dropped to 7.3% of all filings. In 1993, they dropped to 7.1%. In sum, the percentage of businesses accessing the bankruptcy system is decreasing over time, while the percentage of personal failures is increasing. But this important trend does not account for the number of personal bankruptcies that are actually business related. Because of the discharge provisions, among others, individuals with business-related debt may find themselves less favorably treated under the Code than corporate debtors.

It is accurate, however, that certain states have a greater percentage of nonbusiness filings per capita than other states. Similarly, certain states have a higher percentage than others of business failures per number of extant businesses in the state. Neither figure correlates with filing rates in that location. The highest numbers of personal bankruptcy filings per household in 1991 and 1992 were in Tennessee, Georgia, and Alabama. In 1992, there was one filing for every 47 households in Tennessee, and in Georgia and Alabama there were filings in one of every 52 and 56 households, respectively. By 1993, Nevada joined the list, ranking above Alabama. None of these states had the highest percentage increase in total filings. The states with the fewest personal bankruptcy filings from 1991 to 1993 were Hawaii, Vermont, and Maine. In Hawaii, there was one filing for every 348 households in 1991, while in Vermont and Maine, there were filings in one of every 282 and 238 households, respectively. But these states had relatively high rates of increase. Hawaii had the second-highest percentage increase (30%) in filings between 1991 and 1992, and it was the only state where filings increased in 1993.

In terms of business failures, the highest numbers of filings per number of businesses in the state in 1991 appear in Virginia, Georgia, and Arizona. In Virginia, there was one filing for every 59 businesses, while Georgia and Arizona had one filing for every 65 and 67 businesses, respectively. Virginia had the twelfth-highest increase for overall filings in 1991, but Arizona had among the lowest percentage increases for the same period. The states with the fewest filings per business in 1991 were Hawaii, Connecticut, and Colorado. In these states, fewer than one filing for every 256 businesses took place. Yet Connecticut had the sixth-highest increase in filings in the United States in 1991. So although we can distinguish between business and nonbusiness filings, the aggregate numbers do not tell us as much as might be expected, and the breakdown of the numbers on a state-by-state basis shows no easily identified pattern.

In certain regions of the United States, select types of filings are more prevalent, as data from 1991 show. In nine judicial districts, Chapter 13 cases accounted for more than one-half of all bankruptcy cases filed. The largest numbers of Chapter 13 cases were in Tennessee, Georgia, and Alabama. The most nonbusiness Chapter 7 cases were filed in California, Florida, and New York. Puerto Rico, North Carolina, Tennessee, Georgia, and Alabama had the fewest number of Chapter 7 cases in relation to Chapter 13 cases. North Dakota, Vermont, and South Dakota had the greatest number of Chapter 7 cases in relation to Chapter 13 cases. The mega Chapter 11 cases gravitated to the Southern District of New York and the Central District of California. These two districts accounted for 24% of the approximately 125 filings of public companies. The greatest number of Chapter 12 cases were filed in Texas (110), followed by Louisiana (90), California (72), Nebraska (69), and Ohio (69).

The Size of the Problem

Remarkably few data exist on the dollar values involved in bankruptcy cases, but some extrapolation based on the estimates collected by the AO and other sources is feasible. For the one-year period ending June 1991, the AO has estimated that Chapter 7 cases involve $24.4 billion in assets, Chapter 11 cases involve $57.4 billion in assets, and Chapter 13 cases involve $10.5 billion in assets. These figures, however, group business and nonbusiness cases together. It could be that the bulk of the assets in Chapter 7 cases involve business as opposed to nonbusiness Chapter 7 cases. Because business Chapter 7 cases constitute approximately 6% of Chapter 7 cases, the bulk of the assets could be in a limited number of cases. This situation is also prevalent in Chapter 11 cases. More than 86% of Chapter 11 cases involve a business. But depending on how one determines the ten largest Chapter 11 cases (of publicly traded companies) in any year, the assets in these largest cases constitute a disproportionate share of the total assets of Chapter 11 debtors. The AO estimates that the ten largest public cases filed in 1991 had assets of approximately $23 billion. For 1992, the number is even higher, with assets for the ten largest debtors exceeding $35 billion. For 1993, the figure drops significantly, as the ten largest cases had assets totaling "only" $8.6 billion. Other figures, however, show even higher total assets of the ten largest publicly traded companies filing in 1991: approximately $54 billion. If the assets of all Chapter 11 debtors totaled approximately $57 billion, by any measure, the largest cases involve a significant proportion of the total assets. Yet another set of numbers shows that the twenty largest publicly traded companies that filed for Chapter 11 relief in 1992 had assets totaling $66 billion—a number that exceeds the AO's estimate of assets in all Chapter 11 cases in that year.

These measurements do not provide a complete picture of the amount of money involved in the bankruptcy system. But even if we could quantify bankruptcy's monetary impact based on the assets, liabilities, and revenues of debtors under traditional economic measures, the picture would still be incomplete. Other, less easily quantifiable costs are involved in the bankruptcy system. Owing to quantification problems, some commentators believe that the welfare of communities, the continuity of existing businesses, and the preservation of self-worth and human dignity should not be considered within the bankruptcy process. But the inability to measure these interests easily in dollars and cents does not mean that the interests lack value. Instead, what it demonstrates is that our existing economic model is too narrow. If we limit our assessment of bankruptcy's impact to money, we resort to a unidimensional perspective. Therefore, the felt costs of business bankruptcy may not be measurable in strict, neoclassical economic models.

The question of what is currently happening in our bankruptcy system has no easy answer. It is clear, however, that the bankruptcy system addresses an enormity of both quantifiable and nonquantifiable issues for debtors, creditors, and the larger community. So the next question is what the bankruptcy system should seek to accomplish for debtors, creditors, and community.

PART II

Debtors

CHAPTER SIX

Rehabilitating Debtors for Their Sake and Our Own

From a debtor's perspective, one of the goals of bank-ruptcy is obtaining relief from existing indebtedness. Both Seat Co. and Smythe want to eliminate their overwhelming financial obliga-tions, which they see no feasible way of repaying over either the short or long term out of current assets or future income. Within the current U.S. bankruptcy system, this goal is accomplished through the bankruptcy discharge. The result of freeing a debtor from pre-existing obligations is commonly termed a fresh start.

In spite of its long-standing presence within our bankruptcy law, remarkably little is understood about why the fresh start is and should be so important to the contemporary bankruptcy system. Some scholars just reiterate the term *fresh start* in their justifica-tions, saying, for example, that debtors should have an "opportu-nity to begin anew" or a "chance to start over." But such statements do little to explain why a bankruptcy system should have a fresh start at all. Some commentators have addressed the scope of the dis-charge itself, that is, who should get a fresh start.[1] This question, though important, also skirts the issue of why a fresh start should exist.[2]

A legal system could treat debtors in a myriad of ways, and the grant of a fresh start is by no means a prerequisite to having a bank-ruptcy system. In medieval times, when merchants and traders stopped paying their creditors, the benches in the village square where these individuals conducted their business were broken in half, effectively precluding further business.[3] A bankruptcy system could permit imprisonment of individuals for nonpayment, and indeed, such systems currently exist in various countries and were a significant part of America's past. Individual debtors could be required to work for extended time periods to repay creditors, and business debtors could be forced to continue operating until every last creditor was paid in full.

So society confronts a choice when it determines how to treat debtors. And, as with most choices, the range is wide and complex. At one end of the spectrum, debtors could be punished through the deprivation of personal liberty, including death, imprisonment, or house arrest. Denial of personal liberty effectively banishes the debtor from future participation in the world of debt and credit and suggests a society that criminalizes the nonpayment of debt. Indeed, within the criminal justice system, denial of liberty is a primary form of punishment. At the other end of the spectrum, debtors could be completely absolved, treated as if there were nothing wrong with breaching (intentionally or not) obligations to others. These debtors would simply be relieved of their past debts and permitted to retain their present and future assets.

Neither end of the spectrum is particularly compelling in contemporary American society. Severe punishment for nonpayment of debt seems singularly out of place. Because so little consensus exists on whether the death penalty is an appropriate punishment for a serial killer and on whether and for how long drug dealers should be imprisoned, it would be difficult to rationalize such a harsh treatment of those who failed to fulfill financial obligations. Yet complete disregard for nonfulfillment of obligations is also unpalatable. It disregards the harm that nonpayment causes to others and does not prevent that harm from occurring prospectively. It gives debtors an unfair advantage because they profit from resources that were not rightfully theirs. This seems particularly unjust when others work hard to garner whatever benefits they can within the economic system. Escape from indebtedness also comes at a price, as creditors who are not repaid pass their losses on to others. The costs of complete absolution would be borne by everyone in society.

American society is thus torn between two desires: not to punish too severely and not to grant complete absolution. If we as a society reject limitations of physical freedom as a solution, we are drawn to a monetary solution. But whereas money may work as an appropriate solution outside of bankruptcy (where assets are sufficient to repay everyone), it is problematic within the bankruptcy context. It is easy to say that both Seat Co. and Smythe should repay their creditors; that is their punishment for incurring too much debt. But a purely monetary remedy is useless. Neither Seat Co. nor Smythe currently has sufficient funds to repay all creditors and is unlikely to generate such income in the foreseeable future. The search is on, then, for a remedy that is neither physically limiting nor purely monetary.

Forgiveness

The solution to the problem of nonpaying debtors is forgiveness. The fresh start is how society (through the bankruptcy system) mandates that creditors and other members of society forgive nonpaying debtors. This does not mean that all debtors are deserving of complete forgiveness. Indeed, in the next chapter I address how to ascertain which debtors are deserving of forgiveness. But it does mean that forgiveness should play a central part in the bankruptcy drama.

Forgiveness is an immensely powerful concept with a long religious and secular tradition, and its link to debt dates back to the Old Testament, if not before.[4] Forgiveness is appropriate, according to some scholars, if certain preconditions are met: there must be a wrong committed, the wrong must harm another, the wronged party resents what occurred, and the wrongdoer acknowledges the wrong done and takes steps to rectify it.[5] These conditions can be found in the bankruptcy situation. For debtors, the wrong is the nonpayment of legitimate obligations. That nonpayment produces a panoply of injuries. Creditors who are not paid are damaged, economically and perhaps emotionally. And others who pay for the losses indirectly are also harmed. Many injured creditors are resentful of the debtors' failures because debtors have received a benefit for which payment has not been made. Creditors may also feel resentment because debtors overstated their abilities to succeed. Finally, debtors admit to failure and take steps to redress their wrong by accessing the legal system. The system makes that wrong a matter of public record and requires the debtors to submit to judicial scrutiny.

Forgiveness does not necessarily return injured parties to where they were before. Forgiving debt does not mean creditors are repaid what they are owed. But it has the potential to be restorative (rehabilitative) on several levels.[6] It enables those wronged (the creditors) to feel that the disequilibrium created by nonpayment has been at least partially restored. Debtors who have submitted to the bankruptcy process have, in a sense, admitted failure. In a liquidation case, they make their nonexempt assets (if any) available to creditors, and they forgo the right to seek bankruptcy relief prospectively for a prescribed time period. Forgiveness also gives the wrongdoer (the debtor) the opportunity to regain self-esteem and become once again a productive member of society. In a capitalistic economy, we want debtors to reintegrate into the system for their sake and our own. For debtors, reintegration allows the taking of new risks. For society, taking risks is exactly what we want individuals and businesses to do. This enables the wheels of commerce to turn; individuals fend for themselves and do not become a drain on scarce societal resources.

Rehabilitation and Forgiveness: Strange Bedfellows

The suggested explanation raises two significant questions. First, how can the opportunity for rehabilitation be achieved through forgiveness?[7] Second, why is rehabilitation so important? Rehabilitation through forgiveness seems counterintuitive. Why would forgiving the very persons who failed enhance their ability to fulfill their obligations? Consider an example drawn from a real situation.

Suppose a mother whose daughter was killed by a drunk teenage driver decides to forgive the driver. She meets with him, convinces the court that he should be granted leniency, visits him in jail, and spends time with him following his release. It sounds unbelievable, almost unnatural. But the mother's anger would not bring back the daughter, and neither would keeping the wrongdoer in jail in perpetuity. Forgiveness in this situation may help both the mother and the driver. It alleviates, not eliminates, the driver's guilt. This enables him to move on with his life, to become a productive member of society again. And it may also help relieve the mother of her pain. By defusing her anger, she too can move on with her life. And the mother accomplishes this feat by coming to know the teenage driver personally and then forgiving him for his horrific behavior. Certainly, this concept is far easier to describe than to implement. And in certain situations, many people would not be drawn to a rehabilitation approach were it not for a societal requirement.

Rehabilitating debtors does not mean that what they did is good. Rehabilitating a drug dealer or robber is not suggesting that selling drugs or stealing is a good thing. Instead, rehabilitation is an approach for how to identify the wrong and then deal with the wrongdoer. Rehabilitating debtors does not mean that debtors are not responsible for their actions. The opposite is true. Rehabilitating debtors is how we develop responsibility if we can overcome our resentment, anger, and pain. The belief in forgiveness is certainly put to the test in the case of the drunk-driving teenager. But failing to repay debt does not produce the same level or kind of pain and hurt as death of a loved one. If forgiveness is possible in situations considerably more emotionally charged than debt, there is room to find forgiveness in bankruptcy.

How forgiveness assists rehabilitation and promotes responsibility can be explained by a biblical allegory.[8] The story is told of a man who dies, leaving his wife and young sons with his many debts. The widow has no money and no assets, other than a tiny pot of oil. Because she cannot repay her husband's debts, the creditors threaten to take her young sons to be their slaves. Fearing this, she turns to God for help. God tells the widow to borrow all the containers that she and her sons can locate and then to fill all these containers to the top with the oil she has at home. The widow is skeptical because her supply of oil is meager, but she follows God's command. The widow and her children collect all the containers they can find. Then, miraculously, as she fills the containers, the meager supply of oil keeps replenishing itself so there is sufficient oil to fill all the containers. God then tells the widow to sell the oil in the containers. The proceeds generated are enough not only to repay all creditors but to enable the widow to live comfortably thereafter with her sons.

I have always been struck by this story. How easy life would be if everyone in financial difficulty had a readily available supply of a valuable substance that would keep replenishing itself. Creditors would be repaid in full, and the debtor could proceed with life after repayment. In the current climate, we are sorely in need of such a replenishing oil for individuals and businesses. But because we lack divine intervention, we have to look to other avenues—legal avenues—to find solutions to the overwhelming indebtedness that threatens so many.

This biblical story reveals a link between bankruptcy and replenishment. Bankruptcy is a legal method for obtaining replenishment. On one level, I am talking about replenishing creditors—by refilling their coffers with the money they are owed, just as the widow repaid her creditors from the proceeds of the oil. This aspect of replenishment is addressed, at least in part, by a traditional economic model that sees bankruptcy as the answer to the woes of creditors. But replenishment means more than the recovery of money by creditors. The biblical tale does not simply end with the creditors being repaid. God also ensured that sufficient proceeds remained *after* repaying creditors to let the wife and her children live comfortably. Replenishment encompasses a recovery of spirit; it enables the emotional recovery that allows individuals and businesses to start over as productive members of society. That makes all of us feel better: the debtor, the creditors, and the members of society. Bankruptcy's fresh start is the legal analogue to divine intervention.

Developing responsibility through forgiveness has its roots in how people function psychologically. Individuals and businesses make mistakes. And when they make mistakes, society, by forgiving those mistakes, helps them to get back on their feet. We encourage learning, of which risk taking is a central feature, by acknowledging the possibility of failure and providing a way for people to start over, without either forgetting or condoning the underlying behavior.

Consider how children learn to walk. If children who tried to walk were yelled at every time they fell down, few children would want to learn. It would be safer and easier for them to continue crawling. Indeed, the studies of children who are abused or locked in small spaces without an opportunity to fail before they succeed either do not learn to walk at all or do not learn nearly as rapidly as other children.[9] Most children learn that it is okay to fall down; we will be there to help them up. We teach them that failure is a necessary prerequisite to succeeding. We welcome their small, tentative steps, literally and figuratively, toward maturation and integration into society, by forgiving their earlier mistakes and not constantly reminding them of the past. But, equally important in terms of the development of self, we do not walk *for* children. They eventually have to trust their teetering balance until they become more stable. So we teach self-worth and self-respect by acknowledging possible failure. And when the child finally succeeds, we feel good about the process and the child.

The possibility of the failure that accompanies learning discourages many children and adults from taking risks. Because taking risks is precisely what we want people to do, we need a mechanism for dealing with the inevitable failures that are part of the process.[10] Experimentation in the field of science, for example, commonly involves tests that fail; indeed, scientists learn a great deal through the failed experiments, and without the failures, many advances would not have been achieved. Indeed, some of the mistakes have ironically been found to be successes—the drug meprobamate, for example, was tested as an anticonvulsant but was found to be more effective in producing a calming effect—and had scientists shied away from failure, major advances would have been lost.

The bankruptcy process can, if structured properly, become a way of addressing the failures that come from risk taking. It can be a beacon to debtors of all kinds that although failure does occur, the failure is not, in and of itself, the end. The goal is to learn from that failure. Bankruptcy is the helping hand given to children learning to walk.

Why Rehabilitation Matters

The second question posed in the previous section remains: If forgiveness is the route toward rehabilitation, why is rehabilitation so important to the U.S. bankruptcy system? That is, why should anyone other than the debtor care about the debtor's being rehabilitated? Consider criminal law again. Much of criminal law is focused on how to deal with those who have committed a wrong, and punishment, usually in the form of imprisonment, is the standard remedy. Criminal law scholars proffer five basic justifications for punishment: retribution, deterrence (both general and specific), restraint, education, and rehabilitation.[11] These justifications certainly overlap, and the notion of punishment can be explained by invoking more than one of the explanations. These justifications can also be interpreted in different ways and are not uniformly viewed as successful.

The rehabilitation rationale for punishment stands in sharp contrast to the other aforementioned justifications. Rehabilitation is an effort to assist wrongdoers so they can be prevented from repeating their wrongs and can reenter society as productive participants. In contrast, general deterrence tries to ensure that potential wrongdoers will not commit the same act as the criminal. Education serves as a way of signaling to potential wrongdoers that certain specific conduct is unacceptable. Rehabilitation, in contrast, is aimed at the criminal, although it does benefit society by letting prospective wrongdoers know that should they commit a crime, they will receive assistance. Retribution, a mechanism for getting back at the wrongdoer, is backward looking, whereas rehabilitation looks forward. Both specific deterrence and restraint are efforts to stop wrongdoers from doing wrong prospectively by segregating them from others. Rehabilitation, in contrast, assumes that a debtor can and should be reintegrated back into society.

Americans share some understandings about rehabilitating individuals in the criminal law arena, although not about the propriety or success of this approach.[12] When Americans speak about rehabilitating a drug dealer, for example, they have a common belief as to what that means. At a minimum, the dealer should cease selling illegal drugs. People may disagree as to whether and how a dealer can be stopped, but in this context, no one challenges the merits of stopping drug dealing. When we speak about rehabilitating an armed robber, we expect the robber to stop robbing. The question remains as to whether rehabilitation means something more. Rehabilitation, broadly construed, can encompass assisting the drug dealer to treat psychological problems or helping the robber to become educated and participate in social welfare programs.

What it means to rehabilitate debtors is more difficult to determine. Incurring obligations one cannot fulfill is obviously not synonymous with dealing drugs and robbing: dealing drugs and robbing violate the criminal laws, while incurring obligations (absent fraud) does not. We do not want debtors simply to stop incurring debt, whereas we do want drug dealers to stop selling illegal substances and robbers to stop taking what is not theirs. Indeed, we want debtors to be able to *continue* borrowing if they put themselves in the position to be able to repay what they owe their creditors. Hence, at least part of what makes rehabilitation so complicated is that we want debtors to continue what they were doing, but with a different outcome, that is, success as distinguished from failure.

Rehabilitation of the debtor, like that of the drug dealer and the robber, can be broadly construed. If the cause of the debtor's failure is an unstable family situation, for example, or if a business fails because management lacks financial planning skills, then rehabilitation could extend to remedying these deficits. If that is accomplished, then rehabilitation does more than simply provide relief for oppressive financial burdens; it enables the debtor to better his or her situation prospectively. Whether broad-based rehabilitation can and should be accomplished (for debtors and criminals) is a legitimate question. Moreover, even if we could rehabilitate debtors, that success would come at a real economic cost. Rehabilitation, then— for drug dealers, robbers, or debtors—raises the issue of how much of a commitment society is willing to make to assist those who have failed to fulfill their obligations.

For the moment, assume that rehabilitation, at least to some degree, can work. The question remains why debtors' reentries into the credit economy are so critical. Rehabilitation takes place for at least two distinct but interrelated reasons. First, in the context of debtors (and perhaps criminals as well), it makes economic sense. Second, in respect of both debtors and criminals, it is reflective of how a civilized society wants people to be treated.

In the American economic system, individuals and businesses are encouraged to invest in growth. Businesses frequently do this by developing new products and increasing employment opportunities. Individuals contribute to economic growth by, for example, buying an increasing number of products for personal consumption. To achieve this growth, individuals and businesses need and are encouraged to borrow money. When individuals and businesses take this risk, the economy improves. That is how individuals, whether they are self-employed or employed by others, realize their dreams.

Along with investment in the future and the extension of credit, however, come the possibility of personal and business failure. This means that obligations will inevitably go unpaid. Businesses can miscalculate costs and demands for new product. External events, such as rising interest rates or foreign war, can alter business strategy. Individuals, too, are fallible, and illness, job layoff, or a natural disaster can disrupt the best-laid plans. People (as well as businesses) also may be unwittingly overoptimistic about their prospects.

A purely "private" capitalistic model could be adopted for responding to the inevitable failures that occur when risks are taken and goals are not achieved. Under such a system, parties would be treated as fully autonomous, left to sort out their own failures. This hands-off approach, based on a traditional, neoclassical economic model, would enable the strongest and most powerful creditors to determine the best way to recover the greatest amount for themselves. Each creditor would be encouraged to move as swiftly as possible to obtain recovery. Viewed from the standpoint of big, powerful creditors, this approach makes economic sense. It produces the greatest and speediest recovery of what is owed to this group of creditors. For those sharing in the belief that big business is at the heart of any system governing U.S. economic success, benefiting big creditors is a worthwhile goal. They have risked substantial capital; they have the power to control future capital; it is important to keep them happy.

This approach has a short-term economic focus and addresses only a limited number of those affected by a bankruptcy filing. It fails to take into account the myriad parties touched by a bankruptcy case and the economic consequences of their situations. This free-market approach does not encourage debtors to take the risks we want them to take. It does not encourage smaller creditors to lend because they, too, will lose out. With no outside control, the large, powerful creditors may not have an incentive to think in terms beyond their own self-interest.

The big-creditor approach has big appeal in academic circles.[13] It has also been adopted in some countries where creditor recovery is the sole aim of a bankruptcy process. But with a longer-range view in mind, it may make more sense to worry about repaying all creditors, rather than those that are the most powerful. Regrettably, it is difficult to measure the potential economic benefit of encouraging the risk taking of debtors and the repayment of small creditors. But small creditors, at least aggregated, are an important part of the American economic system. And encouraging debtors to invest in the marketplace by taking risks also has long-term economic potential.

Rehabilitation is a goal that says something about American society. In part, society assists debtors on humanitarian grounds. Rehabilitating debtors is part of the responsibility to treat members of
society humanely. It promotes values of human dignity and self-
respect. It also enables people and business to be a part of the ongoing credit economy. As was stated in an 1822 letter to Congress on
the desirability of a bankruptcy law, bankruptcy can be seen as an
"essential attribute of active and humane society. . . . [It is neces-
sary] in vindication of the national humanity."[14] A *New York Times*
editorial made a similar point, albeit in a different context, when it
observed that a "community is only as strong as the care and respect it gives its weakest members."[15] Debtors are among the weak
members of a credit society. If our treatment of them were motivated by retaliation or retribution, we would not be showing care
or respect.

These humanitarian grounds may also translate into economic
benefits. The humanitarian values of self-worth and reintegration
into society are not normally quantified.[16] These goals appear either
unquantifiable or not as economically beneficial as other items in a
capitalistic system. But this is not necessarily the case; the problem
is that we do not know what dignity and self-respect are worth to
the debtor and to society. We want families to become stable; we
want prosperity; we want members of society to have good physical and emotional health. This is economically sound.[17] We want
businesses to invest in long-term growth, to generate more jobs, to
quest after greater prosperity. This benefits everyone because
debtors will feel good about themselves, creditors will gain, and
society will function well. As an economic matter, then, it does not
makes sense to punish debtors in a way that ends up costing everyone—debtors, creditors, and communities—more.

A fresh start, in sum, allows us the opportunity to rehabilitate
debtors. And we care about rehabilitation because it affects both
our economic structure and our vision of ourselves. But discharging
indebtedness means that the cost falls on someone other than the

debtor. Creditors pay a price for rehabilitation, as do members of society. Some of those costs are recouped over the long term. But some of the costs are not recovered in monetary terms. They are recovered through the comfort of a humanely functioning society. For some, nonmonetary compensation may not be enough. For others, nonmonetary compensation is even more valuable than currency.

CHAPTER SEVEN

Finding the Outliers among Us

At the level of broad generality, debtors should be forgiven in order to encourage their rehabilitation—both for their sake and society's. But not all debtors are similarly situated, and some are less likely to benefit from forgiveness than others. Stated differently, some debtors cannot be rehabilitated so they should not be forgiven. And even when we believe we know which debtors can be rehabilitated, deciding how to structure that rehabilitation is no simple task.

Consider the example of learning a foreign language.[1] Some people will never learn, regardless of what and how they are taught, because they lack the desire. And some people find it excruciatingly difficult, indeed impossible, to learn a foreign language, not because they lack either intelligence or desire but because their particular mental hardwiring precludes that type of learning. Finally, a group of individuals may be able to learn, but time, care, and attention need to be given to them. Thus, it is important to be able to distinguish between rehabilitatable debtors (who will get a fresh start) and outliers, those whose conduct or behavior is aberrational (and who will not get the benefits of bankruptcy).

Forgiving Whom?

In thinking about outliers, debtors who intentionally stiff their creditors seem more blameworthy than debtors who encounter an unforeseen calamity. People are suspicious, for example, of corporate officers of defunct businesses who move to Florida, then file for bankruptcy and live in grand style while their former business' work force is unemployed. And people are wary of debtors who buy luxury goods. Some people do not want to give bankruptcy's benefits to the business debtor who cheats unsuspecting consumers out of millions of dollars of deposits for goods never received. Others are troubled by debtors who fail to pay their workers for work completed.

Proceeding to distinguish among debtors based on whether their conduct is likable as distinguished from despicable is a flawed strategy. Although people intuitively sense that some debtors should not be forgiven, that assessment is usually not made on the basis of whether the debtor can be rehabilitated. Rather, the judgment is made by evaluating the fairness of the debtor's conduct, which is basically an assessment of why the debtor cannot repay. If the reason is satisfactory, then the debtor should be discharged; conversely, if the reason is unsatisfactory, the debtor should be denied a fresh start.

In spite of the appeal of this approach, why particular debtors cannot repay does not provide a sustainable basis for distinguishing among debtors. A debtor who does not pay for reasons we find offensive may still be able to be rehabilitated. Moreover, this approach is too subjective a basis for decision making. We are better served by looking at *how* the debtor incurred the underlying obligation. Concrete examples demonstrate that the "why" question, as opposed to the "how" question, is problematic.

Suppose that each of five farmers borrowed money from the bank to buy seed for the next crop. The farmers and the bank anticipated that the crop revenues would be sufficient to service this short-term borrowing. Come time to repay, however, none of the five farmers had sufficient funds. The reasons why they could not repay are very different.

First Farmer planted his seed, but his fields were hit by a plague of locusts, destroying the crop. The money to repay the bank never materialized. Second Farmer also planted his seed. As it was growing, he decided to purchase a new machine that was supposed to make harvesting less expensive by decreasing the amount of necessary labor. Unfortunately, the machine did not function faster than manual harvesting, as Second Farmer had hoped. Had Second Farmer thoroughly investigated the machine, he would have learned that it had not been fully tested. Because the machine failed, Second Farmer's crop was delayed getting to market, and the crop yielded less revenue than he needed to repay his debt. Third Farmer planted, harvested, and sold his crop. Rather than repay the bank, however, he used the money to repay some of his other creditors, who were hounding him. Fourth Farmer planted his seed and harvested his crop, and he had sufficient revenues. But on the way to the bank, he bumped into a group of old friends, and they sat down together to play some cards. Fourth Farmer lost all his money. Finally, Fifth Farmer, unlike the other farmers, never purchased the seed. Instead, he took the proceeds of the bank loan and used them to purchase a new luxury automobile and take a cruise to the Bahamas. In the end, he, too, had no money to repay the bank.

If rehabilitation were not a goal, we could decide that, in a bankruptcy system, the five farmers should all be held responsible for the unpaid obligations and treated identically. In a sense, this would be treating nonpayment as a strict liability crime; the intent of the farmers would be irrelevant.[2] Viewed from the perspective of the creditor bank, this approach makes sense. But these debtor-farmers are distinguishable. First Farmer had no knowledge of what would happen and intended to repay. He experienced an act of God, much like an earthquake or flood, and he had no ability to control his environment, except possibly by electing not to be a farmer in the first instance. Second Farmer made a bad business judgment. He certainly did not intend to lose money on the crop; he wanted just the opposite—to harvest it sooner and less expensively so he could generate even more money. So he took a risk that resulted in a failure which rendered him unable to repay his creditors. At worst, his conduct was negligent because he failed to investigate the harvesting machine thoroughly. If one focuses on the concept of blameworthiness as a function of who exhibited the greater degree of intent, Second Farmer can be blamed for the nonpayment more than the First Farmer. Third Farmer chose not to repay the bank, even though he could have done so. He viewed his other creditors as either exerting more pressure or being more important than the bank. In the ranking of blameworthiness, Third Farmer is more culpable than First Farmer or Second Farmer. But Third Farmer's choices were circumscribed by the realities of his situation. If he did not repay his other creditors, perhaps they would obtain a judgment. Maybe future production would be delayed because of the intrusive creditors' behavior. Fourth Farmer presents yet another situation. Assuming he is not a compulsive gambler, he chose to fritter away the bank's money. Even if he truly believed he would win at the card table, he took an unnecessary and unanticipated risk with the bank's money. It was a different kind of risk from those that Second and Third Farmer took. Unlike Second Farmer's, the risk was not business related. Unlike Third Farmer, Fourth Farmer used the money not for others (creditors) but primarily for his own enjoyment and pecuniary gain. Fourth Farmer is arguably more blameworthy than Third Farmer who is more blameworthy than Second Farmer who is more blameworthy than First Farmer.

Fifth Farmer is most similar to Third and Fourth Farmers, but critical distinctions exist. Third Farmer is arguably less culpable than Fourth Farmer and Fifth Farmer because he did not benefit by lining his own pockets with money. Third Farmer was self-interested in one sense, though: he evidenced a disregard for the bank based on the pressure he was experiencing. Fourth Farmer could have repaid the bank and made money for himself, had he won the card game. But there is an important difference between Third Farmer and Fourth Farmer. Fourth Farmer acted in a manner that might have, but would not necessarily have, deprived the bank of revenue. Contrastingly, Third Farmer knew the bank would not be repaid; the money was going to other creditors. Third Farmer is thus, at some level, more culpable than Fourth Farmer. One could argue, however, that Third Farmer was actually protecting the bank's long-term interest by making sure that irritated small creditors did not shut the business down or delay the harvest through their meddlesome ways.

Whichever spin we put on the first four farmers, Fifth Farmer is the most blameworthy, because he has the worst features of Third Farmer and Fourth Farmer. Like Third Farmer, he knowingly and intentionally deprived the bank of repayment. Like Fourth Farmer, he intended to gain personally (with the car and the cruise). Fifth Farmer had the worst state of mind in terms of the likelihood of benefiting from forgiveness.

Should We Distinguish Based on State of Mind?

These examples reveal that, at some level, we can distinguish between debtors, if we choose to do so, by looking at why they cannot repay. Concepts of intentionality that are essential in criminal law—actual or purported knowledge, recklessness, negligence, and strict liability—produce bases for distinguishing between debtors.[3] The five farmers cover a spectrum of intent. Each end of the spectrum is reasonably clear. Many people sense, perhaps intuitively, that First Farmer should be eligible for relief while Fifth Farmer should not. On what basis are they making this judgment? An assessment based on which farmer acted acceptably is useful in the context of criminal law, where the definition of the crime hinges on the debtor's intent. But the bankruptcy system does not have first-degree indebtedness, second-degree indebtedness, and so on, whereas the criminal law distinguishes between robbery in the first degree and robbery in the second degree. Nonpayment (at least at present) is not a matter of degree; it either exists or it doesn't.

A bankruptcy system thus may be better served by looking at which debtor-farmers are most likely to be rehabilitated, thus moving us toward the "how" question as opposed to the "why" question. To proceed in this manner, we ask which farmer is most likely to learn from his mistakes. If our goal for debtors (as distinguished from debts) is rehabilitation, then why a debtor-farmer made a mistake is relevant only if it affects whether he can be rehabilitated. Stated in terms of a criminal law analogue, if we can rehabilitate the hard-core heroin user as well as the casual social marijuana user, it should not matter why each started using drugs.[4] Whether thieves steal because they need an item or because they want an item is irrelevant as long as they can be rehabilitated. In the context of criminal law, the distinction is used to define the actual criminal conduct and the accompanying punishment. In the bankruptcy context, distinctions among degrees of nonpayment can be made, but they are unproductive.

The first four farmers can be rehabilitated through forgiveness. First Farmer and Second Farmer are most likely to benefit from the opportunity to start over. First Farmer had no control over what happened to him. Second Farmer exercised bad judgment, but his goal was laudable. Third Farmer can also be helped through rehabilitation. Indeed, had he sought bankruptcy relief, the law could (and current American law does) provide that the sums he repaid his general creditors be returned to the estate as preferential.[5] Moreover, further creditor harassment could (and does) stop because of a court-imposed stay.[6] Fourth Farmer is problematic. If we release Fourth Farmer from his obligation to repay the bank, we could be sending the message that it is acceptable to put someone else's money at risk for one's own benefit and pleasure. But if we do not permit Fourth Farmer access to the bankruptcy system, how will he be able to get back on his feet and start over? Will Fourth Farmer accept a helping hand, or is he habitually capricious and irresponsible? This is a predictive judgment, and if the legal system is wrong, the bank and prospective creditors will suffer. Assuming, however, that people are inherently decent, it is more likely than not that Fourth Farmer can be rehabilitated. And, if this assumption proves to be right, future creditors and perhaps the bank as well will benefit.

If Fourth Farmer is given an opportunity to rehabilitate, that does not mean society likes what he did or that it will be forgotten. Moreover, choosing not to distinguish between the first four farmers based on why they cannot repay does not mean there are no differences among them. It means only that they are all capable of being rehabilitated. Although the four farmers who can be rehabilitated (according to the "how" question) are the same four farmers who are considered least blameworthy (according to the "why" question), blameworthiness is not necessarily linked to the ability to be rehabilitated. Fourth Farmer is blameworthy but likely can be rehabilitated.

Fifth Farmer's reasons for not repaying are the least of his problems. Unlike the other four farmers, he incurred debt with no intent to repay. Basically, he borrowed money fraudulently, conduct not evidenced by any of the other farmers. And, unlike state of mind, fraudulent behavior (as distinguished from intent) at the time of the loan's inception suggests that Fifth Farmer cannot be rehabilitated.

Fifth Farmer then exemplifies the kind of behavior that signals a debtor who will not learn from mistakes. This is not an easy group to identify. We are searching for specific behavior that evidences a likelihood that acceptable norms will not be followed. This is not an unusual process.[7] Psychotherapists frequently can forecast later behavior based on conduct or words used early in life. Teachers observing young children playing can often predict who will be a teenage troublemaker. But this assessment is by no means error-proof. Some examples of nonrehabilitatable debtors come to mind. Repeat filers present a potential problem because their continued access to the bankruptcy process suggests that rehabilitation has not worked. Debtors who conceal their books and records, lie on the forms provided by a court, or perjure themselves are not good candidates for rehabilitation. Their ongoing conduct during the case suggests that forgiveness would be wasted.

Looking at Debts Rather Than Debtors

Even if such a debtor as Fifth Farmer could be rehabilitated, there may be specific types of identifiable debt that should not be discharged. These would be debts that are so important to society or to particular creditors that they override bankruptcy's rehabilitative goal.[8] Take alimony, maintenance, and child support obligations. If a legal system so determined, this category of debt could be treated as nondischargeable. That determination would be made, at least in part, because the need for and importance of payment to the recipient outweighs the need for and importance of rehabilitation of the debtor. Moreover, such a policy sends a signal that a society considers payment of familial obligations to be an important responsibility. Notice that the nonpayment is not based on an empirical assessment that putative parents cannot be rehabilitated. Rather, certain values override rehabilitation in limited circumstances.

This inquiry returns us to the earlier discussion on punishment. By not permitting a discharge of some specific obligation, society is moving away from a rehabilitative approach and seeking retribution and deterrence. It is singling out particular behavior and then taking away bankruptcy's principle benefit—forgiveness. Like mass murder, rape, or child molestation, some conduct so offends us that forgiving the debt would make life for the debtor too easy. So we exact the economic equivalent of an eye for an eye: you owe and now you must repay.

Reasonable people could certainly differ as to which debts should fall within the exception to the rule in favor of rehabilitation. Should back taxes, criminal fines, restitution obligations, unpaid student loans, and trust fund obligations all be treated as nondischargeable debts, or do distinctions between these items justify giving only some of them precedence over rehabilitation? The answer to that question will no doubt change with time. At any given point, a society may, as a collective whole, place more value on one thing than another. Once we recognize that some debts (as opposed to debtors) can rightly be removed from the scope of the discharge, we can leave the determination of what those specific debts should be to another day. If, however, the exceptions become too numerous, they could overpower the rehabilitative principle, making the exception the rule and the rule the exception.

Returning to Seat Co. and Smythe

It is useful to assess the eligibility for bankruptcy of Seat Co. and Smythe by examining which farmer each of them most resembles. How do they fare under a determination of debtor eligibility based on their conduct and the nature of their indebtedness?

The Seat Co. scenario does not reveal all the reasons why the company experienced financial failures. There was a problem with international trade, which presumably meant that Seat Co. anticipated certain business results that did not materialize. Seat Co. expected and hoped to make money but did not. It no doubt made bad business judgments. It probably paid some noisier creditors sooner than quieter ones. Seat Co. is thus most like Second Farmer (the one who purchased the machine) and Third Farmer (the one who repaid trade creditors, not the bank). But a part of Seat Co.'s problem had to do with global import and export policies, which it could not control, and in that sense Seat Co. is like First Farmer. Because it least resembles Fourth and Fifth Farmer, Seat Co. is a good candidate for rehabilitation.

Consider a variation on the Seat Co. hypothetical. Suppose, as is apparently the case, that many small businesses like Seat Co. experience cashflow shortages. Unlike Second Farmer, these companies are not short of money because they made bad business judgments; indeed, the opposite is true. They experience the shortfall because all available cash is going back into the business to create future growth. Therefore, in an interim period, a company may be troubled, but it is troubled on the way (one hopes) to greater success. If a group of creditors demanded payment at this particular time and sought to pressure the debtor, then the debtor might be forced to seek relief under the bankruptcy laws. If society's goal is to develop small businesses and encourage risk taking, then the cash-poor debtor seeking to grow should be able to partake of bankruptcy's relief because it can be rehabilitated.

Smythe could not repay for a wide range of reasons. With respect to the car accident, he is akin to the first three farmers. The car accident itself was due to his negligence, but his inability to repay had to do with the size of the damage award in proportion to his ability to pay. He did not stand to gain personally. He was insured up to a limit. It is unclear why Smythe could not repay his credit card debt. Did he spend knowing he could not repay, or did he spend expecting to repay and then discover that he could not? The answer determines whether he is closer to Fourth Farmer or Fifth Farmer. If he went on a buying spree immediately before filing, he more closely resembles Fifth Farmer, and the luxury items he purchased, as specific debts incurred through fraud, might fit within a category of debt that would be nondischargeable. Finally, it is also unclear why Smythe cannot repay his educational loan, although it appears that he intended to better himself and misjudged his ability to repay. This would make Smythe similar to Second Farmer and Third Farmer. So, except for specific debts that could be nondischargeable, Smythe can benefit from the forgiveness the bankruptcy law accords.

The Potential for Rehabilitation

People learn in different ways and over different time spans.[9] Consider once again people learning a foreign language. Some people learn best by reading and studying books; these individuals can pick up an entire language on their own. Others learn auditorily or interactively, by listening to language tapes, by using computer programs with voices, or by speaking in class with a teacher. Still others learn through immersion, actually living in a country in which the language is spoken. Some people need a combination of these methods. Indeed, what works for one person may not work for another.

What this means in the bankruptcy context is that, given the vast differences among debtors, a single approach to rehabilitation is doomed to failure. It is improbable that all debtors learn in the same fashion. Debtors can be individuals (like Smythe) or formal legal entities—corporations (like Seat Co.), partnerships, and business trusts—and wide diversity exists within these categories.

Individual debtors are neither all poor, unemployed individuals (the saints) nor employed, profligate spenders (the rogues). Many individual debtors are employed (like Smythe). Many debtors own homes. Many debtors are not poor according to federal standards of poverty levels. What brings individual debtors into financial ruin is not uniform either. Medical expenses, job interruptions, slumps in local economies, bad investments, family problems (such as divorce, drug abuse, and gambling), overspending, overuse of credit, and lack of insurance for property or health, are all factors that could push debtors over the edge. Diminished stigma, liberalized laws, and reasonably generous exemptions may all encourage access to the bankruptcy system.[10]

Individual debtors also have different types of debts. Some debtors owe credit card companies or credit unions or banks. Other debtors owe friends and family. Some debtors have first and second mortgages; others owe landlords, utilities, and phone companies. Other debtors have business-related debts. Some debtors owe taxes. Some debtors have high medical bills. Other debtors have gambling debts.

Significant differences also exist among nonindividual debtors. When most people think about nonindividual debtors, they focus on the debtors they read about in the newspapers, the well-known mega cases.[11] But most nonindividual debtors are small, non–publicly traded companies. Some have many employees, others very few. Some have twenty-five creditors; others have twenty-five thousand.[12]

In granting forgiveness, the bankruptcy system needs to take into account the diversity among debtors. In addition, we as policymakers need to consider what mechanisms are the legal equivalent of the immersion trip to a foreign country. That is, we need to consider what concrete steps can be taken to effect the goal of rehabilitation.

CHAPTER EIGHT

Effectuating the Fresh Start Policy

In many respects, the current U.S. bankruptcy system recognizes bankruptcy's rehabilitative potential, as many debtors can be discharged. But the current system fails in some key respects, resulting in a diminution of the possibility of rehabilitation. Some of these failures can be more easily identified and remedied than others, although many of the proposed changes come at a cost. And it is questionable whether the benefits garnered from the changes are worth that cost.

From the many changes that could be proposed, I have selected five recommendations that touch on both individual and corporate debtors:

- Enable virtually all individual and business debtors to choose between liquidating and reorganizing
- Extend the limitation on discharge to nonindividual debtors and narrow the list of nondischargeable debts
- Curtail the scope of limited liability for officers and directors of debtor corporations
- Recognize and enlarge the scope of the new value exception to the absolute priority rule
- Provide greater intervention by judges

Liquidation and Reorganization

The terms *reorganization* and *rehabilitation* are, unfortunately, frequently confused and used interchangeably. People speak about the goal of rehabilitation but refer to the chapters of the bankruptcy law that favor restructuring and long-term payout of debt (Chapters 9, 11, 12, and 13) as the reorganization chapters. This implies that only the reorganization chapters are rehabilitative, which is inaccurate. Rehabilitation can be achieved through either liquidation or reorganization.

Under current law, determinations of which debtors can reorganize are made based on whether the debtor is an individual. Corporate debtors can choose whether to liquidate or reorganize, but individuals with consumer debts cannot liquidate if their doing so is deemed a "substantial abuse" of the bankruptcy system.[1] So within the group of individual debtors, those with consumer debts are less able to liquidate than others. And corporations can liquidate for any reason of their choosing, even if creditors and the community would be better off if the business remained in existence. This lack of parallelism is unjustified.

In addressing what constitutes substantial abuse, many courts have determined that the key factor to consider in determining whether a debtor can be permitted to liquidate is the debtor's ability to repay creditors in a Chapter 13 or Chapter 11.[2] Although nothing is wrong with encouraging rehabilitation (which may provide increased recoveries for creditors), it does not follow that rehabilitation occurs only in a reorganization chapter. Suppose, for example, that a single parent is saddled with debts incurred by her former spouse. For this debtor who is seeking to free herself from both obligations and an unpleasant relationship, liquidation is not only more palatable but also potentially more successful. Forcing the debtor to reorganize debts she did not incur will only prolong her recovery. If a consumer debtor can be rehabilitated through forgiveness in a liquidation case, then that opportunity should not be foreclosed.

There is a historical basis for distinguishing between individuals with business and nonbusiness debts. Our forebears wanted to encourage citizens in the New World to take business risks, and creditors understood that businesses might fail.[3] The flip side of the coin was that people expected debtors to repay their personal debts—largely for food and clothing and shelter. Part of the reason for this expectation is that the creditors extending money for these necessaries all lived and worked in close proximity to the debtor.

These historical justifications do not hold up to scrutiny today. Personal obligations are not owed just to the local druggist, dry cleaner, or hardware store whose livelihood depends on the repayment of these sums. Monies are owed to banks, department stores, hospitals, credit card companies, and unions. Many of these debtor-creditor relationships are impersonal. Although individuals may know their banker, they do not know the president of the bank. Credit cards are often obtained through the mail or by phone with no personal contact at all. Lending has become a big business, and there is substantial profit to be made. Lending to consumers is no longer safer and more intimate than lending to individuals in business. Both types of lending involve risks. Both types of loans are important to economic growth. As a society, we want businesses to grow through increased investment just as we want consumers to enhance their participation in the economic marketplace through their buying power.

Until the consumer credit industry lobby took hold, the bankruptcy law did not differentiate between types of individual debtors. The efforts to separate individuals based on the character of their debt can be explained, but certainly not justified, only as a matter of politics.[4] This industry has convinced people that it is losing money. Although it is accurate that the consumer credit industry is losing money through debtor nonpayment, it is also making money from debtors as well as other paying customers. It is more accurate to say that the credit industry is profiting from the lending business but that bankruptcy losses cut into that profit.[5]

Moreover, borrowing does not happen in a vacuum. It is not as if debtors can simply turn a spigot and take whatever amount they want from a lender faucet. Creditors control how much a borrower borrows, the terms of the borrowing, and the time and means of repayment. Creditors who are concerned about the size of their losses in bankruptcy can certainly take steps to curtail them. They could better assess how much to lend. They could charge more for loans to risky debtors, as distinguished from charging more to all debtors to offset potential losses. They could monitor borrowers' behavior. In addition to assessing a debtor's ability to repay at the time of the loan, creditors could oversee the borrower's ongoing situation, curtailing prospective lending or demanding early repayment if the debtor encounters unfortunate circumstances.

If we want to encourage responsibility in debtors, we need to encourage responsibility in creditors. Because creditors profit from extending credit even to those they know or suspect cannot repay, they have a responsibility for the losses that do and will occur. Anyone who has received an offer of a credit card or a credit line in the mail knows only too well how creditors encourage borrowing. Moreover, the credit industry should cease using the bankruptcy system as its collection system. By using the bankruptcy system in this way, creditors are actually rewarding themselves for irresponsibility, as they are freed from the costs of collecting unpaid obligations.[6]

Because creditors have such different incentives from consumer borrowers, the determination of what is right for consumer debtors cannot be made by creditors. If rehabilitation through forgiveness can be justified, then the interests of creditors to maximize recovery through limitations on chapter choice run directly counter to the desired goal. But it does not follow that creditors should be left in the lurch. Instead, protections for creditors have to be identified and promoted through means within the Code other than limitations on the use of Chapter 7.

Two additional hurdles impair the ability of individual debtors (both with and without consumer debt) to exercise choice: geographic proclivities toward Chapter 13 and lawyer counseling.[7] For a host of complex reasons, reorganization is much more prevalent in some areas of the country, which means that debtor choice is limited not just by the Bankruptcy Code. Similarly, lawyers have incredible power to dictate clients' behavior. When clients are scared and troubled, lawyers have the power to influence their decision about what chapter to use. Sometimes lawyers are motivated by what is best for a client. But sometimes they can be guided by monetary concerns or local legal culture. Because a consumer bankruptcy lawyer commonly practices within a limited geographic range before a limited set of judges, lawyers may sometimes have an incentive to satisfy the judge rather than the client.

The lack of consistency in the treatment of individual debtors has led at least one commentator to suggest that Chapter 13 should be repealed.[8] But this drastic solution would affect more than one-quarter of the cases filed. It may be that too many debtors use Chapter 13, and the success of this chapter is worthy of debate. But eliminating the option would harm the very people we seek to help. It seems more useful to consider how to create greater national uniformity. It would be worth focusing, for example, on the role both lawyers and judges play in debtor choice before deciding to eliminate the choice.

Forced reorganizations are unlikely to promote human dignity and self-respect. As a psychological matter, choice is important to individuals. It enables a debtor to become an active participant in determining his or her own destiny, and that facilitates maximum recovery. A debtor may not be motivated to proceed with a forced reorganization because it requires added work and sacrifice. Consider a medical analogy. Historically, doctors gave their patients morphine for chronic pain at regular intervals following surgery. This took pain control out of the patients' hands. More recently, patients have been able to control their own morphine through a pump. These patients were discovered to be much more able than the doctors to determine their own thresholds for pain. Rather than abuse the ready supply of morphine, they used less than the doctors supplied when they controlled how much to use.[9] In the bankruptcy context, we want to create a system that will motivate the debtor to become responsible. We can try to make reorganization more enticing than liquidation, and policymakers have started down that road through the 1994 Amendments by increasing the available debt ceiling in Chapter 13 and clarifying certain home mortgage protections.

As for businesses, from the 1930s through the 1980s, American society has been relatively comfortable according them the option of liquidating or reorganizing. Unlike individual debtors, businesses were not forced to remain in existence if the owners did not want them to continue. A corporation was to be considered inanimate and could not be forced to work. Some bankruptcy judges, scholars, and businesspeople, however, are increasingly concerned that Chapter 11 cases are not functioning as they should. They believe that the reorganization option for businesses should be either eliminated or substantially curtailed early in the bankruptcy process.[10] Problems with corporate reorganization are plentiful.[11] Some people focus their criticism on the low confirmation and consummation rates (approximately 20% of Chapter 11 cases confirm).[12] Others are concerned about the length of time it takes a case to move through the bankruptcy system. Some commentators note that debtors languish in Chapter 11 because creditors do not adequately supervise the debtor. Some cases appear to be inordinately costly, in part because the professionals, who are paid as a priority expense, have no incentive to reach a conclusion rapidly. Some cases involve businesses that, no matter how hard they try, simply cannot succeed in reorganizing. Other cases involve viable businesses with inadequate management. Yet other cases have adequate management but inadequate legal counsel or unnecessarily recalcitrant creditors. Many of these are real problems; others are more perceived than real. But whatever the situation, eliminating the reorganization for businesses is not the answer.

For starters, there is no shared definition of what constitutes success in Chapter 11.[13] For some, it means hefty returns to creditors over the short term. For others, it means confirmation and then consummation of any plan that satisfies the Bankruptcy Code requirements. Some consider success to mean preservation of a business, even if management or ownership changes. Others consider it to mean maintaining jobs for employees as long as possible, even if the business ultimately fails. Before Chapter 11 is discarded, there should be a clear sense of what corporate reorganization is intended to achieve.

To the extent that a shared vision of success in Chapter 11 exists, we need to be clear about why failures occur. Is the goal—reorganization—flawed, or is the means to the end flawed? If the means are flawed, eliminating reorganization does not make sense; instead, the reorganization process should be improved so that it functions more effectively for all parties: debtors, creditors, and communities.

Because of a sense that it is the means and not the end that are flawed, steps are already being taken to improve the Chapter 11 process. If these approaches are adopted and prove successful, they will go a long way toward saying that the end is worthy of retention. All of this is made easier by the growing amount of empirical data available on reorganization cases. Some changes are incorporated within the 1994 Amendments to the Bankruptcy Code. These include a fast track for small-business cases and single-asset real estate cases, direct appeal of orders permitting only the debtor to propose a plan (exclusivity period), and increased conferences with bankruptcy judges to push cases along.[14] Although these amendments are fraught with interpretive difficulties, preliminary empirical data suggest that these provisions are being implemented, and hence one may be able to see if Chapter 11 is improving as a consequence. Consideration should be given to bringing in new management to assist small businesses without disrupting the debtor's control of the plan process. As is being done in a limited number of jurisdictions, consideration should be given to instituting arbitration or mediation procedures to speed up decision making by curtailing costs and litigation, although benefits of this approach need more empirical verification.[15] Finally, ways of increasing the involvement of creditors in the Chapter 11 process need to be found.

One omnipresent concern about Chapter 11 is its costs.[16] The cost that generates the most attention from the media is professional fees. As an absolute number, the amount expended in Chapter 11 on lawyers, accountants, and investment bankers for the debtor, the creditors' committee or committees, the equity holders, and future claimants is large. An article in the *New York Law Journal* pointed out that attorney fees in bankruptcy cases in the Southern District of New York from 1989 to 1992 totaled $770 million.[17]

It is easy to be taken in by the vastness of this number. But the figure includes cases in both Chapter 7 and Chapter 11 and does not distinguish between the costs of large and small cases. Chapter 11 cases, because they cover an extended time period, inevitably cost more than Chapter 7 cases, although Chapter 7 cases hardly qualify as cost free. Additionally, many features of a Chapter 11 generate costs because they take a professional's time: developing a plan of reorganization, negotiating with creditors, writing disclosure statements, soliciting votes, and obtaining confirmation.

To say that bankruptcy fees are high is problematic because no comparable number is provided. What would be the fees for these businesses if Chapter 11 did not exist and they had to restructure outside of court? The numbers also need a context. Suppose Seat Co. had assets of $1 million and professional fees of $50,000; fees would then be 5% of the distribution. Now consider Texaco. Assume total assets of $40 billion and professional fees of $6 million. Six million dollars seems astronomic. But it is less than 1% of the total distribution.

Some professional costs are inescapable. Debtors need counsel. The reorganization process simply cannot be handled without experienced bankruptcy lawyers. Other parties need counsel also, although some have suggested that these fees should be paid not by the estate but by the creditors. Suggestions have been made that attorneys should be paid only at the end of the case. Amendments to the Code try to establish greater uniformity in fees and to award compensation only if there is benefit to the estate, although it is too early to tell whether this new provision will curb cost.[18]

It is possible that the costs of nonlegal professionals—accountants, investment bankers, and other experts—are too high compared with those of the legal professionals. Moreover, in many instances the services provided by nonlegal professionals, unlike those of lawyers, could be shared or satisfied through a panel of experts, an idea suggested by Learned Hand years ago.[19] This type of change is controversial on various levels. It hits at professionals' pocketbooks. It may call for alterations in professional guidelines regarding conflicts and conduct. And, most problematical perhaps, it would require a spirit of cooperation that is contrary to the tenets of the American adversary system.

Suppose that the debtor's books and records need to be reconciled and reviewed. If every interested party hires its own accountant, considerable expense and duplication result. If one accounting firm is retained and then examined by all parties, considerable saving would take place. As another example, suppose that a valuation of a major piece of property is required in a Chapter 11 case. If every party hires its own expert, a range of values will be produced, with each expert espousing the value that is in the best interest of the party who retained him or her. But a panel of experts, beholden to no one, could establish the range of values and demonstrate how the calculations were made. This panel could then be examined by the parties, and the court could ultimately determine value. A panel of two or more experts would be cheaper and more efficient than pitting multiple experts, each of whom is paid by the estate, against one another.

Discharge of What Debts and for Whom?

Under current law, individual debtors can receive a discharge, but certain types of debts are excepted from discharge in both liquidation and reorganization chapters. Because nondischargeable debts limit the debtor's fresh start, the number and nature of these debts matter. Since 1984, the list of nondischargeable debts has grown, and Section 523 now lists seventeen categories of nondischargeable debt. Chapter 13, which historically offered a greater chance for a fresh start than other chapters, precludes discharge of an ever increasing list of debts.

Some of the nondischargeable debts can be justified without much fanfare: alimony, maintenance, and child support, and obligations for fraud or defalcation while acting in a fiduciary capacity. Other debts present a less compelling case (recent taxes and restitution obligations), and some have been added as a consequence of successful lobbying efforts (fees owed a condominium association and drunk driving judgments). The proliferation of nondischargeable debts should stop, at least until the effect of the new additions can be assessed and the existing provisions can be studied. Suppose, for example, that taxes became dischargeable. The government would lose revenue, and bankruptcy might be more appealing to tax dodgers. But individuals would be able to face the future without a significant drain on their prospective income. Moreover, the creeping diminution of the power of the Chapter 13 discharge, which is now blurring the line of demarcation between liquidation and reorganization, should be reconsidered in order to encourage consumer debtors to reorganize.

Although corporations cannot receive a discharge in Chapter 7, they can discharge debts in a Chapter 11 that individuals cannot. This lack of parity produces troubling results. Suppose both Seat Co. and Smythe borrowed money from a bank by intentionally misstating financial information on the credit application. Each borrowed five thousand dollars, which now neither can repay. Assume that both Seat Co. and Smythe decided to reorganize under Chapter 11. Under current law, Smythe cannot obtain a discharge of the bank debt, but Seat Co. can.

One possible explanation for this result is that Seat Co., and perhaps the bank, retains a right, absent a release, to sue the individuals within the corporation (Seat Co.) that committed the fraud. And if the suit is successful, those individuals will have to repay the bank debt. If unable to do so, these individuals could seek bankruptcy relief and, like Smythe, they would not be able to discharge the debt incurred through fraud.

This explanation does not withstand scrutiny. If corporations could be held responsible, then they would be more likely to monitor the individuals in charge. Even if they did not monitor, the nondischargeability of certain debt would send a signal that corporations cannot escape liability in bankruptcy. Not all types of nondischargeable debt are relevant to corporations. A corporation cannot owe alimony, maintenance, or child support, for example. A corporation cannot take out a federally guaranteed student loan. But such debts as those resulting from recent tax obligations, defalcation while acting in a fiduciary capacity, willful and malicious injury, drunk driving on the job, and restitution awards are applicable to corporations.

Suppose the government imposed on a business a $1 million claim for overcharging for reimbursements under Medicare. If the corporation filed for bankruptcy relief under Chapter 11, it could discharge this restitution obligation. Therefore, if unsecured creditors were paid only fifty cents on the dollar, five hundred thousand dollars of the $1 million owed the government would be discharged. This liability would not attach to the corporate officers, directors, or shareholders (absent a specific statute), who would remain free to begin a new business. Compare this result with what would happen if a doctor overcharged the government for Medicare and the government slapped her with a restitution fine of $1 million. This obligation would be nondischargeable under Chapters 7, 11, 12, and 13. If limiting an individual's rehabilitation is justified (which is questionable), it is equally justified in the corporate context.

Curtailing Limited Liability

Under current law, certain individuals can be denied a discharge in Chapter 7; these are the outlier debtors who will not be rehabilitated through forgiveness. Corporations, much like outlier debtors, cannot obtain a discharge in Chapter 7. This is because the business ceases to exist. Under state law, debts of a corporation are *not* the debts of the individual owners, officers, or directors. Therefore, the individuals responsible for the corporation, who do not cease to exist, can start over unimpaired. If limited liability did not exist or were less expansive, these individuals would not be discharged in bankruptcy if they had to seek relief.

Limited liability makes good sense in many nonbankruptcy contexts.[20] But it produces a wide range of anomalous results within the bankruptcy system that lead to concern over whether it should be fully retained in that context. Because limited liability is clearly a matter of state law, one must ask whether federal law (that is, bankruptcy) should take precedence over state law, thereby curtailing limited liability for corporate officers, directors, and shareholders.

Limited liability has already been contractually or statutorily curtailed outside the bankruptcy context. Many lenders, for example, require corporate officers (many of whom are shareholders as well) to guarantee the debt of the corporation. This encourages the corporate officer to act responsibly because if the repayment is not made by the corporation, the lender will try to collect from the officer. If the debt is guaranteed, lenders acquire a new source of repayment: the individual, assuming the corporate officer has sufficient nonexempt assets to repay the debt.

In addition to private agreements curtailing limited liability, statutes and common law doctrines stipulate that certain officers, directors, or shareholders remain personally liable for corporate debts. One example is fiduciary taxes. Corporations are charged with withholding social security contributions on behalf of their employees. This is, in essence, the employees' money. If a company is financially troubled, there is a risk that it will use this money for its own benefit. This use may not be malicious, and the corporate officers anticipate repayment. As a matter of policy, however, this use of funds is unacceptable, and statutes impose personal liability on corporate officers (not directors and shareholders) for willful nonpayment of fiduciary taxes. Such statutes, then, encourage corporate officers to behave as if they are personally responsible for these funds.

Environmental law presents another example. Historically, only businesses were responsible for the environmental pollution they caused. But this approach did not sufficiently discourage polluting, as corporations with large financial exposure for environmental obligations could decide to liquidate under state corporate law, thus leaving the cleanup obligation unpaid. Therefore, as a matter of federal policy, Congress determined that in addition to corporations, certain "responsible parties" should be held personally liable for the costs of cleaning up environmental hazards.

It is worth considering the possibility of curtailing limited liability in certain bankruptcy contexts as well. This could be done by providing that corporate officers and directors cannot discharge in a personal bankruptcy case obligations for which the corporate debtor would be responsible were it an individual. This approach has already been adopted within the current bankruptcy law. Federal law provides that the officers of a federal depository institution are personally responsible if the bank fails to maintain its capital requirements. That provision circumvents limited liability. Because some of these officers and directors decided to file bankruptcy to obtain relief from this personal obligation, the Bankruptcy Code was amended specifically to make this obligation a nondischargeable debt.[21] So, in essence, the federal bankruptcy law reinforced another body of law that cut back on the protection of officers and directors.

Curtailing limited liability in bankruptcy situations diminishes the ability of knowledgeable corporate actors to avoid individual liability. In a sense, this approach serves to equalize corporate debtors and their principals. This is because even wealthy companies with savvy management will be unable to structure transactions that permit avoiding individual liability in bankruptcy. This approach has its downsides. Individuals could be deterred from serving as officers or directors of corporate entities. But individuals now continue to serve despite fiduciary tax liability or even environmental claims. Moreover, American society is litigious, and if the possibility exists to sue officers or directors, it is likely they will be sued. And even if the corporate officials prevail in those lawsuits, success comes at a cost. Further, the cost of liability insurance for officers and directors will increase as the prospects of suit increase, thereby curtailing profits.

New Value and Human Capital

Chapter 11's absolute priority rule (APR) requires that each most senior class of creditors be paid in full (unless they otherwise consent) before junior creditors can be paid. Most of the current debate in case law hinges on whether the contribution of new money (termed new value) is an exception to the APR. The Supreme Court has not addressed this issue head-on, although it has held that the APR does not apply to human capital (labor as distinguished from money). Thus, a farmer seeking to save the family farm could contribute two hundred thousand dollars in exchange for retaining his equity position, but he could not contribute personal services (plowing, milking, or harvesting) valued at two hundred thousand dollars.[22]

Regardless of whether the Bankruptcy Code embraced the exception to the APR as a matter of policy when the Code was enacted, it should explicitly embrace it now. If an owner is willing to contribute new monies to a sinking ship, that evidences a commitment to reorganization and a belief (even if rose colored) that the likelihood of success is greater than the likelihood of failure. The owner is overcoming failure by doing precisely what policymakers want: becoming a productive member of society.

If the new value exception is eliminated, the family farm will fold. But the original owner obviously has money that he could invest. We should encourage him to invest in his existing business as opposed to putting the money in his mattress. The exception to the APR is, in essence, a bet on long-term gain. It is a way of recognizing the intangible value of a business. The ability to reinvest furthers rehabilitation and thus is a risk worth taking. But reinvestment does not mean that the business will necessarily succeed. It is not a guarantee that creditors will gain more over the long haul. It is not a promise of employment for the workers in perpetuity. It is not a perfect salve against the stigma of failure. Owners may have a vision of the future that is overly optimistic or dead wrong. They may have an attachment to something with no marketable value.

The exception to the APR does create a lack of parity among creditors. The debtor's owner can choose whether to reinvest in the sinking ship. But the creditors are not accorded a similar choice. They cannot withdraw their investment and put their marbles elsewhere. In this sense, the rehabilitation is facilitated by curtailing creditors' options and is justified because debtor rehabilitation trumps creditor choice.

Accepting the concept of the new value exception to the APR leaves open two related questions. First, how much equity should an owner acquire for the new contribution? Valuation is a troubling issue in bankruptcy because of the myriad ways value can be calculated.[23] Inevitable conflicts will arise over what a company is worth prospectively, and within a range of values, reasonable people can differ. But the difficulty of ascertaining value, though important, is a problem of means, not ends. If the goal is correct, namely, to permit original owners to reinvest, then determining how much money it takes to retain a certain interest is a matter of fine tuning. Indeed, standardization in the valuation process would be useful throughout the bankruptcy system. It would curtail costs and put debtors, creditors, and investors in a better position to assess risk and gain.

The second and even more controversial question is, How can and should the new value be paid? The law recognizes contributions of new value only in the form of money.[24] If the owner of Seat Co. is willing to invest five hundred thousand dollars of new money into the business, the new value exception to the APR would enable the owner to do so and acquire (or retain) an ownership interest in the reorganized company. The only question would be how much of an interest this five hundred thousand dollars gives the owner. Does it give him a majority stake or a small minority interest, with the majority stake being held by creditors? The answer hinges on what Seat Co. is worth as a reorganized entity. But suppose that instead of money, the owner of Seat Co. wants to contribute his time and expertise, his human capital. Indeed, for individuals unable to borrow additional funds, human capital may be the only asset that they can contribute to the reorganization process. Although the Supreme Court does not share this view, there are good reasons for supporting contributions of human capital. Distinctions certainly can be made between human capital and green money or other assets like real and personal property. One is intangible and involves future commitment (human capital); the others are fungible and tradable and certainly more capable of valuation (money and other assets). One creates an enforceable obligation; the other does not.

Human capital, however, and how we as a society choose to treat it within the legal and economic system, is tied to our concepts of personhood and self-respect.[25] If individuals want to give of themselves, then we should encourage them. Donating one's time or ability is a strong demonstration of a rehabilitative spirit. And permitting the contribution of new money through human capital is not a demand that every debtor contribute labor. Debtors should have a choice, because forcing them to use their human capital, like forcing a debtor to reorganize, would come perilously close to peonage.

A Time for Intervention

Although little empirical data addresses what happens to debtors after filing, intuition suggests that because the reasons for filing are so varied, the legal release from obligations may not be enough to rehabilitate all debtors fully. Some evidence also suggests that the antidiscrimination provisions are not as effective as they could be.[26] Data show that despite the broad discharge provisions, individual debtors are unnecessarily reaffirming obligations with select creditors.[27] Some people have observed that bankruptcy should provide a fresh start, not a head start, but the Code as drafted may actually be accomplishing neither.

Providing true rehabilitation is a critical step. Failing to provide a fresh start in more than name is reminiscent of Derrick Bell's observation about good intentions in American society. As he stated, "We provide food without nutrition; welfare without well-being; job training without employment opportunities; and legal services without justice."[28] We need to have more than good intentions in bankruptcy. We need good results.

Many suggest that bankruptcy should not be the panacea for all social ills. Let bankruptcy resolve just the allocation of limited resources among creditors. Indeed, these people say, if rehabilitation involves job retraining, psychological counseling, financial planning, or educational programs, leave these issues for nonlegal social service agencies. But the law can be, and frequently is, a vehicle for social change.[29] With more than 1 million named and unnamed debtors in the bankruptcy system at any one time, we should not let the opportunity to intervene slip by.

Intervention is not an all-or-nothing proposition, encompassing only costly programs. It could involve something as simple as providing debtors with an opportunity to appear in court and tell their stories.[30] There is a psychological benefit to being able to speak to the judge and one's creditors in one's own words. And storytelling can also benefit creditors. Without meeting a debtor, it is easy for a creditor (and the court) to see only a balance sheet entry. But the dynamic can change when creditors are confronted with the real debtor. This does not mean that creditors should be forced to attend a court hearing, but those creditors who do attend would have an opportunity to hear the debtor's tale.

The government could provide all debtors with financial counseling before they emerge from bankruptcy, and efforts could be made to assist debtors in getting new jobs if needed. Some of these benefits could be provided by linking debtors to existing assistance programs. But American society shies away from governmental intervention for many reasons. First, such intervention can be seen as intrusive and perhaps paternalistic. Second, programs providing financial counseling or business advice to debtors would be expensive. And existing social welfare programs are nothing of which to be particularly proud. Many of these programs do not seem to help most recipients. Some might say they foster dependence, not independence. They are also administratively burdensome. Finally, many people do not want governmental growth. Instead, they want growth of private business, and they believe that problems will ostensibly resolve themselves in a free market economy.

Even if American society were to decide that the bankruptcy system presents a unique opportunity to right wrongs that have befallen debtors, who would oversee such a process? As it is, bankruptcy judges have barely enough time to handle the existing caseload. Indeed, under the Code, they are largely removed from the administrative aspects of cases.[31] In some instances, the judge never even sees the debtor.

A study of how 290 bankruptcy judges spend their time is instructive.[32] Without weighting caseloads based on the types of cases involved, this study found that each bankruptcy judge handled more than 3,200 cases between 1988 and 1989. This figure had jumped from 1,425 in 1980, probably because filing rates had increased by 185% between 1980 and 1991, but the increase in the number of judgeships during the same period was only 25%. The judges did not spend the greatest amount of time on nonbusiness cases. In 1989, for example, Chapter 7 cases accounted for 65% of all filings but only 16% of the weighted cases (weighting was designed to take into account the size and complexity of the cases handled). In sharp contrast, in 1989 Chapter 11 cases constituted 2.5% of all filings but 39% of all weighted cases.

Translating these figures to average judicial time spent is revealing. At a 95% level of statistical reliability, business Chapter 7 cases occupied 40 minutes per case of judicial time, whereas nonbusiness Chapter 7 cases occupied 10 minutes of time per case. On average, judges spent 38 minutes on each Chapter 13 case. Judges spent on average 456 minutes on each Chapter 11 case, with the amount of time increasing with the size of the case.

In simple terms, the greatest amount of judicial time is spent on cases that constitute the smallest percentage of the filed cases—the mega Chapter 11 cases. Individual cases, which constitute the overwhelming percentage of all filings, are allocated the fewest judicial hours. These data can be interpreted in a variety of ways. One possibility is that small cases, particularly no-asset cases, do not require judicial time. Hence, it is quite proper that these cases do not receive a lot of attention. It is also possible, however, that but for the crush of cases and the time-consuming nature of big cases (and the attention that needs to be paid to the number of constituencies in those cases), the individual cases would receive more time.

Implicit policy issues grow out of judicial time allocation. The data reveal that even if judges were willing to meet with debtors, the least intrusive form of intervention previously suggested, they would not have the time. Small cases, whether involving businesses or individuals, cannot get judicial attention given the present crush of cases. Even the appointment in 1993 of new judges and the prospect of more appointments may not be sufficient to offset the time demands suggested by the proposals here. Further, in some sense any expansion of the judicial role into the arena of social services may be thought improper and perhaps not welcomed by the judges themselves. Many people, both on and off the bench, view the judicial function quite narrowly. Even those judges with a heightened sense of the judicial role may not be qualified to assist the many debtors in need.

What other players within the bankruptcy system could expand or alter their role? Arguably, the Office of the United States Trustee could change the focus of its attention from the large cases, which generally are well monitored, to the smaller cases. This group, however, is not particularly trained for social service, at least not with existing personnel. Moreover, as adjuncts to the Justice Department, the United States Trustees may simply be unwilling to undertake the task. Another obvious candidate is debtors' lawyers. However much we may call lawyers "counselors," though, they are for the most part not trained to provide financial or business counseling. Moreover, attorneys in small bankruptcy cases are frequently not paid a great deal of money, and some accomplish what they do by delegating tasks to paralegals.

But other avenues should be pursued. The use of alternative dispute resolution in bankruptcy, which is currently being tried in selected regions of the United States, may help debtors not only to resolve their current disputes but to improve their relationships with their creditors. It makes sense to institute some follow-up studies to see whether debtors who resolved their problems through mediation are better able to break the cycle of failure and poverty than those who did not. Another possibility is requiring debtors to pay for counseling services, as is done in the field of family law for divorce and child custody issues. But most debtors would be unable to pay for the needed service. Another possibility is to try to provide counseling for debtors on a pro bono basis through business schools and schools of social work. But based on pro bono programs in law, professionals show considerable resistance, in practice as distinguished from theory, to these types of programs.[33] Another possibility is to require the consumer credit industry to pay for these programs through a tax calculated on the amount of monies lent. In essence, this would be the lenders' way of paying for the benefits they derive from lending without adequately fine-tuned monitoring and from using the bankruptcy system as their collection agent. Moreover, because the consumer lending industry commonly lends without adequately assessing the borrower's capacity to repay, the suggested approach would help produce healthier prospective borrowers, which would benefit both borrowers and lenders without curbing credit.

I offer no specific program for change. Rather, I suggest a new approach to breaking the cycle of failure. The types of potential programs are almost unlimited. If we want to revive the economy and help small businesses, then helping debtors rehabilitate is one step in the right direction.

PART III

Creditors

_____

CHAPTER NINE

Thinking about Creditors

Viewed from the creditor-focused perspective, bankruptcy seeks to maximize the recovery to creditors. Currently, creditor recovery is accomplished through a collective remedy. When all creditors are forced to share in the available pool of assets, no single creditor garners a disproportionate share.[1] Bankruptcy's collective approach has been described and justified by some scholars as the antidote for the result in the movie *It's a Mad Mad Mad Mad World*.[2] In that movie, each of the characters went on a separate hunt for a treasure on the theory that whoever found it would get to keep the whole thing. But the confusion and costs of trying to collect the treasure outweighed the benefits, and all the treasure seekers ended up empty-handed. Suppose the treasure seekers had agreed to work together. Each treasure seeker would have received less than someone who found the treasure alone, but each seeker would have recovered more than all the unsuccessful treasure hunters in the movie.

This collective approach, when applied to the bankruptcy system, creates a structure that precludes the creditors from individually chasing the debtor's treasure (the available assets). Instead, the creditors work together to both preserve and enhance the treasure and cut back on the costs of trying to recover a piece of it. The loss from the disaster (debtor nonpayment) is then shared among the creditors. As a general principle, this collective approach makes a good deal of sense. Creditors should not have to spend more to get less. Enabling one creditor who is rich or speedy to collect the entire treasure deprives other creditors of the opportunity to recover anything.

The collectivization model (alternately referred to as the creditor model) has flaws, as numerous commentators have pointed out.[3]

Some argue that while it seeks to maximize creditor recovery (that is, to provide economically efficient results), it actually fails to do so. Others challenge the underlying and unsubstantiated premises of the approach, namely, that the goal of all creditors is wealth maximization, that rational people would choose collectivization over any other approach to achieve that end, and that choices are unchanging. The collectivization model has been vigorously challenged, then, in terms of how it addresses both intracreditor issues and issues between creditor and debtor and community.

My goal is not to replay this debate. The collectivization model has problems other than the ones just described: it is at once incomplete and overbroad. It is incomplete in that it explains bankruptcy purely from a creditor's perspective. Bankruptcy involves much more than maximizing creditors' recovery as measured in dollars and cents. Bankruptcy is concerned with rehabilitating debtors, which may not benefit creditors' short-term recovery. American society may forfeit some economic efficiency now for future economic and personal growth, for national humanity.[4] The creditor model is also overbroad because it does not recognize the significant differences among creditors and the many forms those differences can take. Not all creditors reached their predicament in the same fashion, and not all will emerge equally able to withstand the financial losses caused by the debtor's nonpayment.

Yet another flaw in the creditor model also runs throughout the bankruptcy system: this model is premised on a belief in equality of treatment among creditors. The result is pro rata distribution among creditors, a concept at the core of the bankruptcy system's treatment of creditors.[5] But the system fails to recognize the vast chasm between equality of treatment and equality of outcome. A richer, more finely tuned concept of equality is needed.[6]

Equality of Treatment: What Does It Mean?

Equality of treatment among creditors has appeal. It would be unfair to create a bankruptcy system in which the most powerful or most likable creditor was always paid ahead of other creditors. It is far more equitable for creditors to divide up the assets among themselves in proportion to what each creditor is owed.

Assume Seat Co. has $50,000 in assets. Suppose that on the petition date the company owes $100,000 to seven creditors: $40,000 to its bank, $20,000 to one trade creditor who is the major supplier in the industry, $15,000 to the Internal Revenue Service, $10,000 to a tort victim, $6,000 to the telephone company, $5,000 to its employees for back wages, and $4,000 to the local dry cleaner that has laundered all the company uniforms over the past several years. Assume, for the moment, that there are no priority or secured creditors. Seat Co. is balance sheet insolvent.

Suppose the sales manager of the trade creditor is a close friend and neighbor of Seat Co.'s owner. If Seat Co. repaid this trade creditor in full ($20,000), only $30,000 ($50,000 minus $20,000) would remain with which to repay $80,000 ($100,000 minus $20,000) in debt owed to the other six creditors. Suppose the bank and Seat Co. had a long-standing relationship and the bank president exerted considerable pressure on Seat Co. for repayment. Suppose Seat Co. succumbed to this pressure. Absent a rule governing equality of treatment (also termed equality of distribution) among creditors, the trade creditor and the bank would more than eat up the available assets ($60,000 was owed to them collectively), and the bank still would be owed $10,000. The five remaining creditors would emerge from the bankruptcy process empty-handed.

With equality of treatment in place, each of the seven creditors would get a pro rata share (fifty cents on the dollar, because there are $100,000 in claims and $50,000 in assets) of the available assets. A distribution scheme would show each creditor receiving a different amount based on a single formula (table 2). This approach resembles a six-person family dividing up a pie at dessert time. Rather than the parents getting to eat the entire pie because they are older and more powerful, the pie is divided into six pieces so everyone shares in the available dessert. But a pie can be divided in a variety of ways, and how it is divided demonstrates the many meanings

Table 2. Pro Rata Distribution

Creditor	Amount owed ($)	Pro rata payout of 50% ($)
Bank	40,000	20,000
Trade creditor	20,000	10,000
IRS	15,000	7,500
Tort victim	10,000	5,000
Telephone co.	6,000	3,000
Employees	5,000	2,500
Dry cleaner	4,000	2,000
Total	100,000	50,000

of the single term *equality*. In some families, the pie pieces would all be the same size (absolute equality). In others, the pie would be divided based on the appetites and desires of the eaters on the night the pie is served: those who are the most hungry would receive the biggest pieces (equality of outcome). The family could also divide the pie the same way at every meal based on the age and size of the family members. The parents would always receive the biggest pieces because they are bigger, and the remaining pieces could be divided among the children based on their relative ages and sizes (equality of treatment). In the last situation, equal treatment does yield unequal outcomes, but those disparate outcomes are not as nuanced as under the equality of outcome approach. The different meanings of the term *equality* exist on a continuum. At one end of that continuum is absolute equality (six even pieces), and at the other end is equality of outcome (different piece sizes depending on the appetites of the eaters on a particular night), with equality of treatment (uneven pieces determined by a set formula) falling some-where in the middle.

To return to Seat Co.'s creditors, equality of treatment (distribu-tion) does not mean that all creditors are paid identical dollar

Table 3. Absolute Equality

Creditor	Amount owed ($)	Absolute equality ($)	Pro rata ($)	Differential between absolute equality and pro rata (rounded $)
Bank	40,000	7,142.86	20,000	−12,857
Trade creditor	20,000	7,142.86	10,000	− 2,857
IRS	15,000	7,142.86	7,500	− 357
Tort victim	10,000	7,142.86	5,000	2,143
Telephone co.	6,000	7,142.86	3,000	4,143
Employees	5,000	7,142.86	2,500	4,643
Dry cleaner	4,000	7,142.86	2,000	5,143
Total	100,000	50,000	50,000	0

amounts. Instead, what it means is that all creditors receive the same percentage of what they are owed, in this case 50% of their claim, even if they vary in size and power.

In contrast, under a system of absolute equality, Seat Co.'s seven creditors would divide the $50,000 in available assets evenly among themselves, with each creditor receiving $7,142.86 ($50,000 divided by seven). That would be like dividing the dessert pie into six even pieces (table 3). Applying absolute equality, some creditors (the bank, the trade creditor, and the IRS) would receive less than what they would be paid based on a pro rata distribution, while others (the tort victim, the telephone company, the employees, and the dry cleaner) would receive more. If each of the seven creditors had been owed $10,000, then each would have been paid the same percentage (71.43%) of the $50,000 of available assets, that is, $7,143. In this situation, absolute equality would have been synonymous with equal treatment. But in reality, absolute equality is problematic because creditors are usually owed hugely differing sums. Pro rata distribution recognizes these differences.

Lessons on Equality Learned from
Nonbankruptcy Law

The current U.S. bankruptcy law adopts (with the exception of secured and priority creditors) a system that most closely resembles equality of treatment (see table 2). Stated in the language frequently employed in constitutional law, the current bankruptcy system and the collectivization model apply notions of formal equality. This is better than a system based on absolute equality. But equality of treatment rests on a shaky premise, namely, that all creditors are the same. This assimilationist stance is inaccurate. Look at Seat Co.'s creditors: some are big businesses, one is a small local store, some are individuals, and one is the government. These creditors will experience their losses differently. For some of the creditors (the bank, the trade creditor, and the IRS), a loss of under $50,000 will hardly be noticed. For others, a loss of the same amount or less affects whether they stay in business (the dry cleaner) or make their mortgage payments (the employees and the tort victim). The situations giving rise to the obligation of the debtor to the creditor also differ dramatically. The bank, the trade creditor, the telephone company, and the dry cleaner intentionally lent money to the debtor. But the IRS, the tort victim, and the employees were, in essence, involuntary lenders, or "reluctant creditors." This group (with the possible exception of the IRS, which does assume a certain degree of nonpayment based on years of tax collection) did not expect to take the risk of nonpayment. These creditors were not in a position to determine how to handle the loss *ex ante* because they did not expect to be owed any money.[7]

There are thus material downsides to equality of treatment. Suppose there are two children, both ill from the same disease.[8] One of the children is close to death while the other child, whose life is not threatened, is in temporary mild pain. Suppose that only one dosage of medicine is available, which could save the gravely ill child's life. If the medicine is divided under an equal treatment approach, each child would receive half the available medicine. This would be akin to a pro rata distribution to creditors owed an equal amount. In view of the vastly different conditions of the two children, however, it makes sense to treat them unequally. If the desirable outcome is that both children survive, then there needs to be inequality of treatment. The gravely ill child needs all the medicine; the mildly ill child can survive just fine without any medicine.

Now suppose that women who want to be firefighters have to pass the same test of physical strength as their male counterparts. Assume that the test requires the prospective firefighter to carry a 250-pound person down a sixty-foot ladder. This test adheres to the principle of equality of treatment because, regardless of gender, all candidates take the same test.[9] But equality applied in this fashion yields unequal results: women will rarely, if ever, become firefighters because they will not be able to pass the test, given the disparity in size and strength between men and women. Unless the requirements for becoming a firefighter are changed for women, equality produces inequality. To achieve equality, men and women would have to be treated differently.

Some will argue that if the goal is to provide competent firefighters, the test standards should not be lowered simply to give women access to this job. The risks to the public from weak firefighters are too great. This point is valid if, in fact, carrying a 250-pound person is the sine qua non of excellence in fire fighting. If the essential requirement of firefighting is anaerobic skill, then women's inability to meet the set criteria would lead to the conclusion that women should not be firefighters. I suspect, however, that anaerobic strength is not the only criterion for determining who will be a good firefighter and that lifting a 250-pound person, though not insignificant, is not something a firefighter commonly does. Perhaps the weight test could be better correlated to the real-life experience of firefighters. Women firefighters may bring qualities other than strength to the job, and perhaps the testing of all potential firefighters (men and women) should include an assessment of these skills. Suppose that in addition to strength, potential firefighters were tested for agility, aerobic ability, speed, reflexes, knowledge of fire safety rules and procedures, response to stress, capacity for compassion, and ability to communicate with bereaved individuals. Using the new criteria, many women could perform at least as well as, and perhaps better than, their male counterparts.

This type of example has prompted people to reconsider what is and should be meant by *equality*. Since the 1980s, there has been a strong movement away from both equality of treatment (formal equality) and absolute equality and a toward a model based on equality of effect (outcome).[10] This is a more fact-sensitive approach. This shift focuses attention on the differences among people rather than the similarities; it addresses the end result rather than the means used to reach the result. In the case of ill children, it means not dividing the medicine evenly even though both children are ill. For the firefighters, it means instituting a test that takes into account women's lack of physical strength.

Outcome-based approaches may be costly. Creating and administering two separate tests for firefighters or developing a more sensitive test can be expensive. Also, in a world of limited job opportunities, equal outcome may deprive some qualified men from obtaining jobs that will now go to women. This is not the place to debate the efficacy of affirmative action programs that create equality (for women and minorities) and inequality (for white men) at one and the same time.[11] But the debate concerning the meaning of equality has important implications for how to treat creditors within the bankruptcy system.

With limited exceptions, the current legal system does not distinguish between creditors based on their size, the impact nonpayment will have on them, or the origin of the indebtedness. These are serious omissions. This failure does not mean that we should discard the equal treatment model altogether. It should remain as the starting point. But there needs to be a way to deviate from this approach and introduce notions of equality of outcome. This change would dramatically alter how creditors are treated, and its cost has to be measured against its benefits.

Establishing Priorities

The suggested shift is not as radical as it first appears. Although the current distribution scheme is premised on equality of treatment, striking exceptions to this general approach already exist. Certain groups of creditors are accorded priority over the others. Assuming sufficient money is available, priority creditors are repaid in full. The higher the priority, the greater the likelihood of repayment. Return to Seat Co.'s seven creditors and consider which, if any of them, should move to the front of the pack and on what basis. We could say that the involuntary creditors (the employees, the IRS, and the tort victim) should step to the front because they did not intend to become creditors. Or we could look at which creditors are sufficiently large and well enough off financially to be able to withstand the loss of less than $50,000 (the IRS, the bank, the trade creditor, and the telephone company) and then give priority to those who cannot (the employees and the dry cleaner). Whatever approach we take, a priority system differentiates between creditors and moves away from a system of equality of treatment.

Priority Creditors

Under current law, two of Seat Co.'s seven creditors are entitled to priority: the employees and the IRS. Each employee is entitled to a maximum of $4,000 for unpaid wages earned within ninety days of bankruptcy. For simplicity's sake, assume that Seat Co. owes each of five individuals $1,000 for wages earned within the ninety-day period. The next priority is the IRS, for $15,000 in back taxes. For simplicity's sake, assume the unpaid taxes are for recent returns. The five remaining creditors are nonpriority creditors, who share pro rata after repayment of the priority expenses. These unsecured creditors (with total claims aggregating $80,000) share in the $30,000 of remaining assets after the $20,000 in priority claims are paid. The remaining five creditors will thus receive 37.5% of what they are owed.

Table 4. Distribution with Priorities

Creditor	Nature of claim	Amount owed ($)	Amount distributed, taking priority into account ($)	Differential between payout with and without priority ($)
Employees	Priority	5,000	5,000	2,500
IRS[a]	Priority	15,000	15,000	7,500
Bank	Unsecured	40,000	15,000	−5,000
Trade creditor	Unsecured	20,000	7,500	−2,500
Tort victim	Unsecured	10,000	3,750	−1,250
Telephone co.	Unsecured	6,000	2,250	− 750
Dry cleaner	Unsecured	4,000	1,500	− 500
Total		100,000	50,000	0

[a]This table does not take into account that, in Chapter 11, payments to the IRS can be stretched out over six years.

Notice how, as one might expect, the creditors obtaining the priority (the employees and the IRS) are treated substantially better than they would be if there were no priority system (table 4). Correspondingly, those not accorded a priority (the bank, the trade creditor, the tort victim, the telephone company, and the dry cleaner) are treated less favorably than they would be if all creditors shared in the pool of available assets. The differences may not appear to be substantial in absolute dollar amounts, but the amounts may matter to the creditors. The loss of $1,250 in payout under the priority system for the tort victim, for example, is important if the victim has unpaid medical expenses and is unable to work. In contrast, the telephone company's diminished payout (a decrease of $750) will barely be noticed. Any sting to the telephone company is further mitigated by the tax benefits it can garner through the bad debt deduction (which enables it to reduce its taxable income). Tax benefits, however, do not help the tort victim pay her own creditors now.

Secured Creditors

Thus far, the bank has been treated as an unsecured creditor, as if it holds no collateral securing Seat Co.'s obligation. But suppose that the bank holds a security interest in one of Seat Co.'s pieces of equipment, which is valued at $10,000. Assume also, for simplicity's sake, that Seat Co. has sold the equipment and is holding the proceeds in a segregated account for the bank. For bankruptcy purposes, $10,000 of the bank's $40,000 claim is secured, and the remainder, $30,000, is unsecured. The Bankruptcy Code requires creditors to bifurcate their claim into a secured and an unsecured claim if the collateral is worth less than the debt.[12]

Under existing law, Seat Co. must distribute the proceeds from the equipment sale to the bank before other creditors, including the priority creditors, are paid. In essence, then, secured creditors have a priority over all other creditors to the extent of the value of their collateral. Again, priority creditors (of which there are two) will be paid ahead of other unsecured creditors (of which there are five when one includes the unsecured portion of the bank's claim, which is paid from unencumbered assets). Of the $50,000 in cash available for distribution, $10,000 goes to the bank's secured claim and $20,000 to the priority claims. Thus, $20,000 in cash is available for distribution to unsecured creditors with claims of $70,000. This yields a payout of approximately 28.6% on unsecured, nonpriority claims (table 5).

Administrative Claims

The final nail in the unsecured creditors' coffin is the first-priority expense, administrative claims, which include professional fees. This category of claims also encompasses any costs incurred during the course of a case that are not repaid in the ordinary course. As the popular press and academics have frequently pointed out, administrative expenses, as an absolute number, can be very high.[13] Assume Seat Co. has retained an attorney and an accountant

Table 5. Distribution with Priorities and Secured Creditors

Creditor	Nature of claim	Amount owed ($)	Amount of payout (rounded $)	Differential between payout and pro rata after priorities (rounded $)
Bank (secured)	Secured	10,000	10,000	6,250[a]
Employees	Priority	5,000	5,000	0
IRS	Priority	15,000	15,000	0
Bank (unsecured)	Unsecured	30,000	8,571	−2,679[a]
Trade creditor	Unsecured	20,000	5,714	−1,786
Tort victim	Unsecured	10,000	2,857	− 893
Telephone co.	Unsecured	6,000	1,714	− 536
Dry cleaner	Unsecured	4,000	1,143	− 357
Total		100,000	49,999	± 1

[a]The bank's total differential between payout and pro rata after priorities is thus $3,571, based on a combination of secured and unsecured claims.

and that their respective fees (which must be approved by the bankruptcy court) aggregate $10,000. The consequences of this priority are immediately noticeable. After the bank receives its proceeds ($10,000) and the attorneys, employees, and IRS are paid their respective priorities (aggregating $30,000), only $10,000 remains to distribute to nonpriority unsecured creditors. This is $40,000 less than the amount that would have been available had all creditors been treated on a pro rata basis (see table 2). Unsecured creditors with claims totaling $70,000 will share in $10,000 in assets, producing a payout of approximately 14.3% to unsecured creditors. Had other legitimate administrative expenses (such as payment to the creditors' committee counsel and payment of expenses for members of the creditors' committee, which is now permitted under the 1994

Amendments) been included in this model, the percentage payout would have been even smaller. Indeed, in some cases, secured and priority claims eat up the entire estate.

Who Are the Real Winners and Losers?

The consequences of a payout to unsecured creditors with all the priority expenses in place, including administrative expenses, would be very different from those of a payout in which all creditors (including secured and priority) were treated on a pro rata basis (without regard to their status), which would yield a payout of 45.5% (table 6). With priority status in place, the trade creditor, tort victim, telephone company, and dry cleaner are all hurt compared with pro rata distribution. Despite being secured, the bank is so undersecured that it would do better being treated on an unsecured pro rata basis ($18,200 versus $14,290). Were the bank oversecured, its situation would be reversed.

The real economic winners with all the priorities in place are the professionals, the employees, and the IRS. Secured creditors are bankruptcy's other winners. Do these particular parties deserve to be in bankruptcy's winners' circle, or are other creditors more deserving of the coveted priority treatment?

Professionals

The first priority accorded to professionals can be justified on the theory that these individuals, so essential to facilitating the bankruptcy process, will not work unless they are paid. Moreover, unlike many of the debtor's creditors, the professionals arrive after the fact to attempt to right the tipping ship. Arguably, the other creditors would receive even less were these professionals not retained to effectuate the bankruptcy process.

Almost everyone would agree that achieving success in bankruptcy, howsoever defined, requires input from outside professionals.

Table 6. Distribution with All Priorities in Place

Creditor	Nature of claim	Amount owed ($)	Payout amount pro rata (45.5%) ($)	Payout amount with priority/secured status in place ($)	Differential between payout with existing system and pro rata payout ($)
Bank (secured)	Secured	10,000	4,550[a]	10,000	5,450[a]
Attorneys/ accountants	Priority (post-petition)	10,000	4,550	10,000	5,450
Employees	Priority	5,000	2,275	5,000	2,725
IRS	Priority	15,000	6,825	15,000	8,175
Bank (unsecured)	Unsecured	30,000	13,650[a]	4,286	−9,364[a]
Trade creditor	Unsecured	20,000	9,100	2,857	−6,243
Tort victim	Unsecured	10,000	4,550	1,429	−3,121
Telephone co.	Unsecured	6,000	2,730	857	−1,873
Dry cleaner	Unsecured	4,000	1,820	571	−1,249
Total		110,000	50,000	50,000	± 50

[a]The bank's pro rata payout amount is $18,200 once secured and unsecured debt are combined. Its total differential between payout with the existing system and pro rata payout is −$3,914.

Pro se individual filers commonly experience problems achieving their goals in bankruptcy.[14] Indeed, outside bankruptcy, debtors can and do obtain professional advice, so in this sense, the world of bankruptcy is not adding a type of expense that otherwise would be nonexistent. Proceeding without professionals would be like performing self-surgery after a doctor diagnosed the need for a gallbladder operation.

Although the administrative expenses are high and consideration should be given to curtailing them, that is not the question here. The issue is whether professional fees should be accorded a first priority. The concerns about the high priority would diminish were the size of the payments to diminish. It is easy to suggest, particularly in a climate generally hostile to lawyers, that the professionals should not be so well paid in bankruptcy cases. This conclusion ignores a distinction between transactions pre- and post-petition. Many pre-petition transactions with a debtor are voluntary: the parties choose to deal with each other, and then they end up sharing in a disaster. But a professional engaged by the debtor was not a part of the disaster. And the professional's decision to be engaged in a case is not synonymous with consenting to share in the disaster. Indeed, it is because of the disaster that the professional has to be retained in the first instance. A professional in the bankruptcy case should not be required to render services at bargain basement rates because everyone else is suffering a loss. By way of analogy, suppose a company hires a bad contractor and, as a result, its office building is not well constructed and cannot be timely completed without hiring a new contractor. It would be absurd to suggest that the new contractor should be put at financial risk for the sake of a problem that this contractor did not create.

This argument supports payment to professionals. But it does not address whether the need for professional expertise mandates a first-priority payout. If other parties are more worthy of repayment than everyone else, then professional fees should fall to a lower priority. Whether this would cause the better qualified professionals to leave the bankruptcy field is an issue that would have to be assessed empirically. Indeed, most professionals wish to avoid a return to the time when bankruptcy law practice was not well regarded and was considered by most firms as unseemly, like family law or criminal law.[15] The quality and professionalism of the bankruptcy bar have risen since then. Professionals are unlikely to leave what they do in significant numbers because of a somewhat greater but not disproportionate risk. Maybe a lower-priority status would increase their incentive to see that the higher-priority creditors are paid, as their own payment would be contingent on this repayment.

Employees

Justifying a priority payment to employees (as distinguished from management) for a limited proportion of their back wages is not difficult.[16] First, this is a group that may not be able to withstand a financial loss because they operate with little cushion and would be unable to repay their own creditors if they are not repaid. Second, they did not enter into a debtor-creditor relationship with the failed company; they entered into an employer-employee relationship. Employees do not perceive of themselves as lenders. Third, if employees are not paid, they are unlikely to continue working. Because a work force is critical to a reorganization effort, it makes sense to pay these workers, as their labors will inure to the benefit of *other* creditors. Indeed, some courts even permit these priority expenses to be paid before a plan is confirmed although this approach has no explicit statutory justification.

The effort to protect employees actually extends even further. The current bankruptcy priority system protects, up to a predetermined cap, pensions, severance, and health care benefits earned before bankruptcy. Indeed, some of the hottest debate regarding bankruptcy reform since the mid-1980s revolved around the priority to be accorded unpaid pension benefits.[17] Although pensions and severance are not traditional wages, they are significant to recipients who may have relied on their receipt in choosing jobs throughout their lives. Moreover, many recipients are now unable to purchase from an outside source (at a reasonable price) what they expected to receive from the employer. One cannot help but sense that employers should be stopped from depriving present and former workers of at least some of their earned benefits.

Taxes

The adage that only two things are certain in life—death and taxes—holds true in the bankruptcy context. Priority to state and federal taxing authorities is premised, no doubt, on the theory that the government cannot forgo revenues it requires all citizens and businesses to pay. Moreover, the government needs the revenues to provide services to a wide range of citizens, and a shortfall would deprive others of needed benefits. A desire for a deterrent also comes into play. If everyone could rush into bankruptcy to receive a discharge of taxes, many people might do just that.

But in a universe of scarce resources, we have to reconsider whether such a high priority for the government is warranted. Think of the government as one large entity. Losses at one end (from, for example, nonpayment of taxes and unemployment benefits) have to be offset against gains on the other end (current and future taxable income from various businesses and individuals including but not limited to the debtor). So suppose Seat Co. decides to liquidate because it has insufficient sums to fund a plan of reorganization. Under the priority system, Seat Co. will pay the government the $50,000 it owes in back taxes as a priority. The government is ahead by $50,000. But this is deceptive. Suppose that when the government is paid, small unsecured creditors go unpaid. When this happens, these creditors' businesses fail. Suppose the dry cleaner who serviced Seat Co.'s plant fails. If the dry cleaner pays only $10,000 in taxes annually, the government is still $40,000 ahead. But suppose the failure of the dry cleaner results in five lost jobs, as other dry cleaners do not need more workers. These individuals would have paid some taxes, and now they need to draw unemployment benefits. Assume that these benefits and lost taxes total $10,000. The government is still $30,000 ahead. But the five workers can't meet the payments to their creditors and can't pay their insurance for health and property. Suppose one worker has a heart attack and another damages a neighbor's car. Assume the medical expenses total $10,000 and the car is damaged to the extent of $5,000. The medical expenses will be subsidized by the government, and an insurance pool, run by the state, will pay for the property damage. The government's gain is down to $15,000, and that sum will continue to decrease in the event of other drains on government resources. In summary, if the government is paid as a priority, it will have more over the short term. Bankruptcy's ripple effect, however, will eat away at that gain, and what appears to be a victory for government repayment will yield less glorious results over the longer haul as the costs of the priority system are felt.

The government, unlike employees, is able to sustain a loss at least over the short term. This is not to say that the government has infinite resources and can always just print more money. This type of thinking promotes deficit spending and a growing budget gap. But in terms of wealth redistribution, the government is better positioned to recapture bankruptcy losses than employees or some of the other creditors. In addition, paying the government to reduce prospective nonpayment of taxes assumes that people are copycats and will flock to file bankruptcy just to avoid paying taxes. Assuredly, some individuals or businesses will take advantage in this fashion, but most will not. As it is, American society has a voluntary tax system, and most Americans pay.[18]

Ways of repaying the government other than in cash (even if payments could be stretched out) should be investigated. Perhaps future earnings could be taxed at a graduated scale until repayment for back taxes is made. Perhaps the government could take long-term promissory notes from the debtor. In a noncapitalistic system, the government could take over ownership of troubled businesses. Although American society may shy away from such overt government intrusion into private enterprise, the government has interfered in seemingly less offensive ways to promote certain businesses and industries. The government bailout of Chrysler is an example.[19] Governmental positions on foreign trade affect industry success. Tax deductions, tax depreciation rules, and investment tax credits all foster particular results, and although they do not shift ownership from private industry to the government, they exemplify market manipulation. So some tax incentive program in the bankruptcy arena has both precedent and potential.[20]

Secured Creditors

Of all the priorities, treatment of the secured creditor is one of the more problematic. Some scholars question whether security interests should even exist or, if they do, whether they should survive a bankruptcy.[21] The bankruptcy law already limits the rights of secured creditors. A secured creditor's claim is bifurcated into secured and unsecured claims based on the value of the collateral on the date of filing. Most secured creditors can be crammed down, which means they can be forced to accept a repayment plan not of their own choosing. Finally, the secured creditors' position can be subordinated to other secured creditors who are willing to lend to the debtor, assuming there is sufficient collateral. These examples reflect significant inroads into the position of secured creditors in bankruptcy. Except in the context of lien avoidance, however, the value of the secured lender's collateral is preserved and protected in bankruptcy. Moreover, there is a distinction between curtailing post-petition security interests in bankruptcy and eliminating them altogether.

If a lender is concerned about a borrower's defaulting, it may not lend without collateral. If it does lend and the company fails, realization on the collateral could mean that little or nothing would be available for distribution thereafter to unsecured lenders. This result is not unfair, some argue, because the unsecured lenders could spend the time and money to investigate a debtor's net worth before extending credit. They could elect to deal with the debtor only on a COD or purchase-money basis. For small lenders, however, the cost of the credit check in time and money may not seem worth it even though the potential for loss is sizable. The effects of secured credit can be felt even more strongly by those lenders who could not protect themselves even if they wanted to do so. Involuntary creditors like the IRS and the tort victim are in this category.

Rather than eliminate secured debt, we should identify and then remedy those limited situations in which the secured lender becomes too powerful and controls the reorganization process to the detriment of all other creditors, the debtor, and the community. Such secured lenders may include single-asset real estate lenders and mortgagors. Both were further strengthened by the 1994 Amendments.

In certain parts of the United States, with downturns in the real estate market, single-asset debtors (the asset being a piece of land and perhaps a building) seek to restructure the secured lender's debt. When the lender is undersecured, the debtor may try to classify the large unsecured claim separately from other unsecured claimants. There is considerable debate over whether this separate classification is permissible.[22] If the undersecured portion is not separately classified, the secured creditor controls both the secured and unsecured classes, which means controlling the reorganization process. If debtors were permitted to place the undersecured portion of the secured creditor's claim in a separate class, unsecured creditors would gain some leverage.

Unlike the interests of other secured lenders, the interests of mortgagors cannot be stripped down in Chapter 11 and Chapter 13 cases. Hence, if the value of the debtor's home falls well below the value of the debt, the mortgagor is entitled to be treated as a fully secured creditor. This approach was justified on the theory that mortgagors would cease lending on homes if they were not assured of payment, a result that would harm debtors. There is some reason to believe, however, particularly following the *Durrett* controversy, that this is an idle fear.[23] If individuals could adjust, if not modify, home mortgages, the lender's power would be curtailed.

Another possible change is increasing the flexibility of the methods of repaying the secured creditors. If secured creditors are viewed as partners of the debtor in a long-term business venture, then the focus should shift to longer-term payments. Secured creditors could take their interest payments in equity rather than cash to reflect a commitment to the debtor. Debtors with no free assets could negotiate to convert a portion of the lender's debt into equity. Lenders would become more like co-partners with the debtor and less like commodities brokers living for the short-term trades.[24]

Although the U.S. bankruptcy system starts with a premise of equality of treatment, all is not equal among the creditors in the kingdom of debt. It is time to rethink both the meaning of equality of distribution among creditors and the justifications for priority treatment.

CHAPTER TEN

Rethinking Equality of Distribution among Creditors

The Bankruptcy Code rests on a policy of equality among creditors, but actually in place is a system of partial inequality through the priority system and preferred treatment of secured creditors. If the specific unsecured claims that are nondischargeable are added to the mix, equality of treatment seems even farther away. This is because if a debt is not discharged, the creditors holding those claims can look to future as well as current assets to recover, thereby bettering their chances of full recovery. Although some inroads into a system of pro rata distribution are wise, the justifications for differing treatment under current law do not withstand scrutiny.

Equality of treatment fails to recognize the marked diversity among creditors, including the significant differences in how they became creditors and the consequences to them of nonpayment. "Unsecured claims" is a catch-all category involving wide-ranging obligations. It includes the claims of creditors who extended credit voluntarily in large and small amounts. It folds together large and small businesses—Seat Co.'s supplier of belt material, owed five hundred thousand dollars, and its supplier of stationery products, owed fifty dollars. Employees, owed back wages for which there is no priority, and individuals injured through negligence or recklessness while on Seat Co.'s property are also lumped into the category of unsecured claims, as are nonpriority tax claims, utility bills, and obligations to landlords for unpaid rent.

Composing a Creditors' Committee

From a purely distributional vantage point, it makes sense to place in the same pool a large corporate creditor owed $5 million, a medium-sized business creditor owed $50,000, and a small individual creditor owed $500. The biggest and strongest creditor cannot muscle all the assets for its own benefit and deprive the weaker and smaller creditors of everything. This approach could be called grouping for distributional purposes. But the existing bankruptcy system forms groups for other purposes as well.

From the group of unsecured creditors, the United States Trustee selects the official creditors' committee. This committee represents the interests of the entire unsecured creditor body during a Chapter 11 case. It provides a check on the debtor's powers. Although the success of committees has been questioned (because they frequently are not formed in small cases and are inactive in others), the concept is sound. If Seat Co. has five hundred creditors, they cannot all sit down at the table and negotiate with the debtor regarding a repayment plan. A committee should save money as each creditor does not need to retain separate counsel. The problem rests with how that committee is chosen and operates.

Under the bankruptcy law, the United States Trustee appoints (based on the dollar amounts owed) the seven largest creditors willing to serve as the official unsecured creditors' committee.[1] The Code provides that the Trustee must choose a "representative" committee from among the largest creditors, which has been interpreted to mean appointment of a wide range of types of unsecured creditors. Among Seat Co.'s five hundred unsecured creditors, for example, the seven-member creditors' committee could be composed of four trade creditors, each owed more than $500,000; one insurance company owed $400,000 for past-due premiums; one bank with a large undersecured claim equal to $300,000; and a union seeking recovery for unfunded health care benefits totaling $100,000. This committee includes different types of unsecured creditors and hence satisfies the need for a representational committee—at least at one level.

The Code defines the constituency of committees narrowly, with only the largest, albeit diverse, creditors being picked. The Code considers a creditor "large" based on the amount owed, not the net worth of the creditor itself. So it is possible that a small business owed a huge sum could sit on a creditors' committee with a large corporate entity that is also owed an enormous sum. Conversely, a creditor whose corporation is large could be owed a small amount. In practical terms, the creditors with the largest claims in dollars tend to be the largest creditors in terms of net worth, as their size is what enabled them to lend so much to one debtor. Creditors owed small amounts can be but are not necessarily small in net worth.

Although the largest creditors (in amount and size) certainly want to maximize recovery for all creditors (because the large creditors will receive the biggest shares of the pie under a pro rata distribution system), their needs may differ substantially from those of smaller creditors. Although the sums owed the members of the creditors' committee are large as absolute amounts, the repayment of these amounts may not affect the creditors' livelihood in either the long or short term. Seat Co.'s trade creditors, insurance company, bank, and union, for example, can withstand the losses.

Suppose these committee members are all convinced that the debtor's continued existence is the best way to ensure maximum repayment. Continuity provides at least some of the creditors with the possibility of future business. Assume the committee negotiates a 50% payout plan with payments to be made over a period of five years without interest. A trade creditor owed $500,000 would be paid $50,000 per year for five years. In the grand scheme of things, this $250,000 is a sizable payout, and it would appear that the committee had been extremely successful. But the consequences of this arrangement are different for the dry cleaner that Seat Co. owed $5,000. This small creditor is owed a small amount. From the dry cleaner's perspective, though, the amount owed is large. Under the plan, it will be repaid $2,500 over five years, or $500 per year. For the dry cleaner, a five-year payout is too long. It needs the money now to pay for its rent, equipment, wages, and taxes. Otherwise, the dry cleaner will fail. The creditors' committee may have negotiated a plan that yields the greatest amount possible, but the equality of treatment will yield unequal results. By lumping creditors together based on their status as unsecured claimants, the bankruptcy law ignores equality of outcome.

Separate Classification and Treatment

The implicit assumption that the largest creditors (in amount and, correspondingly, size) have the same needs and considerations as smaller creditors is flawed. There are several ways of accomplishing greater flexibility in the treatment of unsecured creditors, ideally without adding excessive costs or time to the bankruptcy process. Creditors' committees could be reconstituted to include creditors owed lesser amounts or at least a representative of that group. Alternatively, assuming that smaller creditors are willing to serve (which is debatable), an additional committee could be created for them. The second plan, however, clearly would increase costs, and the proliferation of committees generally has already led to added administrative burdens in cases.[2] Another option is to permit greater flexibility in both classification and payout for plan confirmation purposes. The Code now provides that creditors owed small amounts can be separately classified for administrative convenience, and creditors with slightly larger amounts can reduce their claims so they, too, can be treated separately.[3] It is unclear, however, whether the class of unsecured creditors could be bifurcated into two or more classes and, if so, whether the creditors in these separate classes must be treated equally in terms of ultimate payout.[4] Another possibility is to permit different payouts for different creditors within a single class, an approach that is not permitted (except by creditor consent) under existing law.

Separate classification has been tested with wide-ranging results in the context of single-asset cases where the debtor puts the lender's undersecured claim in one class and other unsecured creditors in another. In some cases, the treatment of the two classes of unsecured claims is different, with the lender's claim being stretched out while the other unsecured creditors receive a greater immediate payout.

Consider what would result from implementing a system of distinct payments to creditors within the same unsecured class. Suppose that Seat Co. has eight creditors. It owes four creditors $1 million each and four creditors $50,000 each. It intends to treat these two groups differently. Seat Co. proposes to pay each of the four large creditors (in terms of amount owed) $40,000 in cash plus shares of stock in the reorganized debtor valued at $160,000. These large creditors would be receiving the equivalent of twenty cents on the dollar ($200,000 out of $1 million owed). Suppose Seat Co. proposes to pay each of the four small creditors (in terms of amount owed) $40,000 in cash. The small creditors would receive 80% of what they are owed ($40,000 out of $50,000). In terms of cash payments, the large and small creditors are treated the same, but in terms of relative percentages, the large creditors are receiving substantially less, even taking into account the stock distribution (20% versus 80% payout). In this example, there is equality neither of treatment nor of outcome.

Suppose, instead, that the large creditors are to receive $40,000 in cash, stock in the reorganized company valued at $260,000, and a promissory note for $550,000 payable in one lump sum in ten years ($500,000 in principal and $50,000 in interest). Suppose payment to the small creditors remains at $40,000 in cash on confirmation. Now, both groups of creditors are getting identical payouts as a percentage of what they are owed ($800,000 of $1 million versus $40,000 of $50,000). But the type of payout (cash, stock, and notes versus cash only) is different. From the perspective of the small creditors, the inequality yields a far preferable outcome in that they receive what they need: cash. Contrary to the view of one well-known scholar,[5] many small creditors have no interest in a long-term investment in the debtor because they can barely make their own payments to creditors. The large creditors would also prefer a cash payment because with cash they can choose their own future investment. Although they could perhaps sell the stock and the note (most likely at discounted value), because of these assets they are clearly more linked to the debtor and its future than the small creditors. Indeed, many large unsecured trade creditors and banks recognize (although they do not discuss) the equity-like nature of their investment. In essence, this approach adopts the view that larger creditors are committing to a debtor long term. Knowing this ahead of time, voluntary creditors could assess the degree to which they want to be involved with the debtor. Thus, singular classification and disparate treatment of unsecured creditors may be workable as long as the percentage payout among the classes of like creditors remains constant.

Within the current system, there is a question as to whom creditors' committees represent. Some committees seem to assume that whatever is good for committee members must be good for all other unsecured creditors. But other creditors are not similarly situated. Suppose an employer decided to form a committee composed of employees to address issues of worker welfare. If the employer appointed only the most senior employees to the committee, the committee would not necessarily be the voice of all workers.

Although separate classification or treatment has appeal, it is not yet sufficiently fine-tuned. It does not provide a basis for distinguishing among unsecured creditors except in the most general of terms: amount owed. But the impact of nonpayment on particular creditors also provides an important dividing ground. Suppose three creditors are each owed ten thousand dollars. Based on dollar amount, they are identical. In a pro rata distribution, they would receive the same amount. Even under the separate classification or different payout approach suggested previously, they would be treated identically as small creditors, based on the amount owed. But these three creditors could be very different. One could be a large Fortune 500 company for which a loss of ten thousand dollars is hardly noticeable. For this large company (which will write off the debt for tax purposes), it is not even cost effective to hire a lawyer to collect the amount or oversee the bankruptcy. Another creditor could be a small company for which ten thousand dollars is a very large receivable, and collecting the money could be necessary for the company's survival. For this small company, counsel would seem critical, although in reality counsel may not be able to do much. Finally, suppose that ten thousand dollars is owed to an individual who worked for the debtor as an independent contractor. This individual needs the money to pay for food, clothing, and shelter for herself and her family. Under current law, all three creditors are treated equally, and this is justified on the theory of equality of treatment. As just proposed, all three creditors could receive identical treatment (50% payment), but the payment could be structured differently. The individual and small business could receive five thousand dollars in cash now while the payout of the same amount to the large business could be stretched out over five years. Even with this variation, however, the individual and the small business could suffer terribly because they would still be unable to repay their obligations. Equality of treatment, even as modified, would produce inequality of outcome.

An approach needs to be found that enables the creditors to achieve equality of outcome. Under such a system, a creditor in need would be repaid more than creditors less needy. Generally, small businesses and individual creditors could be paid more than large creditors that were owed the same amount. Suppose the individual and small business in the previous example were each paid the full amount of their claim in cash (ten thousand dollars), and the large business creditor received two thousand dollars. If this approach were adopted in every situation, innumerable problems would arise, as the less well paid creditors would understandably revolt over the redistributional effect. But such a system could be implemented on a limited basis. This could be accomplished through the creation of a rebuttable presumption.

A New Rebuttable Presumption

Under the new presumption, any unsecured creditor, large or small in either size of entity or amount owed, could challenge the standard pro rata distribution as it applied to him or her. The distribution system would continue to operate based on equality of treatment (subject to the more elaborate understanding of equal treatment with separate classification and payouts), but a creditor could rebut the presumption of equal treatment upon a showing of irreparable injury. A rebuttal would then enable the creditor to recover based on equality of outcome rather than equality of treatment.

This approach could be implemented by creating an accelerated priority for creditors irreparably injured and deleting one of the other less justifiable priorities. Creditors claiming such priority status would bear the burden of proof at a hearing before the bankruptcy court. They would need to show, with reasonable certainty, that failure to receive different treatment would produce irreparable injury. If the court was satisfied that the creditor rebutted the presumption, the court would then determine the appropriate remedy. Full and immediate priority payment is one option, but a court could also provide the successful rebutting creditor with partial accelerated payment of some lower amount with the balance to be received at the time and in the manner proffered to the other unsecured creditors.

The determination of what constitutes irreparable injury in this context would not be easy. Examples of irreparable injury would certainly vary dramatically and would include imminent collapse of a business, mortgage foreclosure on the creditor's home, or inability to acquire needed medical care. But *injury* is not a self-defining term, as the following example demonstrates.[6]

Suppose four creditors each lent Smythe one thousand dollars. They all seek to rebut the presumption. First Creditor, a good friend, wants to be repaid so she can buy luxury goods for herself. Had she not lent Smythe the money (or had she been repaid), she would have been able to make such purchases, having saved and invested prudently. Second Creditor is Smythe's next door neighbor. Since the loan, her spouse has become very ill, and without obtaining repayment or taking out a home equity loan, she cannot put food on the table. Third Creditor is Smythe's co-worker. A profligate spender, he needs to be repaid so he can pay his own rent because he has no savings. Fourth Creditor is a finance company that had mailed Smythe a credit application, which it subsequently approved without much investigation.

Third Creditor may be the most needy (he could be rendered homeless), but he did contribute to his own downfall. First Creditor is among the least needy but, unlike Fourth Creditor, did behave in a prudent manner that will go unrewarded—a particularly troubling result if the improvident Third Creditor recovers and she does not. Second Creditor, who could not control her situation, needs food as distinguished from shelter. Although she could obtain a home equity loan to tide her over, such a loan would increase her obligations; she would be out of pocket by two thousand dollars, not just one thousand dollars. Fourth Creditor has little going for it; it is in the business of lending and chose not to investigate Smythe's application (perhaps in exchange for a higher interest rate). Distinguishing among these creditors is hard and can be done only through a subjective assessment. With that caveat, an argument can be proffered that only Second Creditor and Third Creditor will suffer irreparable harm if they are not repaid. Although one may not feel badly for Fourth Creditor, First Creditor evokes sympathy—but not enough to rebut the presumption. If a court allows too many rebuttals, there may not be enough money to go around. This is a realistic concern. Being a rebutting creditor does not guarantee payment; instead, it guarantees an order of payment if funds are sufficient. If there is a shortfall, the available amount is divided pro rata among the successfully rebutting creditors, which is a return to the very approach we are avoiding.

Given the high standard of proof, the interpretive complexities, the difficulty of convincing the court of the creditor's plight, and the remedial uncertainty, these types of requests from creditors would and should be infrequent. A rebuttable presumption is a remedy for a specific, narrow set of circumstances. Moreover, it is unlikely that creditors would overextend credit solely on the hope that they could rebut the presumption later. A good analogy is the present state of the law regarding the equitable remedy of an injunction (which would require the wrongdoer to do or cease doing something). Courts have articulated specific standards that must be satisfied in order to obtain injunctive relief. The movant (the party seeking the injunction) must establish the following four elements: (1) likelihood of success on the merits, (2) irreparable injury to movant absent the injunction, (3) no substantial harm to others if the injunction is granted, and (4) relief is not contrary to public policy. But as with the definition of harm in bankruptcy, harm in the injunction context is measured on a case-by-case basis. Although some parties seek injunctions when they are not necessary, most situations do not fall into that category. Injunctive relief is not a common judicial remedy, and courts have increasingly imposed sanctions on both clients and attorneys who bring frivolous suits.[7]

At first glance, it seems that creditors as a whole would be disinclined to adopt this suggested approach, particularly as one or more creditors could obtain a greater distribution than others and receive it earlier to boot. But creditors could be convinced of the merits of the system. First, some creditors are willing to look beyond their own self-interest. Moreover, creditors may appreciate the concept of the rebuttable presumption because it would be available to them if they needed it prospectively. Additionally, if creditors were aware of the possibility that a limited pool of creditors would receive preferential treatment, they could factor this into the initial assessment of whether to do business with the debtor and at what price.

In a sense, this mechanism for rebutting the presumption of equality of treatment is the creditor's analogue to the fresh start. It recognizes that a creditor may make a mistake in lending and that the price of that mistake should not be a permanent loss of the creditor's business or home. This rebuttable presumption would enable creditors to recover not only for their own benefit but for society's as well. Keeping these floundering creditors afloat may also inure to the benefit of the organizing debtor by, for example, ensuring that a certain product remains available. Hence, the approach indirectly furthers debtor rehabilitation.

Looking at Initiation

Equality of treatment, in addition to downplaying differences in the amount that creditors owe and in the impact of nonpayment on them, ignores how each debt was initiated. This, too, needs to be considered. Suppose Seat Co. had three creditors, each owed ten thousand dollars. Trade Creditor, which is in the business of selling a product and had an opportunity to check Seat Co.'s credit, sold goods valued at ten thousand dollars for which it has not been paid. If Seat Co.'s credit rating had been cause for concern, Trade Creditor could perhaps have sold the goods on a COD basis or taken back a purchase money security interest to protect itself against nonpayment. Because Trade Creditor sold on an unsecured basis, it took the risk of nonpayment, and the cost of that risk is probably built into its overall pricing system. The real world is never as simple as the examples. In reality, Trade Creditor may have needed the sale, even if there was a risk, because it had a weak cash flow. Or perhaps Trade Creditor could not afford the necessary credit check and sold to Seat Co. based on unverified information. Trade Creditor could be new in the business, wanting a sale to show other would-be buyers that it is an active and competitive participant in the marketplace.

Suppose Tort Creditor is owed ten thousand dollars because he was injured as a result of Seat Co.'s failure to install a certain precautionary shield on the assembly line. Assume Seat Co. is insured only for accidents over one hundred thousand dollars and self-insures for lesser injuries. Tort Creditor paid for his own medical bills but needs reimbursement soon. He is also concerned about time lost at work and certainly does not want the inconvenience that accompanies his injury. Tort Creditor is different from Trade Creditor. He did not bargain to be injured. He had no way of measuring Seat Co.'s solvency before he got hurt. It probably never occurred to him to check Seat Co.'s insurance deductible. Tort Creditor has no business motive, other than earning a salary, for entering into Seat Co.'s employ. Intuitively, Tort Creditor seems more deserving of repayment than Trade Creditor, although neither will suffer irreparable injury if payment is not made.

Inside Creditor, one of the debtor's owners, is owed ten thousand dollars because he lent the company money several years ago. Although he expected repayment, Inside Creditor had privileged information about Seat Co. that enabled him to assess whether and when repayment was likely. Inside Creditor could demand repayment when he sees the business headed for trouble and perhaps negotiate favorable repayment terms. Certainly, Inside Creditor is different from Trade Creditor and Tort Creditor. Of the three unsecured creditors, Inside Creditor seems the least sympathetic in terms of generating support for repayment.

Although these three creditors are distinguishable, the question is whether the bankruptcy law should treat them differently for purposes of distribution and if so, on what basis. One possibility is to reclassify all creditors based on whether they are voluntary or involuntary creditors and then to provide better treatment for the involuntary creditors. Indeed, involuntary creditors could be made a priority in addition to or in lieu of other existing priorities. If this were done, it would reflect the sentiment that involuntary creditors are more worthy of payment than voluntary creditors because they did not assume the risk of nonpayment, and the amount of money available to voluntary unsecured creditors would decrease.[8]

But the classification into voluntary and involuntary is not as simple as it first appears. In the example, Trade Creditor and Inside Creditor are voluntary creditors whereas Tort Creditor is an involuntary creditor. Similarly, victims of mass torts, like asbestosis or defective intrauterine devices, would be treated as involuntary creditors whereas banks, suppliers, and landlords would be classified as voluntary creditors. But other, less obvious kinds of involuntary creditors do not elicit sympathy in equal amounts.

The U.S. government, which has to pay for environmental cleanup of a toxic waste site, becomes an involuntary creditor of the debtor. It will provide the cleanup for the benefit of society, even if the debtor is not in a financial position to repay. The government is also an involuntary creditor when a debtor does not pay its taxes. Under the voluntary tax system, the government does not assess the creditworthiness of the citizenry. Rather, it assumes payment will be made and then seeks to collect when payment is not forthcoming. Doctors or hospitals that provide medical treatment on an emergency basis, without requesting payment or proof of insurance upfront, can become involuntary creditors. So can employees.

Dividing creditors based on whether the obligations were incurred voluntarily or involuntarily thus lumps too many creditors together. Tort victims, the government as pollution rectifier and as taxing authority, and doctors and hospitals are not all affected by nonpayment in the same way. Some involuntary creditors—like some voluntary unsecured ones—are better able than others to withstand the loss. An individual tort victim who can no longer work is different from the IRS. The doctor who is not paid may be in a position to recover from other patients and hence withstand at least this loss.

Perhaps, then, a distinction should be made between tort victims and other involuntary creditors. Tort victims could perhaps be treated as priority creditors or alternatively as unsecured creditors entitled to better treatment than other involuntary unsecured creditors. Some commentators have suggested that the tort claimants should be ranked equal with or superior to secured creditors.[9]

But not all tort victims are the same, either. Some torts result in monetary rather than physical injury. Business interference and slander, for example, are torts that do produce injury, including monetary and psychic harm, but not bodily injury. Also, individual tort victims are different from victims of mass torts, and not all mass tort victims are equally situated. In the previous example, Tort

Creditor was not injured as a result of a mass tort. He suffered from an industrial accident, and although others on the assembly line could also have been injured, the problem is somewhat isolated.

In contrast, mass torts raise a serious issue of how to address the potential, commonly unanticipated harms that are a by-product of industrialization and advancing medical knowledge. As more and different products are developed and as researchers learn more about the long-term links between the environment, chemicals, and health, seemingly safe products can become weapons of death. This is not a bankruptcy problem; instead, it is a problem that falls into the bankruptcy arena when the unanticipated financial obligations cannot be met.[10] The bankruptcy system may be an arena to resolve these problems. But because elevating involuntary creditors would come at a cost, the size of the problem should be assessed. How often are mass torts an issue, and what inroads will elevating tort victims make to the ultimate payout to creditors and the credit markets that extend new money to businesses prospectively? Treating mass tort victims more favorably in bankruptcy situations would not solve the national dilemma relating to mass torts. But it would provide a resolution in the limited confines of the bankruptcy system.

Even within the category of involuntary mass tort victims, significant differences exist. The victims may have experienced a personal injury due to unanticipated harms that no one, neither the debtor nor experts in medical science, could have foreseen. Other mass tort victims could have suffered harm because the debtor's principals foresaw the problem but decided it was cheaper to keep selling the defective product (and pay for the injuries) than to pull the product from the marketplace. In the first case the debtor is not implicated, while in the second it is.[11]

From the perspective of the victim, the debtor's (or its principals') state of mind may matter in terms of culpability. From the creditors' perspective, extra payment to the intended as opposed to unintended tort victim passes the cost of the debtor's bad behavior onto the unsecured creditors. If the intended harm is to be addressed more beneficially (from the vantage point of the victim), the debtor—not the creditor—should assume that burden.

If limited liability were lifted in situations involving the knowing sale of a defective product in the name of economic efficiency, the unfairness of discharging these obligations in bankruptcy would be substantially curtailed.[12] The injured parties could pursue the principals, assuming they had assets. This system would also not appear to disrupt the credit markets. Treating the intentional tort victim better than the unintended tort victim would probably not happen often, as I suspect that most mass tort situations are not caused by bad actor debtors seeking economic efficiency at the expense of human well-being.

A revised bankruptcy system could also distinguish between involuntary creditors based on which creditors provided the greatest assistance to the debtor and society and could then reward those contributors with a greater payout. Both the government, in its role as rectifier of pollution, and the doctor helped the debtor and the larger community. The government cleaned up a hazard that could have damaged the debtor, its workers, and the community exposed to the pollutants. The doctor provided a needed medical service without which the debtor would have died, and the debtor's survival helps not only the debtor but his family and community as well. Although the government as taxing authority is helping the debtor at some level by providing governmental services, the benefits are more remote and less personal to the debtor. Tort Creditor, from the previous example, is not helping the debtor, except perhaps to alert the debtor to lax safety standards that, if corrected, would prevent future injury to other workers. But to repay the government (in its capacity as pollution controller) and the doctor but not Tort Creditor or the government (as taxing authority) is to produce results that differ from those reached according to the other suggested bases for classification: the impact of nonpayment on the creditor and the voluntariness with which the creditor entered into the lending relationship.

Among the various ways of classifying involuntary creditors identified thus far, none seems completely satisfactory. Treating all involuntary creditors as a priority is overinclusive. Classifying the involuntary creditors erodes equality of distribution without a persuasive, unifying, or consistent explanation. Despite this problem, it is hard to justify treating all involuntary and voluntary creditors equally. Although curtailing limited liability is a partial salve, it is not an all-encompassing solution.

Adding to the Rebuttable Presumption

A further possibility is to expand the basis upon which the presumption of equal treatment could be rebutted. In addition to irreparable injury, the presumption could be rebutted if a party demonstrates that it will be treated in a grossly unfair manner in the debtor's plan. This added defense resembles the controversial doctrine of substantive (as distinguished from procedural) unconscionability used in contract law.[13] To demonstrate substantive unconscionability, the moving party would need to demonstrate two things: (1) the party is an involuntary creditor, and (2) the proposed treatment under the plan is unconscionable (taking into account how the injury was incurred) as it applies to the creditor. If the court is convinced by the moving party's proof, then the presumption of equality of treatment would again be rebutted in favor of more beneficial treatment for the involuntary creditor. This could mean accelerating payment, elevating this one involuntary creditor (or a group of creditors, if a class is created), to a higher priority (perhaps at the level of secured creditors) or altering the payment package.

The irreparable injury and the substantive unconscionability bases for rebuttal are different in crucial ways. Proof of irreparable harm focuses on the creditor's need for payment in order to survive the bankruptcy. Relief on this basis would be infrequent, and the economic state of the creditor would need to be dire. Proof relating to unconscionability, however, does not require that a creditor show dire financial consequences; indeed, the financial consequences could be irrelevant. Instead, the involuntary creditor would show the extreme unfairness of the situation giving rise to the creditor's claim.

Suppose, for example, that Seat Co. produces a seat belt made of a fabric that it knows to be flammable. Suppose that it calculates that car accidents involving fire are not the norm, and hence, while some people undoubtedly will be burned, most people using the belt will be just fine. Now assume that a driver whose neck and chest were badly burned sues Seat Co. and obtains a judgment of $2 million. Assume that Seat Co.'s insurer pays all except the twenty-thousand-dollar deductible. The nonpayment of the twenty thousand dollars will not cause the driver irreparable injury. The medical bills are all paid, and the "extra" money is to compensate the victim for pain and suffering. Assume that Seat Co.'s plan of reorganization contemplates a payout of ten cents on the dollar to all unsecured creditors. Secured creditors would be paid in full. If the driver wanted to recover more, he could allege substantive unconscionability and perhaps prevail. If limited liability were lifted against the offending corporate officers (and if they had the financial wherewithal to pay), the strength of the substantive unconscionability could diminish.

Now consider the injured pedestrian in the Smythe scenario. Suppose the pedestrian, who is still owed $2 million, has no medical insurance of her own and no prospects of future employment owing to her paralysis. Assume that Smythe has five thousand dollars in nonexempt assets to distribute after payment of priorities. Assume that his other creditors are the government as tax collector (also an involuntary creditor), the government as lender for student loans (a voluntary creditor), three credit card companies, and several trade creditors. Under equality of treatment, the creditors will share equally. The involuntary creditor could probably succeed under an analysis of either irreparable injury or substantive unconscionability and could recover a greater portion of the available assets.

The suggested change does come at a cost. Administrative costs (in both time and money) rise when a streamlined system becomes more case-by-case oriented. Ease of administration, which justifies many imperfections in the law, cannot be ignored, as under the suggested system judges would be called upon to determine irreparable injury, substantive unconscionability, and the appropriate remedy. Is this a situation where the theoretical justification for change is right but the difficulties of implementation outweigh the merits?[14] Possibly. But if the rebuttable presumption is used infrequently (and real sanctions are imposed for misuse) and melded into the existing priority system in exchange for another priority, then the attendant costs should not increase substantially. And the system-wide gains through prevention of other failures could offset some of the added burdens.

But there are also costs to the nonrebutting creditors. When one creditor is paid earlier and more, other creditors lose. Most likely, the risk of loss will fall disproportionately on bigger businesses, as they can withstand losses. Big businesses would end up supporting the smaller creditors that would be devastated by loss and hence able to rebut the presumption of equality of treatment. It is possible, of course, that a big business that lent a large amount would seek to rebut the presumption. But it is more likely that bankruptcy would damn the successful creditors twice: once through the fresh start for debtors and next through the rebuttable presumption for unfortunate creditors.

This situation signals that bankruptcy is out to get the big guys, which is troubling. Large creditors, unlike many small ones, do have the capacity to recoup losses by passing them onto others and withstanding the lag time between the loss and the recoupment. And unlike many small community-based businesses, large businesses can decide not to extend unsecured credit in large amounts. Because larger creditors have these options, it is easier to foist more burdens on them, reallocating loss from unstable businesses to more stable ones.

This argument recalls the earlier discussion of debtors. We want to save debtors, for their sake and society's. Similarly, we want to save creditors, usually small ones, because they took a risk that not only did not succeed but has the potential to cause their own demise. But if too many costs are foisted onto large creditors, they may stop lending, which in turn could damage debtors who need credit to function. Therefore, rebuttal of the presumption of pro rata distribution should be narrowly construed, applied in only the most compelling of situations. That will preserve stability while providing flexibility.

In a sense, the argument has come full circle. The American bankruptcy system tries to help debtors by rehabilitating them through forgiving their failures. If creditors all collapse because debtors are saved, society has not made much progress. Many creditors (both large and small) can sustain some loss and will then pass that loss onto others through higher prices. But, for a limited number of creditors, the loss will lead to irreparable injury.

The bankruptcy system needs to help creditors as well as debtors. The strategy just proposed seems to be helping everyone, at the expense of solvent or marginally solvent creditors. At some level this is true, although secured creditors, who have adequate collateral, are not affected. But certain benefits come from helping smaller creditors, and these benefits are easy to forget in the rush to maximize creditor recovery. These are the benefits that come from a shared belief in long-term national growth. A more fine-tuned approach to unsecured creditors enriches American society, both economically and emotionally. Equal treatment is not synonymous with equal outcome.

CHAPTER ELEVEN

Two Thorny Issues Concerning Creditors

Two additional issues concerning creditors merit attention: the definition of a creditor and the buying and selling of claims. Aspects of the first issue affect consumer and business cases; other facets of both issues are of particular importance in large corporate Chapter 11 cases. Chapter 11 cases may constitute only a small portion of bankruptcy cases, but because of the number of creditors affected in large cases, the perceptions of how these creditors are treated influence the entire bankruptcy process.

Who Are the Creditors?

The discussion in the previous two chapters concerning equality of distribution among creditors assumes that we know who a debtor's creditors are and how much they are owed. In many cases, this presumption is correct. An unsecured creditor of Seat Co. that supplied rivets is owed a specific sum for the rivets delivered. The utility and telephone companies also have fixed claims. The employees' unpaid wages or pension contributions can be determined with certainty. The credit card companies can establish what Smythe owes based on actual purchases.

But the situation is frequently not so clear. A dispute about the quality of the rivets shipped might call for an adjustment of the amount owed. A claim of the Internal Revenue Service may be disputed based on the parties' respective approaches to calculating income and deductions. So, on the date of filing, a debtor could know the identity of its creditors but be unclear about the actual amounts some of these creditors are owed.

Some disputes can be resolved relatively easily. Once the parties confer and review the applicable books and records, they can reach a consensus as to the amount owed. In individual and small business cases, good books and records may not be maintained. Reconciling the books and records of the debtor with those of each creditor—particularly in the mega cases, with numerous creditors—can become an arduous, costly, and time-consuming task.

Under the current bankruptcy system, the debtor and its counsel usually work with each creditor to reach a resolution. In some larger cases, debtors retain an outside organization to assist in the administrative aspects of this chore. The bankruptcy court is available to resolve disputes that the parties cannot independently settle. In several regions of the United States, aspects of the claims resolution process can be changed from an adjudicative process (involving the court) to one involving mediation or arbitration. Such an alternative dispute resolution mechanism apparently saves time and money for debtors and creditors, although prospective empirical assessment would be merited to assess this. Alternative dispute resolution also frees up judicial time, a significant by-product considering the scarcity of this resource. Alternative dispute resolution is not flawless, however; details regarding the choice, payment, and ethics of the mediator or arbitrator, and regarding the process of obtaining and enforcing mediated or arbitrated decisions, still need to be ironed out.[1]

Quite apart from the obvious benefits of an alternative dispute resolution mechanism, there is an added benefit from making bankruptcy less adversarial. For some debtors and creditors, meeting in a nonlitigious environment will open the door for better communication. Without using lawyers as their mouthpieces, a debtor and creditor can talk together. They can express anger and perhaps sympathy. They can tell their stories in their own words. This approach may not be particularly useful in resolving disputes between large, impersonal corporate entities with little at stake in terms of personal relationships. But a disputed claim between an individual debtor and her local druggist may be better resolved face to face.[2]

It is easy to trivialize the process of claims resolution, which appears to involve merely bookkeeping reconciliation. But the size of the creditors' ultimate distribution hinges on the resolution of claims. In addition, the only creditors entitled to recover are those with allowed claims.[3] Although a debtor can set aside certain funds for undisputed, unliquidated, or contingent claims, it is far easier to reach consensus on the amount of the liabilities.

Suppose Seat Co. owes its trade creditors $4 million. Suppose also that Seat Co. has $1 million in assets available for distribution over the next three years to unsecured creditors under a plan of reorganization. The government, however, asserts a tax claim against Seat Co. of $1 million. If the tax claim is allowed, it could become an administrative expense. Alternatively, it could be a nonpriority, unsecured claim. Or it could be disallowed in its entirety. This determination materially affects the distribution to unsecured creditors. If the tax claim is considered a priority expense (and assuming no stretch-out), the $1 million available to unsecured creditors would be dissipated, and distributions would fall from the anticipated twenty-five cents on the dollar to zero cents on the dollar. If it is an allowed nonpriority claim, the total of unsecured claims increases from $4 million to $5 million, thereby reducing payments from twenty-five cents on the dollar to twenty cents on the dollar. If it is disallowed in its entirety, unsecured claimants receive the anticipated twenty-five cents on the dollar.

Disputes concerning the amount owed only begin the necessary inquiry. In some claims, not just the amount but the very existence of the claim is uncertain. That is, there is uncertainty as to whether any liability exists. Suppose that before Smythe's bankruptcy, a car that he repaired crashed. The driver claims that the accident was due to Smythe's shoddy work and threatens to bring a lawsuit. Assume that Smythe seeks bankruptcy relief before any such suit is filed. According to the Bankruptcy Code, the driver is a creditor on the date of filing although it is unclear at the time of filing whether

Smythe is actually liable. In bankruptcy parlance, the driver's claim is both unliquidated and disputed. Before the driver is entitled to recover, the claim must be "allowed," which requires a determination of the underlying liability or, if that is too cumbersome and time consuming, at least an estimation of the liability.[4] Another example occurs in the context of a guarantee. Suppose Seat Co.'s owner guaranteed the bank's debt. The owner is a creditor of Seat Co., but the amount owed on the guarantee depends on whether the bank is being repaid by Seat Co. If the bank is fully secured, there will be no liability on the guarantee. In bankruptcy parlance, the claim of the guarantor is contingent and has to be fixed before it can be paid as an allowed claim.

In the examples given so far, the uncertainty as to either the amount or the existence of a claim is a problem of incomplete information. It is clear who the parties are, and resolution of the uncertainty is possible within a reasonable time frame. In other situations, however, it is unclear whether there are creditors and, if so, who they are, let alone how much they are owed.

Consider the problem of mass torts. Suppose that Seat Co. is a debtor in Chapter 11. Before the case was filed, in the course of manufacturing its product, Seat Co. released a noxious substance that, unknown to anyone at the time, was carcinogenic. It was later discovered that anyone exposed to this substance can develop lymphoma, a cancer that is usually treatable if caught early. Although the management of Seat Co. does not believe that the company is liable, a court would likely hold it responsible for the consequences of exposure to the noxious substance. Suppose that, on the date of Seat Co.'s bankruptcy filing, 10 out of its 500 current workers have developed lymphoma and are being treated. The affected workers are creditors of Seat Co. because they both were exposed to the noxious chemical and developed lymphoma before Seat Co. filed for bankruptcy. Even if the amount owed to these individuals is undetermined, it is quantifiable. The pre-petition *affected* workers are not the problem. The problem is the 490 current workers who were exposed to the contaminant but are not now ill. Suppose one worker develops lymphoma during the Chapter 11 case. Is this individual a creditor with an administrative expense claim, because the illness arose post-petition? The then-remaining 489 workers are also a problem, because it is not known if any of them will develop lymphoma. Suppose no one shows any symptoms during pendency of the case. Are they creditors, or "future claimants"?[5] And what of the hundreds of former workers—some of whom retired, others of whom were fired, and others of whom resigned—who were exposed? If any of these former workers had developed lymphoma before the bankruptcy, they would be creditors. And even more troubling, what happens to those in the local community who were exposed to this substance when it was emitted? Are they creditors? And what of the children, born and unborn, whose parents were exposed to this noxious substance that could have affected their health now or in the future?

The problem of determining who will be injured becomes a bankruptcy dilemma. Although state and federal courts are plagued by similar issues, a bankruptcy necessitates immediate, concrete, and workable solutions. Yet again, the bankruptcy system is forced to address a significant nonbankruptcy problem. And how these issues are resolved has critical implications for a bankruptcy case. If all the future claimants are treated as creditors of Seat Co., their claims can be discharged in bankruptcy. The company can reorganize without the threat of massive prospective tort liability hanging over them. In contrast, if the future claimants are deemed *not* to be creditors, the debtor's fresh start will always be impaired because these future claimants will be able to sue to recover.

Notice the arbitrariness of this system. If someone becomes sick pre-petition, he or she is a creditor, the claim is discharged under a plan, and the person may recover less than one hundred cents on the dollar. If someone becomes sick during the pendency of the case, he or she may be considered a post-petition creditor entitled to payment in full as a priority administrative expense. If someone who was exposed to the contaminant did not develop the illness during the pendency period, he or she will become a claimant entitled to payment in full if this person contracts the attributable illness and if the debtor's assets are sufficient to pay when the time comes. But by then, the company may have liquidated. Thus, absent judicial intervention, if an individual is fortuitous enough to contract a fatal disease later rather than earlier, he or she will be paid in full if there are sufficient assets. Conversely, if there are insufficient assets, the individual is unlucky in not having started to die sooner. But of course, individuals cannot control when they get sick. The company cannot predict if and when the exposed individuals will get sick. The company also cannot predict if and when its economic well will run dry.

In such a case as Seat Co.'s, actuaries could be retained to determine, within some range of certainty, the number of possible victims and how much these individuals will need to be compensated when they contract lymphoma. What the actuaries can't tell is who these victims will be: Will the next victim be the shop manager, the maintenance worker, the office administrator, or the vice-president of sales? Will it be the child living across the street or the teacher at the local elementary school? If we knew which, as opposed to how many, people would become ill, would that help us? If we knew how many people would become ill, we could estimate the amount of Seat Co.'s exposure. Seat Co. could then set up a fund that would generate sufficient proceeds to pay future claimants. This fund would make it possible, for some purposes, to treat prospective victims as creditors *now*. Seat Co. could move into the future, free of the extensive tort liability, and the future claimants would know that should they become ill, they might have a source to look to for payment. This system has been tried in existing cases despite the absence of express statutory authority and is contemplated in current and future cases based on amendments made to the Code in 1994.[6]

But this approach has problems. The actuaries could miscalculate. The fund could be either over- or underfunded. Future claimants are not hurt by overfunding. But other creditors will bear the risk. If the fund is overfunded, existing creditors will have turned over a disproportionate share of their recovery to fund nonexistent future injury (this problem could be mitigated by a future kickback provision). If it is underfunded, as has happened in the real world, prospective creditors may find themselves unpaid, and the company may have insufficient revenues to fund the shortfall. Finally, there is a due process problem.[7] Normally, a party whose rights are being affected in a bankruptcy case is entitled to notice. Notice enables people to assess the debtor's proposed plan and object to it if need be. But future claimants do not know that they will become claimants, so they are not in a position to speak. This problem could arguably be circumvented by having the court appoint a representative to act on behalf of future claimants. Obviously, such an appointment adds yet another cost to the bankruptcy process.

The U.S. government may have to set up a system for addressing the problem of mass torts. If a national tort victims' fund existed, then perhaps, as now happens in environmental cases, the government would step in to provide assistance and assume the role of creditor. But absent such a massive program, it makes no sense to leave the tort victims and all other creditors unsatisfied with the result. Bankruptcy law has to adopt a carpe diem mentality. Until a better global solution is developed, future claimants should be deemed creditors and paid, through a trust mechanism, alongside other unsecured creditors.

This approach diminishes the pie of available assets. Future claimants' recoveries will affect the existing creditors, the same group whose claims may be diminished through the new rebuttable presumption. It is possible, however, that the new solution will increase the worth of the troubled company, as a new purchaser might have paid less for the business if the existence of future claims had been uncertain. Failing to deal with present and future tort victims does not make the problem go away; instead, it shifts the loss to future creditors and equity holders. The question, then, is whether it is better to deal with the problem now or to leave it for future generations to resolve. Although the global solution to mass torts will need to await the future, the bankruptcy system has a unique opportunity, indeed almost an invitation, to resolve the problem now.

Buying and Selling Claims

Thus far, the discussion has incorporated the assumption that all creditors entitled to payment in a bankruptcy case are the same creditors the debtor owed before bankruptcy. Primarily in large cases, however, the stock, bonds, and debt of financially troubled companies have begun to be traded.[8] In these instances, investors (usually outsiders and noncreditors) agree to buy the obligations of existing creditors or equity holders for cash. The new investors are willing to purchase such claims because they believe in the long-term success of the debtor's business and have the financial wherewithal to stick with the debtor over the long haul. They anticipate a significantly greater distribution (in stock, notes, or cash) than the amount they paid the original claimants. Sometimes the investors believe that by acquiring sufficient debt or equity they can control the debtor's reorganization and obtain the debtor itself at a bargain-basement rate. Although some courts have criticized this "trading in claims," nothing explicit in the Bankruptcy Code prohibits this behavior, provided adequate disclosure is given to the original creditors or equity holders regarding what they are giving up in exchange for what they are receiving. This practice, however, needs to be reevaluated.[9]

Suppose Seat Co. is a publicly traded company with $30 million owed to three thousand unsecured creditors. Some creditors want to be paid in cash now because they need to pay their own creditors or purchase new equipment to speed manufacturing. Other creditors want a short-term resolution of the situation for tax reasons. Yet other creditors, such as banks, may want or need immediate cash in order to remain in compliance with federal regulations that require maintenance of sufficient reserves against bad debts. Regardless of need, smaller creditors find cash a more palatable form of payment than securities or notes because they have no interest in being the debtor's equity partner and, in any event, are unfamiliar with or do not have access to the market for trading.

Assume Hydra Company offers to pay Seat Co.'s unsecured creditors twenty-five cents on the dollar in cash immediately. Hydra advises these creditors that under the debtor's proposed reorganization plan, they would receive at least forty cents, but confirmation is at least a year away, and the payout would likely take the form of stock and notes. Confirmation could also stall or fail, which would render future payment problematic at best. Assume that all the creditors agree to the buyout by Hydra. So Hydra buys $30 million in claims for $7.5 million. Now the debtor owes Hydra, as a substitute creditor, $30 million. No pre-petition unsecured creditors remain.

To confirm a plan of reorganization that allows the equity holders of Seat Co. to retain any interest (and hence not violate the absolute priority rule), the unsecured creditors must either be paid in full or consent to different treatment. A reorganization plan must be accepted by more than one-half in number and two-thirds in amount of the allowed claims.[10] So through the buyout, the control of the reorganization effort, which once belonged to the three thousand unsecured creditors, shifts to Hydra, which holds all the claims of the unsecured class.

Hydra runs certain risks. The debtor could fail to reorganize, and the company would then liquidate. Hydra could find that the claims of priority creditors leave nothing for unsecured creditors. Previously hidden liabilities could come to light. Or some creditors could decide not to sell to Hydra, making it questionable whether Hydra holds half the number of unsecured claims. This question hinges on whether Hydra's purchase counts as one large claim (in which case it is one creditor with one vote) or whether the character of the original claim is retained for voting purposes (in which case Hydra has three thousand votes for the three thousand claims it acquired).[11]

The original check-and-balance system in Chapter 11 was intended to give a debtor an opportunity to start over while according the *existing* creditors an opportunity to share in the debtor's future and to oversee the reorganization process. The debtor's fresh start would not occur on the backs of creditors. In that context, the absolute priority rule made sense. Junior classes of creditors (including equity holders) should not be paid until more senior creditors are paid. With Hydra's buyout, there is no longer any need to protect the original creditors on a go-forward basis. An underlying premise of bankruptcy policy was that existing creditors, who had done business with the debtor and perhaps wanted to do so in the future, had a stake in the outcome. The original creditors also needed to be protected from the debtor's potential power to disenfranchise them in bankruptcy, particularly because their interests were diffuse and varied. If the original creditors are replaced with an outsider, the Code is protecting the sophisticated investor that is fully capable of protecting itself.

Hydra is a different type of creditor, one not contemplated by the Code. It differs from other unsecured creditors in amount owed, impact of nonpayment, and initiation of the indebtedness. The amount Hydra is owed is significant in itself ($30 million) but probably not in comparison to the investor's overall net worth. The loss of $30 million will not impair Hydra's livelihood. Unlike all creditors other than those owed post-petition administrative expenses, Hydra did not incur its obligation pre-petition. Indeed, Hydra had nothing to do with Seat Co. before the bankruptcy. It had an opportunity to look at a situation with hindsight, employ an investment strategy, and then act.

Should the absolute priority rule have the same force when the original creditors are not the ones being directly protected? On the one hand, without the absolute priority rule, entities like Hydra would not offer to buy out creditors because it would be too risky. Because a buyout is beneficial to many of the original creditors, the retention of the rule in some form makes sense. On the other hand, Hydra benefits from a rule not designed to protect a sophisticated investor fully capable of assessing risk, and protections are, like people, not necessarily fungible. Some deviation in the absolute priority rule may be in order when the original creditors are long gone. The interests of the original debtor need to be balanced against those of the acquiring creditor, whose stake in the debtor is quite different. In the field of corporate takeovers, newcomers are permitted to step in, but existing management is armed with certain defenses to protect its turf.[12] Similar defenses for the debtor would have to be developed within the bankruptcy system when the creditors' interests are acquired. This does not mean that Hydra would fail in its efforts to control Seat Co. But some of Seat Co.'s power in the reorganization process would be restored. Perhaps debtor exclusivity could be extended or the voting requirements altered somewhat when trading in claims takes place.

Hydra's offer to creditors produces two particularly troubling results. First, it puts pressure on the original creditors to act. Original creditors may worry that if they do not accept Hydra's offer, they will not achieve a distribution, even long term, of twenty-five cents on the dollar. Because the creditors may be acting individually rather than collectively in response to Hydra's offer, individual creditors may be rushed into dealing with Hydra without reviewing alternatives, which costs time and money. For better or worse, one of the things that normally occurs in a bankruptcy case is a breathing space. This time is viewed as a benefit to debtors, but it also benefits creditors, which can collectively contemplate the debtor and its future. Hydra's offer, however, taps into creditors' fears (creditors might think, "I don't want to be the lone holdout" or "I don't know whether I'll be able to get more down the road even if I put pressure on Hydra or Seat Co.") and curtails the time for reflection.

Moreover, the creditors most likely to be pressured are those that are small. Sophisticated creditors that are owed huge amounts may be able to process quickly the information about the debtor's proposed plan and Hydra's offer and to perform a risk-benefit analysis. But a creditor owed several thousand dollars is not going to make that assessment. For the smaller creditor, the lure of green money now is strong and the fear of the unknown is great, and Hydra can take advantage of that.

The second troubling result of Hydra's acquisition of claims is that it could diminish a nonacquiring pre-petition creditor's power substantially. Suppose that Supplier is owed $3 million. Of the original claimants, Supplier was the seventh-largest creditor, with the largest single creditor being owed $5 million. Suppose the unsecured creditors are owed $25 million in the aggregate. When Hydra appears, all the creditors cash out their claims except Supplier and one other creditor with a claim of $1 million. This leaves Supplier with the next-largest claim after Hydra. At this point, Hydra has acquired $21 million in claims, Supplier retains a $3 million claim, and the remaining creditor has a $1 million claim. Hydra's claim is large enough in dollar amount (more than the two-thirds of the amount voting) for Hydra to control the plan process; if the debtor does not propose a plan satisfactory to Hydra, that company will vote down the plan.

Hydra has one possible problem if it decides to promote a particular plan and control the debtor. A plan needs to be approved by more than one-half in number of the claims. With only three creditors, Hydra needs Supplier or the other remaining creditor to vote its way (assuming that Hydra's purchase is treated as only one claim, which is questionable). If obtaining the requisite number (as distinguished from amount) of votes proves difficult, Hydra may have to buy out the recalcitrant creditor or creditors at a higher rate to ensure that it has enough votes. If Hydra buys out the $1 million claim for forty cents (rather than twenty-five cents) on the dollar, then Supplier has lost all leverage. Before Hydra's buyout, Supplier was a powerful force in the debtor's reorganization. Afterward, Supplier fades into oblivion, particularly if Hydra ups the ante to the creditor owed $1 million. It is possible that the plan Hydra supports is good for Supplier. In that case, Supplier is weeping crocodile tears. But Supplier may have a different agenda; for example,

Hydra may want to sell off Seat Co. piecemeal whereas Supplier wants to help the company survive intact.

One additional issue is raised by Hydra's late buyout of the recalcitrant creditor. Is it fair for Hydra to pay a holdout creditor more than it paid the other creditors without warning all creditors in advance that if they held out, they might be entitled to more? This unfairness could be remedied by requiring such a purchaser as Hydra either to disclose the possibility of increased payouts up front or, alternatively, to commit to pay more money to early-selling creditors if the price increases down the road. If these solutions are not implemented, the concept of equality of distribution is dramatically overturned.

In spite of the concerns surrounding the buying and selling of claims, significant factors militate in favor of permitting such entities as Hydra to acquire debt or equity. Because at least one primary goal of bankruptcy is to protect creditors, nothing is wrong with Hydra's buying out the pool of unsecured creditors. If three thousand creditors want to cash in their claims for an immediate payout of twenty-five cents on the dollar, it would be intrusive and paternalistic to stop them, assuming they understand the alternatives through adequate disclosure. Additionally, entities that are willing to assume long-term risk should be able to partake in a greater share of the benefits than other creditors because they may experience greater financial exposure and time delay in obtaining repayment.

Moreover, many of the concerns about trading claims and equity can be addressed through adequate disclosure of the trading arrangement. All costs of this disclosure process should be paid by the acquiring creditor. This includes the costs for the counsel of the debtor's and creditors' committees to review the proposal and oversee the process. The disclosure to potential sellers should be complete and understandable, recognizing that not all creditors are sophisticated investors. The court should conduct a hearing on the adequacy of disclosure and oversee the buy-sell process to ensure compliance. Because the investor is effectively controlling the reorganization without the benefit of a court hearing on confirmation, what is happening is analogous to a sale of all of the debtor's assets outside a plan. Court monitoring will ensure that the marketplace does not overtake the safeguards of the reorganization process.

In addition, creditors with newly acquired claims, such as Hydra, should not necessarily be protected in the plan process in the same way as traditional unsecured creditors. So, for example, the amount of disclosure normally required to assist creditors in determining whether to vote for a plan need not be as extensive when a class of claims has been acquired. In this case, such a purchaser as Hydra has already made certain financial assessments and has satisfied itself that an investment in the debtor is wise. Limiting disclosure in this context would save time and money. Second, it is highly questionable whether Hydra's expenses (for counsel and accountants) should be treated as a priority expense. Unlike other unsecured creditors, which need to obtain professional guidance in a Chapter 11 case in order to protect their interests, Hydra does not need protection. It can afford its own counsel, and no doubt hired same in assessing whether to make the initial investment. The estate should not have to subsidize professional guidance for a company that, at this point in the case, is purely self-interested.

Even if the complex issues concerning the meaning of equality among creditors are resolved, the creditor-related problems discussed in this chapter remain. But the issues raised here recall some larger themes of this book: the vast number of parties affected by a single bankruptcy case and the question of the role and function of bankruptcy law in contemporary American society. In this context, it is imperative for a bankruptcy system to take the interests of community into account.

PART IV

Community

CHAPTER TWELVE

The Interests of Community

Wrapped into the inquiry of whether community interests should matter in bankruptcy are numerous complex questions, including, What is meant by *community?* and, Which communities matter? The idea that community matters is subject to considerable debate.[1] Some people believe that the bankruptcy system involves only the resolution of the financial relationship between a debtor and its creditors. For these individuals, the issue of community is invisible. To return to the "duckrabbitpond," they do not see the pond. Others recognize the issue but do not believe it is of relevance to the bankruptcy system.[2] For this group, the interests of community detract considerably from the goal of maximizing recovery to creditors and equity holders. Finally, some people recognize the relevance of community but do not believe that the costs of taking it into account merit its becoming a participant in the bankruptcy process.[3] These three positions (invisibility, limited utility, and cost-prohibitive utility) differ, but they yield the same outcome, namely, that bankruptcy should not concern itself with community. The already abundant and ever-growing theoretical bankruptcy scholarship based on economic models almost universally excludes reference to community for one or more of the foregoing reasons, and the few references that exist are relegated to footnotes or alluded to in passing with palpable disdain. Bringing the import of community to light offers an opportunity to change not only bankruptcy law itself but the direction of and approach to bankruptcy scholarship.

An analogy to nonbankruptcy law is useful. Consider the problem of sexual harassment. Some people have challenged its very existence, and men and women may well perceive its presence or absence differently.[4] Indeed, a female member of the military recently testified at a congressional hearing that she was forced to take a psychiatric test when she accused a commanding officer of harassment.[5] Others believe that eradicating sexual harassment may be politically correct but that the concept itself is substantively vacuous. Still others believe in eradicating sexual harassment but consider it either impractical or cost-inefficient to do so. The preliminary focus of any effort to eradicate sexual harassment must be to convince nonbelievers that it exists and should be taken seriously. Only then is it possible to address the finer points, that is, how sexual harassment should be addressed in homes, schools, and businesses, and how society can and should deal with both the harasser and the victim.

Suppose a male construction worker whistles at a woman passing the work site and then proceeds to look at her with "elevator eyes." Some people do not believe that what the worker did was sexual harassment. Others believe that what the worker did was sexual harassment but that his actions are not sufficiently important to warrant much attention. The worker himself may be unaware of the debate about his conduct. Or the conduct may be improper but impossible to stop without terminating all construction, which is clearly impractical and cost-prohibitive. Whichever explanation is true, the offending conduct is not taken seriously, and the victim's perspective is not given much weight. If our goal is to curtail sexual harassment, we need to begin by making people see both that it exists and that it is important, to the victim and to society.

Confronting Invisibility

Persuading people to see what they believe is invisible is no simple task. It forces them to reconsider some fundamental values and to recognize that existing positions can be changed. For many people, recognizing the import of community in bankruptcy requires uprooting basic philosophical tenets. Rather than view and value individuals as autonomous and the debtor-creditor relationship as a private transaction between two parties designed to maximize wealth, we need a view that rests on the belief that people are interrelated on a variety of levels and that interconnectedness has value, even if it cannot be measured in economic terms.[6] While not disregarding autonomy, this view permits social responsibility to trump private interests in some situations.

The answers to questions related to community cannot be found in U.S. bankruptcy law. They are located in such disciplines as philosophy, political theory, economics, and sociology.[7] They are found in people's personal beliefs and experiences. The answers plumb individuals' understandings of the world in which we all live. In this sense, a discussion of community resembles the earlier discussions of the meaning of the fresh start and equality of distribution among creditors. Those discussions revealed that bankruptcy reflects deep philosophical beliefs but is not the source of those beliefs. Given the fundamental nature of the issues being addressed in the context of community, it is important to recognize that reasonable people can differ. It is legitimate to ask why Seat Co.'s lending bank or trade creditors should care (or why society should make them care through legal means) whether the community of Blytheville, Arkansas, is destroyed when a plant is shut down or pollutants are left in the soil. It is reasonable to ask why a credit card company based in Texas should care (or why society should make it care through legal means) whether Smythe's bankruptcy in Maine is devastating to him and his family. The actual participants in the bankruptcy process may not even be aware of the implications of their situation for their communities. Bank lenders, trade creditors, and credit card companies may simply want to be repaid what they are legitimately owed. The bank lender and trade creditors did not lend to the Town of Blytheville; they lent to Seat Co. Similarly, the credit card company extended credit to Smythe, not his relatives. These creditors, then, do not envision themselves as responsible for the consequences of the loan and its nonpayment. If community matters, then creditors will need to be convinced that they should care about what now seems irrelevant to them because they may be paying for it, at least over the short term.

Whether or not we want to admit it, our actions (and inactions) can and do affect the larger environment. We experience interconnectedness at innumerable levels. We intersect with others in our families, our neighborhoods, our workplaces, our houses of worship, our towns and cities, our schools, our hospitals, our governments. Some of our connections are physical, others are emotional, and still others are intellectual. Some are important to us; others are merely incidental contacts. Unless we retreat from the world, we are constantly affecting each other—economically, physically, emotionally, spiritually, intellectually, politically.

These interconnections can be considered the representations of the innumerable communities in which each individual lives. Although the communities differ, each person is part of communities close at hand and communities that are further removed. The family, for example, is usually a close community. The workplace is another frequently close community. The town may be an important but not as intimate community, depending on both the time one spends in it and one's connection with all its inhabitants. City, state, and federal governments are also communities, although people's relationships to them are attenuated, both geographically and psychologically. Individuals may be involved in politics but may not know their senator personally. They may care about tax increases and welfare benefits for those less privileged but may not know the commissioner of the IRS or the secretary of health and human services.

Some of these communities overlap. Sometimes the interests of a community conflict with those of another; at other times, they are consonant. Parents who work outside the home experience this sense of overlapping communities on a daily basis. The needs of their home, including that of providing care for a child, may conflict with the needs of the workplace, and both communities are important. Within contemporary society, the needs of both communities cannot be fully and easily met.[8] In contrast, some children may see an overlap between their community of friends and their school community, and those two communities may mesh well. For children who are bussed into a different school district, however, the communities of friends at home and at school do not mesh well.

In the world of bankruptcy, community can take many forms. First, the debtor has communities. An individual debtor's communities can be family, workplace, or church. A corporate debtor's communities can be shareholders, the town where the business is located, and the workers in the factory. Creditors and equity holders each have their communities as well. The creditors themselves collectively form a community, as do the equity holders. And each individual creditor has its own communities, which include family, shareholders, or partners. Bankruptcy also touches broader communities: the community in which a business is located, the community into which the debtor's assets can be relocated if they are sold in the bankruptcy case, the community within an industry, or the communities affected by decreased or increased tax revenues. The list is as vast as the array of human interactions. And every bankruptcy case affects community.[9]

Without question, it is far easier to pretend that community is not affected. But once we have recognized the interests of community, we are forced to handle the issues that just flew out of Pandora's box. Communities affect people in different ways. And people's actions or inactions touch different communities differently. Therefore, while the community of Blytheville is not as intimate as the community of shareholders in the small family business of Seat Co., the larger community is not irrelevant. Instead, Seat Co. has varying degrees and types of responsibility to the wide range of communities that its actions or inactions touch. Analyzing this responsibility encompasses an explanation of the communities' need for individuals and the individuals' willingness and need to help others.

The Circle of Responsibility

In discussing debtors, I addressed society's responsibility to individuals, which in turn produces increased individual responsibility. This responsibility is largely effectuated through the forgiveness granted by the bankruptcy discharge. In discussing creditors, I addressed the responsibility of some creditors to shoulder the financial burdens of others. But the increased costs may ultimately be passed onto members of the larger society, including the government. And some of these people or entities pass the costs onto still others. The third kind of responsibility involves the individuals' responsibility to community. Unlike responsibility from the outside in (society to debtors) or among private parties (one group of creditors to another), community interests focus on responsibility from the private parties out (debtors and creditors to the larger community).

This last piece of the equation of responsibility completes a circle revealing that responsibility is based on reciprocity.[10] Society owes a duty to individuals, individuals owe duties to each other, and individuals owe something back to society. Each party benefits by someone else's being responsible for it. In turn, each party is responsible to someone or some group apart from itself. If any one piece of the circle fails in its duty, the reciprocal nature of the responsibility breaks down.

Communities help individuals in a wide range of ways. They provide safe environments in which to raise children; they create opportunities for creativity; they provide assistance in times of distress; they supply badly needed services like water and police protection. They also enable debtors to obtain a fresh start through the creation of bankruptcy law. And communities also need individuals' resources and time. To recognize that a community exists and to treat it as irrelevant is to ignore the consequences of inattention, namely, failure.

Suppose that the members of a local community decide that the children of the community should be able to play basketball on weekends. Unless individual adults commit to set up the program, organize the teams, oversee the practices, referee the games, and provide the awards dinner, nothing will happen. If the parents do not want to do this themselves and they still want the program, then they need to donate the money necessary to hire the individuals who will perform these services.

A marriage, too, creates a community. Unless the partners in that marriage work at the relationship, it will not sustain itself. Although some of the sustenance in a marriage can come from money, other aspects of survival of the marital community require time and attentiveness. If an individual who is married recognizes the bond but does not think it matters, then the marriage is likely to fail.

Now consider a larger community. A small town has a lovely main street lined with small shops: a dry cleaner, a bookstore, a luncheonette, a pharmacy, a hardware store, a newsstand, a gas station. All the townspeople like the small town. It is the place where they see their neighbors; it is the place where the shopkeepers know them. If someone has forgotten to bring her wallet, she can still take what she needs and pay the next day. The town is the place where everyone learns that Mrs. Johnson's son is getting married and that Mr. Myerson's gout is getting worse. But if the townspeople do not frequent the shops on Main Street and instead choose to shop at bigger (and cheaper) chain stores some distance away, the community of Main Street will be dissipated. If the stores and their convenience and ambiance are important, then people in the community need to support the town by patronizing the stores and perhaps paying somewhat more for the goods they purchase. They need to commit resources and time to the community.[11]

The continuity of the three communities just described has value, although that value is not always measured in traditional economic terms. Saving a basketball program or a marriage clearly has benefits. It makes people feel good about themselves, and that benefit allows them to function well in society. And keeping stores open in a small town also matters: the town provides a pleasant place to live. Although pleasantness of surroundings is not commonly factored into the traditional neoclassical economic model, the long-term consequences of human unhappiness with a place are not insignificant.

These noneconomic values are hard to see in a world dominated by talk of market economics. In decrying modern medicine's focus on business rather than caring, one doctor articulated the debate poignantly: "Because individualism and competition are increasingly celebrated, the principles of the marketplace now permeate our personal lives and even capture our judgment. When we spend our waking hours scheming about how to win, it becomes difficult to keep in touch with fundamental human needs. . . . We forget that there is more to being civilized than material goods and individual rights. There is ethical behavior, respect, dignity and caring."[12]

The Individual's Need to Help

It is not enough that communities need individuals; individuals must be willing to help communities. Individuals help communities because, at their core, people are altruistic and are willing to forgo certain self-interests to accomplish larger goals. This statement about human nature is hard, if not impossible, to prove. Many variables in a complex society affect what we do and why. Perhaps if people returned to a state with no modern developments (like that described in *Lord of the Flies*), they would eat each other and abandon the children who were too weak to survive, although I remain skeptical. But we do not live in a primitive state; we live, more or less, as civilized people within a civilized society. Extrapolating from the state of nature to how people behave today is pure conjecture. It seems far more helpful to look around at how people behave now. Ultimately, I am no more able to prove that people are inherently good than detractors will be able to prove that people are inherently bad. All I can hope to demonstrate is that the picture is not as bleak as some imagine it to be.

It is true that everywhere people do bad things. People are constantly killing others, stealing from both friends and strangers, and abandoning children with no apparent regret. This group, however, is not the majority of human beings. Look at other events that happen every day. People care for their children. Teachers work hard to educate students despite terrible surroundings, a lack of funds, and low status as professionals. People generously give of their time to talk to the elderly and the sick. People accept jobs with low pay because they like the work or because it has, in their view, social utility. People do not hit those standing ahead of them in line. People listen to friends in need. People, even those who are not wealthy, donate to charities.

Clearly, some of this "good" behavior is beneficial to the person who performs it. People may feel better if they assist others. People may act in certain good ways (for example, they may refrain from stealing) for fear that if they do otherwise they will be injured (shot or imprisoned). People may give because they want the social accolades that come from largess. Indeed, caring for others does not mean giving up one's sense of self. Altruism and self-interestedness can, up to a point, co-exist.

But people's true nature is demonstrated in situations where they cannot plan ahead. Suppose an individual finds a hundred dollars on the floor of a local grocery store. The money could never be identified, and the finder would not be arrested for keeping it. Would most people keep the money? Or would most finders turn in the money to the store in case a customer reported losing anything (reserving the right to recover it for themselves if the money went unclaimed)? Or would the finder question fellow customers to see if something had dropped out of one of their wallets? Turning the money over to the store is not an economically rational decision. It does not maximize individual wealth. So if the individual is returning the money, something other than self-interestedness is motivating the decision. If the finder is concerned about whoever lost the money, then the finder is acting altruistically, forgoing maximization of personal wealth because the loss to someone else outweighs the personal gain.

The finder's behavior could be rationalized in economic terms. The finder figures that if he were ever to lose money, he would want the individual who located it to give it back. So it is in his long-term self-interest to behave in a way that will encourage others to behave similarly. But it is also possible that the finder behaves as he does because he thinks that it is a good thing to help others.

This approach to human behavior can be contrasted with another story. An individual was driving in a deserted area at night. As luck would have it, he got a flat tire. When he went to change it, the driver realized that he had no jack. He waited several minutes, but no cars were on the horizon. All he could see for miles was farmland, and in the distance was a lighted farmhouse. Having no choice (and no mobile phone in the car), the driver set out for the farmhouse. After walking for several minutes, he paused and thought to himself, "I could get all the way to the farmhouse, and no one could be home." Lacking alternatives, he kept on walking. Several minutes later, he thought to himself, "Even if the farmer is home, maybe he won't have a jack." But he kept on walking. Several minutes more went by, and the driver thought to himself, "Even if the farmer has a jack, which he probably does, maybe he won't let me borrow it." This thought plagued the driver. With each additional step, he wondered whether the farmer would lend him the jack. He thought to himself over and over, "The farmer will slam the door in my face; he'll tell me to leave his land; he'll refuse to help me after I've walked all this way." The driver worked himself into quite a tizzy. A short time later, he reached the farmhouse and knocked on the door. Within a minute, a farmer came to the door and opened it. But before the farmer could even say a single word, the driver raised his fist, wrinkled his brow, and shouted angrily, "You can just take your jack and stick it."

In this story, the driver sees people as self-interested and uncaring. But I envision a different story. The driver arrives at the farmhouse fully expecting that the farmer will give him some help. Indeed, the farmer not only will offer to let the driver borrow the jack but will drive the stranger back to his car and help him change the tire. If it turns out that the farmer is unwilling to lend the jack, the driver can deal with that unfortunate circumstance when it happens. Moreover, one selfish farmer (who will no doubt exist) should not lead inevitably to the conclusion that all farmers (or all people) are self-interested and unhelpful. Instead, the conclusion should be what is undoubtedly true: no system will work for everyone or every situation.

Think of a farmer who agrees to give the driver the jack. It is possible to see this act as selfish rather than altruistic. The farmer figures, like the finder of the money, that he would want someone to give him a jack were he stranded. Hence he behaves as he does to protect himself prospectively. Moreover, it may be more economically efficient, from a societal standpoint, for the farmer to give the driver the jack, because finding and paying for a tow truck would cost significantly more in time and money. But these two justifications for the good behavior assume that the farmer had an opportunity to make these assessments before the fact. I doubt that, as he stood at the door responding to the driver, he assessed his own position in this way.

It seems much more likely that the farmer would look at the driver and make a quick assessment as to whether he (the farmer) was at risk of injury. (For example, was the driver who he said he was? Was his story believable? Did the driver resemble a recently escaped felon from the local penitentiary?) Assuming the farmer did not see himself at risk, he would lend the driver the jack because he wanted to help him in a time of need. At some level, the farmer would recognize that the driver could walk off with the jack and not return. From the farmer's perspective, that risk is outweighed by the benefits of providing some assistance. If this positive portrait of human nature is an accurate one, then individuals may well be willing to attend to communities in order to help those communities survive.

How Far Does Responsibility Go?

The critical question remains of the extent of the responsibility from individuals to communities. Suppose that Smythe is walking down the street and sees a child drowning in a lake. Rather than stop, Smythe keeps going. Because no one comes to the child's aid, the child drowns. If the child's parents were to sue Smythe under tort or contract law, they would not be able to recover. Smythe had no contractual relationship with the child, and U.S. tort law does not create an affirmative duty to assist someone (as distinguished from the existing duty not to harm someone).[13] Indeed, Smythe could be subjected to liability if in the process of rescuing the child he accidentally and carelessly injured her. The "no-duty-to-rescue rule" is justified, at least in part, by the belief in the autonomy of each person. That is, it would be intrusive, as a matter of social policy, to force an individual to rescue another when the rescuer did not choose to do so.

Even if we believe that a duty should run between Smythe and the drowning child,[14] creating a new duty is problematic. We may want Smythe to save the child because it is the right thing to do. But that is different from saying that Smythe is legally responsible if he doesn't save the child in every situation. Suppose that Smythe could not rescue her without considerable risk to his own safety. Suppose that Smythe could rescue her if he were to forgo his visit to a dying friend in the hospital before visiting hours ended. Suppose Smythe simply wanted to get home to his family for dinner. Suppose, finally, that the child did not want to be rescued. Clearly any duty to rescue would need limits. In choosing those limits, one would be making certain value judgments. One could decide, for example, that one's own life is more important than that of the drowning stranger. Perhaps seeing a dying friend is more important than saving an unknown drowning person. Perhaps a job interview is less important than saving someone's life, and perhaps going bowling is not as important as saving a drowning child.[15]

Aside from the problem of identifying who should be saved and how that assessment should be made, it is fair to suggest that changing from a no-duty-to-rescue rule to a duty-to-rescue rule would change the way people behave. If people had a responsibility to rescue and a liability for failing to rescue, individuals would need to be on the lookout for others in danger. This would take time and attention. People might try to limit their exposure to others for fear that they would have to act. If the possible exposure to liability makes people unwilling to take risks for fear they will be sued, then expanding the zone of responsibility would run counter to what the rule would be trying to achieve.

The duty to rescue has real implications for how Americans think about themselves and their society. During a state examination for admission to the bar, for example, a test taker started to have an epileptic seizure. Several other test takers (prospective lawyers) rushed to the aid of this individual, who was eventually removed from the room and taken to the hospital. When the incident was over, the rescuers asked for extra time to complete the examination because they had lost precious time tending to the stricken test taker. Their request was denied (though their scores were reviewed later), and the individuals were instructed to return to their seats and complete the examination within the allotted period.[16] The result is consistent with the no-duty-to-rescue rule. But the people that society wants as the compassionate dispensers of justice may well fail the bar exam because they cared about another person.

The Corporate Context and the Role of Duties

Responsibility is not limited to situations involving individuals. A long-standing debate in corporate law concerns the question, To whom does the corporation owe a duty? Most people take for granted that corporate officers and directors owe a duty to shareholders. They are the individuals or entities who have invested in the company; they are the ones who are at risk financially. But this issue is not nearly so clear cut.[17] Some commentators have suggested even perfectly solvent corporations have a duty to act as socially responsible citizens. Rather than operate purely to profit shareholders, a corporation should take the interests of community into account. Although views differ considerably as to what that commitment to the larger community means, it is clear that the commitment is an effort to break down the artificial distinction between what is private (the interests of shareholders) and what is public (the interest of community).

This issue became more pressing in the takeover era of the 1980s. During that period, more than half the states passed "constituency statutes." These statutes, which corporations can elect to adopt for their own use if they choose, stipulate that corporations owe a duty to a broadly defined arena of people and entities. Under the typical constituency statute, businesses owe a duty to employees, customers, suppliers, creditors, and the local community. Although the effect of these statutes has not been great because of a lack of corporate adoption, they raise a critical issue. Is the sole goal of the corporation to produce profit, or is that goal qualified by other goals?

Constituency statutes and the suggested movement away from a pure profit motive as the raison d'être for corporate law have been criticized on numerous bases. First, they depart from the idea that corporations are creatures of contract, privately created by parties. Second, to be effective, these statutes would need to be based on federal rather than state law. Third, some people are concerned that investors would shy away from socially conscious companies in favor of those investing to make a profit.

More recently, a suggestion has been made that corporations teetering on insolvency owe a duty to their creditors.[18] Under traditional corporate law, a corporation owes a fiduciary duty to creditors only when that corporation is insolvent. Up until that point, the corporation's allegiance is to its shareholders. Therefore, in bankruptcy, a debtor (ostensibly insolvent) becomes a guardian of the interests of the enterprise and has an obligation to protect the interests of creditors. That is one reason why the absolute priority rule provides that creditors must be paid before equity holders.

Community Interests in Bankruptcy

It is unsatisfactory to determine either that no communities matter in bankruptcy or that all communities matter. On the one hand, obliterating the interest of community would have such implications as the no-duty-to-rescue rule or a corporate structure motivated solely by profit. On the other hand, an overriding interest in community would have such implications as a duty-to-rescue rule or a corporate system that eradicates the motivation of investors. Thus, we need to take some but not all communities into account. But assessing which communities matter in formulating bankruptcy law is immensely difficult.

The universe of communities within the bankruptcy process includes the named participants—the debtors, creditors, and equity holders—and the unnamed participants. These are the families of debtors and creditors. They are future tort claimants. They are affected workers. They are local businesses that are not owed money. They are the communities where the debtor is located. They are the communities where a debtor's acquirer may relocate the debtor's business.

These various communities are like the ripples that occur when a stone is thrown into water. Every debtor is a pebble, and when the pebble hits the water, concentric circles are formed. The circles closest to the pebble are the smallest but the strongest. The outermost circles are the largest in size but weakest in form. In fact, there are an infinite number of ripples, but we can see only those closest to us. Moreover, the circles eventually hit the opposite shore, affecting the bank of the pond, even if the impact is imperceptible to the naked eye. Many people, including a significant number of bankruptcy scholars, think about bankruptcy as addressing only the circles closest in—creditors and the economic welfare of society based on that creditor's recovery. Seeing the other ripples requires a shift from the narrow to the broad, from the short term to the longer term.

Some people have trouble making this shift. For many people, suggesting that community counts is like waving a red flag in front of a bull. People see a social welfare state. Or they see communism. Or they see moral majoritarianism. Or they see eradication of individual rights. Or they see noneconomic behavior. Or they see an overbearing judiciary that doesn't understand the doctrine of separation of powers. Or they assume that community interests will be more significant than all other interests. This picture is a misperception.[19] It is true that in some cases community interests will be more important than other interests. It is equally true that in other situations the interests of the debtor will outweigh those of community. In still other contexts, the interests of creditors will overshadow all other interests. Until the hands are dealt and the game is played, no one knows who will be holding the trump cards.

Saying that community matters is not a prescription for a social welfare state. Sacrificing individual gain is not always necessary. Taking community into account also does not mean that all economic modeling should be discarded as flawed. Contrary to the views of some critics, the interests of community are not always aligned with those of the debtor. Society will not always save the buggy-whip maker, the proverbial name for the company that should become extinct because it has outlived its usefulness. What consideration of community means, instead, is that American society needs to expand its understanding of what Americans value and to develop a more expansive economic analysis.

In his now-famous study of American farming in the 1950s, updated in the 1970s, anthropologist Walter Goldschmidt looked at the consequences of agribusiness (large corporate-owned farming).[20] He evaluated two communities in California, one with small owner-operated farms and the other with corporate-owned and -managed farms with contract farming. Goldschmidt found that the small farms were not energy- or production-efficient in the short term. Based on these criteria, agrifarming was superior. But the quality of community life in the town with farmer-owned and -run farms far exceeded that of the town with agrifarming. Streets, sidewalks, parks, schools, and religious and political involvement were all better in the community with non-mega-business farming. Assume several small individually owned farms are experiencing financial difficulty (picture a local flood). One option is for the farms to reorganize in Chapter 11 with the farmers retaining ownership. Another option is to force the farmers to sell their land and equipment to a farming conglomerate, with a distribution of the proceeds to secured and unsecured creditors. This choice affects the local community. That effect does not mean that a court should invariably decide to save the small farmers' farms, as such a decision would create other inefficiencies—in energy and production. It could also materially harm banks and trade creditors (at least in the short term). But what it does mean is that the farm should not necessarily be sold simply because doing so will benefit creditors.

Consider the problems currently confronting Asbury Park, New Jersey.[21] A contracting company named Carabetta Enterprises was both a general and limited partner of Ocean Mile, an entity under contract to redevelop a significant portion of beachfront property in Asbury Park. Ocean Mile failed to fulfill its commitments to redevelop Asbury Park. Years thereafter (the project was to have begun in 1986), a settlement agreement was reached between Ocean Mile and the city under which the developer had to either come up with new funding within a limited period or, among other things, resign as the developer. The debtor Carabetta (it filed for Chapter 11 relief in 1992) sought to void that settlement because it diminished the value of its Chapter 11 estate by curtailing the prospects of proceeding with and obtaining profits from the redevelopment.

Meanwhile, the City of Asbury Park was deteriorating. Since 1992, Ocean Mile had not paid taxes on numerous parcels of beachfront land, and it owed the city approximately $1,450,000 in back taxes. Because the redevelopment never commenced, new businesses never arrived, and old businesses moved or closed. Historic buildings and memorabilia from Asbury Park's notable past were lost or sold. As the ultimate punishment, dwindling taxpayer revenue was being spent to defend the city.

The interests of the community of Asbury Park are not consonant with those of the debtor Carabetta. The debtor's interest in retaining the rights to redevelopment conflicts with the needs of the city and its citizens to cut their ties with Ocean Mile and Carabetta as quickly as possible to salvage the dying community. Recognizing the impact of the bankruptcy on Asbury Park does not mean that the interests of the debtor or creditors are necessarily subordinated. But it does add another element to the equation.

Taking community interests into account in the bankruptcy arena is not the same as the newly developing moral and political theory that has been coined communitarianism. Communitarianism, generally speaking, is a theory premised on the importance of community and the responsibility that individuals have to better society.[22] Communitarians believe that the social good takes precedence over individual liberties in many situations and that contemporary society pays far too much attention to individual liberties, thereby destroying the social fabric. Mandatory drug testing, sobriety checkpoints, and increased thresholds for obtaining divorces are three examples of issues that communitarians support, believing that in these cases individual liberty is outweighed by the need for a safer, more stable society.

Some aspects of communitarianism are consistent with the considerations of community proffered here. I agree that individuals and businesses do not act in a purely selfish and autonomous manner, neither affected by nor affecting the world around them. People have a societal responsibility that requires a shift from short- to longer-term perspectives. The considerations of community impact and of communitarianism both foster a movement away from rights-based thinking and toward responsibility-based thinking. Both approaches recognize and accept some self-sacrifice.

My suggestions regarding community impact, however, differ from the communitarian agenda in material respects. Unlike communitarians, I do not mandate the supremacy of community or create an agenda for how families or businesses should conduct themselves. The approach developed in this book applies to only a limited subset within society: individuals and businesses touched by financial distress who seek relief under the federal bankruptcy laws. This book was not intended to provide a prescription for how the American economy should operate or how financially healthy individuals and businesses should comport themselves.

Communitarians proffer a theory based on equalitarianism, whereas my approach is an antidote to an assimilationist stance. I suggest that wealth should and can be redistributed in bankruptcy, but any system for making those divisions must recognize the marked diversity among creditors. Moreover, I recognize the right of secured creditors who have obtained collateral to protect their interests.

Which Communities Count?

Saying that community counts still leaves open the question of which communities a bankruptcy system should consider, and standards are required in order to find and define community within existing bankruptcy law. Establishing standards, however, means that visible community interests will go unheeded. Even if the process of fixing the standards is procedural in nature (composed of rules, burden of proof, and the like), it is substantive in outcome (affecting the bottom-line question of which communities count). In some ways, determining the cognizable parties in litigation raises similar issues.[23] When a wrong has been committed, courts (and lawyers) commonly address who can be sued. Sometimes the answers are simple. If Jonathan damages Mary's tree, Mary can sue Jonathan. They have a direct relationship. But suppose Mary's children also liked the tree and felt damaged by its destruction. Suppose Mary's neighbors were also upset because the tree's destruction eliminated much needed shade and diminished home values. Could the children and neighbors also sue Jonathan? And suppose an arborist society, concerned about tree preservation and the environment, heard about the destruction. Could it, too, sue Jonathan? With these "questions of standing," the law defines the parameters of who has standing to sue, and that determination, though procedural in nature, is substantive in impact.

Three key concepts taken from questions of standing, particularly in public interest cases, are useful for determining which communities should be recognized within the world of bankruptcy: "nexus," "injury," and "redressability."[24] First, the communities that matter are those in which an identifiable nexus exists between the debtor's bankruptcy and the community. That nexus can take a variety of forms. It can be, for example, an ecosystem nexus, a vocational nexus, or a social welfare nexus.[25] Second, if the nexus indeed exists, then there must be some real and palpable injury that is or will be felt by the community as a consequence of the debtor's bankruptcy. This injury does not need to be economic (although it certainly can be), but it cannot be conjectural or hypothetical. Third, the injury must be capable of being redressed in the debtor's bankruptcy case. Some injuries caused by a bankruptcy will not be able to be remedied by, for example, adjusting the treatment of the parties within a plan of reorganization. In this case, the injured community will go unrecognized. Only if all three conditions are satisfied will the community in question have a place at the bankruptcy table.

Suppose a small airline is in financial trouble and seeks bankruptcy relief. The airline proposes to do three things: shut down service to Blytheville, exchange its current fleet of ten small prop planes for three large (but very noisy) jets, and move its base of operations from Little Rock to Hope. The debtor's secured and unsecured creditors are in favor of all of the proposed changes, as they will streamline operations and generate the additional revenues needed to fund a distribution of thirty cents on the dollar to creditors in a three-year plan of reorganization. Several groups, however, express concern over what the debtor proposed. The community of Blytheville is worried that if the airline shuts down, there will be no air transportation into or out of Blytheville. This will inconvenience the residents and will make mail delivery slower than it already is. And companies that are based in Blytheville, like Seat Co., will have a harder time obtaining supplies. What they do receive will be delayed and cost more. Some residents outside Little Rock are concerned that when the carrier moves to larger planes, the noise over their homes will be significant. Moreover, real estate prices will drop and day-to-day living will be disrupted. Finally, the City of

Little Rock is concerned that if the airline headquarters leaves the capital, other businesses may follow suit. The local tax base could go down. Moreover, the fifty workers at the headquarters will either lose their jobs or need to relocate to Hope.

Most of these concerned communities can satisfy the first condition of the test, namely, an identifiable nexus with the debtor. The residents and businesses in Blytheville, the owners of land near airports, the government in Little Rock, and the airline's workers all have a connection with the debtor. But suppose a real estate firm that sells houses near the airport wants to object to the change in plane sizes, which would lower property values and decrease the firm's sales and commissions. This group is only marginally related to the debtor.

The aforementioned communities will all experience some injury, although the degree of injury varies somewhat. The community with no air service, the neighbors with new noise pollution, and the workers displaced from Little Rock are most affected. The real estate brokers concerned with decreased land values and the City of Little Rock, while affected, have injuries that are much more conjectural. The movement of the company's headquarters to Little Rock may produce only a slight blip in that city's economy, and perhaps better businesses will replace the small headquarters that departed. The land values may drop, but perhaps that drop is only temporary. If land is scarce and the community is desirable, then the values may increase, particularly if something is done to cure the noise during peak periods.

As for the third condition, all the real injuries to the three most affected communities could be remedied through the bankruptcy. The debtor could be forbidden from confirming a plan that shuts down all service to Blytheville. The new planes could be rerouted to minimize noise, and some of the older planes could be retained for service during noise-sensitive periods. The displaced workers could be offered severance or relocating bonuses. Or they could be retrained for other jobs in Little Rock. So, the test successfully identifies three communities that matter in the airline's bankruptcy. The treatment of these three groups may benefit one of the less directly affected groups, the brokers. This three-pronged test, however, is only a mechanism for determining what community interests are important enough to be considered at the bankruptcy table. Agreeing to consider a community interest does not mean that that interest will prevail.

The three-pronged test does limit the number of communities that a court takes into account, and in some situations, this could be troubling. Suppose, for example, that a buyer for Seat Co.'s assets wants to close the plant in Blytheville and open a new plant in Durham, New Hampshire. Seat Co. has no identifiable relationship with Durham. So under the proposed test, the community interests of Durham would not be taken into account, at least directly, in Seat Co.'s bankruptcy case. It could be, however, that the loss to Blytheville is Durham's gain. And if the community of Durham is in greater need than Blytheville, then the sale of the assets and relocation of the plant benefits a community other than the community where the debtor is located. This argument does assume, somewhat problematically, that communities are fungible.

It is true that the proposed test favors the continuity of existing communities. But the existing community will be less successful in balancing its interests against those of the other parties (the debtor and the creditors) if some other community can be shown to benefit. So if the debtor and creditors support the sale of Seat Co.'s assets, one of their arguments could well be that their proposal benefits Durham.

The next step is to examine how, as a practical matter, community interests can be brought into the bankruptcy arena. To do this, it is necessary to evaluate how current bankruptcy law deals with community interests.

CHAPTER THIRTEEN

Which Communities Matter within the Bankruptcy System?

In this chapter I explore four ways current bankruptcy law addresses the import of community, although a bit of revisionist history is at work because the label *community* as used here was not an identifier known to the courts or Congress.[1] The approaches in the following examples, while instructive, are incomplete. If community interests are to be taken seriously within the bankruptcy system, current law needs to be changed.

Textualism and Judicial Opinions

Although decisions on bankruptcy issues are necessarily rooted in the Bankruptcy Code and Federal Rules of Bankruptcy Procedure, judges are commonly called on to interpret existing provisions in situations clearly not contemplated when the Bankruptcy Code was enacted. In some of these situations, courts have recognized the role of community. On the surface, it may appear that judges are purely guided by textual language, in this case the applicable Code provisions and rules. Many judges specifically state that the outcome in a judicial decision is based on the language of the Code.[2] Indeed, some scholars who have studied the Supreme Court's decisions in the bankruptcy area have commented on the high degree of textualism these decisions reveal. One article on this subject is even titled "Of Commas, Gerunds and Conjunctions."[3]

It is easy to be fooled into thinking that textualism is truly a guide for decision making. But despite the text, judges' decisions on bankruptcy and other issues are frequently influenced by their judicial philosophy and their personal sense of what a particular provision means in context. Because such a text as the Bankruptcy Code does not literally speak, the particular language of the text frequently can have several interpretations, and the language must be placed in the context of other provisions within the same text. Therefore, although some people believe that true meaning (of a religious text, for example) can be divined from the words themselves, many people remain convinced that meaning is elusive and ultimately personal. It is more accurate to state, then, that courts, including most particularly the Supreme Court, employ what could be termed mock textualism rather than textualism. That is, they engage in policy making masquerading as textualism.

This is not to suggest that personal philosophy is terrible. Indeed, the potential for wise decision making rests on a judge's ability to move beyond the text and think about what the "right" choice is.[4] Activist judges can recognize that sometimes what the text says and what it means are two different things. Decision making that recognizes the possibility of interpreting the text (rather than accepting it at face value or saying one is accepting it at face value when the face value is by no means clear) is thus not mock textualism. Instead, these courts are deciding cases by looking at the meaning that lies behind the text. The process these judges employ could better be termed contextualized decision making.

Contextualized decision making scares many people. It reveals that decisions are not as clear-cut as may first appear. It permits judges to look at the specific facts before the court and then interpret and apply the text in light of those facts. It allows judges to be influenced by the impact of a bankruptcy on the various participants in the process. It allows courts to consider community interests in assessing how to interpret the Code, although the word *community* may not appear in the decision rendered.

Concerns about contextualized decision making, including concerns about consideration of community, can at least be partially assuaged by overcoming the seeming appeal of textualism. Despite beliefs to the contrary, textualism or mock textualism does not provide certainty. If textual meaning were clear-cut, lawyers and judges would not spend so much time debating meaning. Although some decisions, including those from some members of the United States Supreme Court, express disdain at the apparent inability of individuals to see the true meaning of the Bankruptcy Code, most law is malleable. Indeed, for several years I tried to predict the outcome of Supreme Court cases dealing with bankruptcy. I figured that if the watchword of the decade was textualism, I should be able to predict outcomes by looking at the Bankruptcy Code. But my predictions were frequently wrong, not because I failed to consider the text but because what most justices read the text to mean differed from what I read it to mean. Certainty was not enhanced by textualism.

Moreover, as much as some people would like to believe in objective decision making, all choices are, at some level, subjective. In the real world, justice is not dispensed from on high. It is dispensed from the mind and the heart.[5] Lawyers engaged in bankruptcy practice know this intuitively. They are frequently sensitive to who is hearing a particular matter. They are usually cautious about telling a client what a judge will decide. The trade-off for certainty is decision making that is more sensitive to facts. Contextualized decision making recognizes that decisions are made for the actual situation a court is addressing. A text, while seemingly free standing, generates its true meaning when it is read in light of real cases and real people.

Contextualized decision making is not an abdication of precedent.[6] Indeed, prior decisions and legislative history can help guide the decision maker. Even in a system of precedent, however, there must be room for individualized justice.[7] The complaint that tough cases make bad law reveals a concern that sometimes facts push a decision one way or another. That is not bad. What is bad is a system of decision making so rigid that it cannot bend at all.

Consider contextualized decision making in the context of family rules. Suppose the rule is that children must be in bed, with lights out and television off, by nine o'clock in the evening on school nights. The rule makes sense as a generalized matter. Kids should be rested before the school day. As any parent well knows, however, some situations call for a variation of the rule. Suppose a child's mother has been out of town, and the child wants to stay up to greet her upon her return home. Suppose the child is desperate to see a worthwhile television show that will not be repeated at another time. Suppose the child isn't tired on one particular day because she had a nap in the afternoon. Suppose the local hockey team could win the Stanley Cup for the first time in more than fifty years, and the game is televised. The variation of the rule does not make the basic rule irrelevant or open the floodgates to unprincipled decision making.

Consider an example of contextualized decision making in bankruptcy. In 1993 a Texas bankruptcy judge was asked to reconsider an earlier decision he had made on venue.[8] The case involved several radio stations located in Utah. The debtor filed its Chapter 11 case in Texas, where the debtor's owner was located. That location was a permissible place for the filing under existing law. But the debtor's actual business, its primary secured lender, its creditors, and its employees were all located in Utah. In deciding to transfer the case to Salt Lake City, the judge emphasized the importance of having a judge familiar with the debtor's community make the decision about the debtor's future. He observed that a local judge would be in the best position, based on common sense and life experience, to assess the likelihood of the debtor's success. The Texas judge noted, with some displeasure, the failure of a retail chain whose bankruptcy was filed in New York but whose stores were in Texas. The Texas judge believed that the New York judge was oblivious to the grave consequences of store closures on a small Texas community. Perhaps the result would have been different had a local judge handled the bankruptcy case.

The decision about transferring venue from Texas to Utah is not unprincipled. It is an example of contextualized decision making on two levels. First, under existing law, the court was required to balance competing factors in determining where a case should be heard.[9] More important, the Texas court considered the interests of community to be one of those factors even though the existing rules on venue nowhere mention community by name. And the decision goes further by recognizing that context matters.

Railroad Reorganizations and Beyond

According to the railroad reorganization subchapter of Chapter 11 of the Bankruptcy Code, railroads cannot be liquidated; they can only be reorganized.[10] This implies that railroads have a special role in society. Clearly, the preservation of railroads cannot be just for the benefit of the railroad's owners. Other businesses have owners who also want their respective businesses to survive. Instead, this subchapter suggests that the continuity of rail service is important to the larger community.

In subchapter IV of Chapter 11, several specific provisions indicate that in any railroad reorganization, the court must take into account the "public interest."[11] A railroad debtor, for example, cannot abandon its railroad track unless such abandonment is consistent with the public interest. A railroad's plan of reorganization cannot be confirmed unless it is consistent with the public interest.

These provisions date back to the days when railroads were the primary means of transportation in the United States. If a railroad failed, an entire segment of the country could be cut off from commerce. And because one railroad's track was linked to that of another railroad, a shutdown or abandonment of track would have a ripple effect on other parts of the country. In addition, individual travel would be substantially delayed or curtailed. The other existing forms of transportation were considerably slower, more dangerous, and frequently more costly. Although there has not been an abundance of case law directly addressing the meaning of the "public interest" in railroad cases, the existing cases make clear that the balancing test in railroad reorganization cases is not just between the interests of debtors and creditors but also involves community.[12]

Although the Bankruptcy Code uses the phrase "public interest" and I use the term "community," these concepts are not so divergent. A dictionary definition of public interest speaks about the well-being of society. Obviously, what is in the public interest is a matter of considerable debate both within and outside the legal community. Whether and when it is in the public interest to preserve troubled companies is clearly an important question. But even to refer to the public interest in the context of railroad reorganizations suggests that traditional neoclassical economics alone did not and does not govern the fate of railroads. A court is bound to look at a larger universe and weigh that interest with those of the other affected parties.

An obvious question is why concern for the public interest should be limited to railroads. At least in contemporary society, railroads are not so unique that the protections given them should not be replicated elsewhere in the Code for other situations. If the provisions within subchapter IV have the narrow goal of protecting community access to transportation, then at a minimum the consideration of the public interest should extend to the more modern forms of transportation that, if curtailed, would also substantially affect a community.

Suppose, for example, that a small, private bus company services rural communities in Arkansas.[13] This company is losing money and wants to reorganize under the Bankruptcy Code. To achieve a successful restructuring, the bus company will need to shut off its less profitable services to some locations, including Blytheville. But, for the community of Blytheville, bus service is essential. Without transportation, it, too, will fail. If the case of the bus company is evaluated based on what will yield the greatest return to existing shareholders and creditors, assuming no new investor is waiting patiently in the wings, the bus company should shut down the Blytheville routes. If all that matters is repaying creditors, an appealing plan is to restructure the healthy parts of the bus company, give the secured lenders (the bank and the bus manufacturer) a repayment commitment, pay unsecured creditors more than they would get in liquidation, and call the case a success. But if this approach is taken, many people in Blytheville will not be able to get to work. Seat Co.'s workers will be unable to reach the plant. Those who cannot drive will be unable to go into the town to purchase food and medicine.

If, however, the service to Blytheville is maintained and the bus company is to reorganize as a profitable company, someone will have to pay for those choices. The restructuring could take several forms. Money originally allocated to unsecured creditors (and possibly equity holders) of the bus company could be spent subsidizing the unprofitable routes to and from Blytheville. Alternatively, the local or state government could advance monies to fund a portion of the reorganization if the plan of reorganization contained a commitment to continued service to Blytheville. Or investors could be found to purchase the assets and start a new bus company that provides service to the affected areas. The community in Blytheville is as deserving of attention in the bankruptcy context as the community where a railroad is located.

Consider an example beyond the arena of transportation. Suppose that a local private hospital cannot make ends meet. Asking a court to consider the public interest in determining the fate of this hospital is similar to requiring a court to consider the public interest before abandoning railroad tracks. A hospital, like a railroad, keeps the community alive. On strictly economic grounds, preserving the hospital may make no sense. Supporting a small hospital in rural America may be too costly, and it may well be better to transport patients to a larger regional hospital.

The noneconomic consequences of consolidating medical facilities must be probed, however. Some patients will die on the way to the regional hospital because of the delay. And when patients are hospitalized outside their own community, it may be difficult (in some cases impossible) for family and friends to visit. Attention from friends and family helps the healing process, decreasing the length of hospitalization and improving subsequent recovery. But when family members are far away, their ability to participate in the patient's medical care becomes problematic, leading to decreased communication with caregivers and increased anxiety. For those able to visit, the time and expense of travel to the regional hospital disrupt work and family life. An expanded economic model should consider these less obvious costs to families and communities, and they should be weighed against the gains generated through consolidation.

Economist Richard Thaler noted that people do not always make rational wealth-maximizing decisions, and he set out to investigate how consumers actually behave, as opposed to how certain economists hypothesize that they behave.[14] He studied people's responses to the following two questions: (1) Would you pay two hundred dollars to decrease the chances of dying by one in ten thousand? and (2) If I paid you two hundred dollars, would you be willing to increase your chance of your dying by one in ten thousand? Most of the respondents were unwilling to pay the two hundred dollars in response to the first question. In response to the second question, however, most respondents were unwilling to give up even a one-in-ten-thousand chance of living in exchange for two hundred dollars. At least in theory, the responses should have been consistent with one another. If decreasing the likelihood of survival isn't worth two hundred dollars, then receiving two hundred dollars for giving up that chance is economically rational and produces wealth maximization. But respondents were not willing to relinquish that small chance of survival even though it made economic sense. People behave, as Thaler expresses it, quasi-rationally.

One facile response to the hospital scenario is to suggest that it is not a bankruptcy problem. Just let the U.S. government reconfigure the nationwide health care system. Perhaps instead of shutting down, the local hospital could be retooled. It could give up its surgery and sophisticated equipment and instead focus on medical emergencies, primary care, clinics, and at-home care. More seriously ill people, once stabilized, could be transported to bigger hospitals equipped to handle their problems. New methods of communication for families and medical providers could be arranged through videoconferencing, and special busses could be arranged for transportation to the regional hospital. This all makes sense—in the abstract—but that is where economic models fail.

The suggested retooling will take time and planning. The local hospital is insolvent today. And people are not going to stop getting ill while the government sorts out a solution to the health care problem. As in situations involving mass torts or environmental pollution, a national solution is needed, but in the interim the current needs of real people must be addressed. This is where bankruptcy comes in. Bankruptcy provides a solution for a given situation, recognizing that the larger solutions will have to wait for another day.

An example involving a small hospital reveals the ability of the bankruptcy system to act as a problem solver.[15] Following an outpouring of support for the hospital from the community, a court could confirm the hospital's Chapter 11 case based on a community-focused approach to the Code provisions. Assume that the court permitted a bifurcation of the unsecured claims into separate classes so that the government, holding an enormous claim, could not delay the reorganization process. Such a court would be applying contextual decision making by interpreting the claims-classification provisions of the Code with the concept of community in mind. This approach also adopts a hopeful approach to the question of whether the reorganization is feasible.

But the outpouring of support for this local hospital, which services the poor, should not dry up the minute the case is closed. Success of a local hospital would demand an ongoing commitment postbankruptcy by all members of the community—doctors, nurses, patients, charities, and the government. This approach recognizes that people need communities and communities need people.

Labor Contracts

Seat Co., in the original scenario, went into bankruptcy to obtain relief in part from an onerous collective bargaining agreement. And Seat Co. hardly stands alone in that regard. Well-known larger companies have filed bankruptcy at least in part to resolve labor difficulties. Continental Airlines and Wheeling-Pittsburgh are just two examples of companies whose management believed that the companies could be profitable if they were not wed to their existing labor contracts.[16]

Even before the Supreme Court's decision in *Bildisco*, a case that changed (some would say clarified) the manner of dealing with collective bargaining agreements in bankruptcy, courts viewed labor contracts differently from other executory agreements.[17] Although a debtor always had an opportunity to reject an executory contract based on the debtor's best interests, the standard for rejecting labor contracts was higher. That is, a company could escape its obligation to manufacture product, rent warehouse space, or buy advertising time more easily than it could relieve itself of its obligations to existing workers. Like railroads, then, the interests of workers were considered sufficiently important to be treated specially.

The *Bildisco* decision generated considerable debate, and Congress stepped in to provide a new statutory provision dealing exclusively with collective bargaining agreements. This section, known as Section 1113, provides that in order to reject a collective bargaining agreement, the needs of debtors to reorganize must be balanced with the workers' desire to have some sanctity to their labor contracts. Specifically, a debtor must show that the balance of equities clearly favors rejection before it can abrogate a collective bargaining agreement, and, except in exigent circumstances, it cannot terminate the agreement unilaterally. Understandably, courts have struggled to interpret this test and have debated what precisely needs to be balanced and what equities the court should consider.[18] In a sense, this test is a legal articulation of the need for a court to take the interests of community into account. At first, it seems that the only relevant interests are those of the debtor and the community of workers. But the test goes beyond that.

Suppose a debtor manufactures IBM-compatible computers and entered into its labor contract when it was the largest manufacturer. Accordingly, its profits were high; the wages and benefits it paid were correspondingly high. Suppose that numerous new manufacturers, including those from abroad, have entered the marketplace, the price of computers has gone down, and there is a temporary but real shortage of computer chips. If the debtor does not obtain wage concessions, it will have to shut its doors. This event will have several consequences. Not only the unionized workers but also numerous other workers—such as sales staff, designers, secretaries, and bookkeepers—will be without work. The marketplace will be considerably disrupted, as other manufacturers may not be able to fill the void immediately. Work in progress will depreciate significantly in value because completed product will be worth considerably more. The local community will suffer because the tax base will erode as people move away and seek other employment.

Assuming the debtor is accurately describing the situation, a court addressing the debtor's ability to abrogate its collective bargaining agreement will look at all these factors in balancing the equities. It will not limit itself to comparing the loss to workers if the contract is rejected with the gain to shareholders if the business survives. The court will be assessing the interests of community, although the word *community* appears nowhere in Section 1113.

Health and Welfare Interests

The corporate context is not the only one in which community interests are relevant or recognized. Among the key provisions of the Bankruptcy Code is the automatic stay, which prohibits parties, including the government, from taking action to recover against the debtor. Despite the breadth of the stay, the government is allowed to proceed to enforce any nonmonetary judgment as long as the goal is to further the government's police or regulatory power.[19] The Bankruptcy Code does not specifically define what is within this power. Both the legislative history and the case law, however, suggest that the government can pursue actions for preservation of health and welfare. Once again, the word *community* does not appear. But the lawmakers and courts are not talking about the debtor's health and welfare. They are talking about a significantly larger universe.

Suppose, for example, that an individual debtor, like Smythe, has been polluting by dumping used motor oil into a local pond. Suppose the government issued a restraining order to stop the activity and obtained a monetary award of $1 million to clean up the damage. Although the exception to the automatic stay would not let the government collect the $1 million, the restraining order would not be subjected to the automatic stay. When the government's activity is in the interest of the larger community (as distinguished from being purely in the government's interest, as collecting money for its own coffers would be), that action can continue, notwithstanding a bankruptcy.[20] Consider another example. Suppose that Smythe had been convicted of arson and sentenced to jail. This exception would permit the government to proceed with incarcerating Smythe even if he sought bankruptcy relief. The government's incarceration of Smythe may not benefit him, and it certainly does not enable creditors to get repaid faster, if at all. Instead, it protects the community from the danger Smythe poses to it.

The automatic stay also works to protect more private communities, such as that of the debtor's family. For example, in Chapter 13, the stay extends to not just the debtor but selected co-debtors.[21] This provision recognizes that a creditor's action against a member of the debtor's family, the most likely co-debtor of the individual debtor, would affect the debtor's ability to reorganize because the debtor would try to protect the family member. Therefore, the Code steps in to protect those extended "community" interests.

Another example is the Bankruptcy Code provision stating that if a home is jointly owned by a debtor and another party, that home can be sold only if certain stringent preconditions are met: the property cannot be partitioned, sale free of the co-owner's interest will yield a sufficient economic return, and most important for this discussion, the benefits of the sale must outweigh the detriment to co-owners.[22] In all likelihood, the co-owners specifically protected by this provision are the nonfiling spouses of debtors who could lose the family home or be forced into bankruptcy themselves without this provision.[23] The provision is thus an explicit recognition of the interests of noncreditors who would be adversely affected by a bankruptcy. Again, however, the word *community* is not in evidence.

Methods of Proceeding

One way to enhance the role of community in bankruptcy is to rely on judicial activism. Although activism should continue, it presents certain drawbacks as the sole method for ensuring that community counts. First, not all judges are activists. Hence, inclusion of community would be sporadic and nonuniform. Second, even judges inclined to consider community may be a reluctant to substitute their judgment for that of Congress in terms of determining what is important in the bankruptcy context. These judges would prefer to see explicit reference to community before they actively or overtly consider it. This preference is generally confirmed by the history of Section 105.

Section 105 permits courts to act in whatever ways are necessary to effectuate the Code, and courts have repeatedly invoked this provision when they sense that the Code produces an unfair result. But even judges willing to apply Section 105 freely must have some basis for granting the indicated relief.[24] Judges cannot, as the appellate courts reviewing bankruptcy cases have repeated, act based on free-wheeling equity. The equitable powers derive from what is actually in the Code. For example, unmarried couples trying to file jointly have generally not been successful in getting a court to interpret Section 302 broadly, even with the assistance of Section 105.[25] This is because the use of Section 105 would be overriding what is in the Code explicitly and creating equity without the benefit of supporting legislative intent.

If community is to be recognized, some specific amendments to the Code are needed. Changes I propose—modification of the confirmation standards and inclusion of a balancing test—draw on the current approaches for treating railroads and labor contracts. The proposed changes are not based on the Code's treatment of health and welfare considerations, which are much more limited in scope (that is, no stay) than those concerning railroads and labor (which involve balancing). Because it will be difficult to assess what community interests are implicated without considering each case specifically, a flexible approach is more suitable. In addition, a definitional section and a provision related to burden of proof should be provided in the Code.

Specifically, Sections 1129, 1225, and 1325 should be amended to stipulate that consideration of community is a prerequisite to confirmation of any reorganization case. This is a lesser standard than that which exists for railroads because Section 1173 (dealing exclusively with railroads) provides that no plan can be confirmed unless the public interest is satisfied. What is proposed generally is a standard that mandates that the public interest be taken into account (balanced) in determining whether a reorganization plan can be confirmed. If other interests trump the interests of community, then the plan still could be confirmed. Under the suggested amendment and in contrast to the railroad provision, a plan could be confirmed even if it was *inconsistent* with the public interest as long as the public interest had been considered and was outweighed by other competing interests.

Following the lead-in language to Sections 1129, 1225, and 1325 ("The court shall confirm a plan if . . ."), the following specific provision should be added: *"The plan takes the interests of community into account unless the balance of equities clearly favors denial of these interests."* The burden-of-proof section, added to each confirmation provision, would read, *"In any hearing under this subsection, (1) the community has the burden of establishing that it qualifies as a community; and (2) the party or parties seeking confirmation have the burden on all other issues."* Additionally, the term *community* would be defined in Section 101: *"Community means those persons, including the government, with a nexus with the debtor for whom (1) there is substantial injury caused by the bankruptcy filing and (2) that injury is redressable through the reorganization process.*"

This proposal reveals certain choices. The word *clearly*, taken from the balancing test in Section 1113 regarding collective bargaining agreements, creates a presumption in favor of community interests that is reinforced in the suggested burden of proof. Deletion of *clearly* would readjust the presumption and enable the debtor or creditors to make a lesser showing if their interests were to supersede those of the community. The definitional section comports with the earlier discussion of what communities matter, although it includes the word *substantial* to ensure that only those communities with a real and serious stake in the outcome are considered. The suggested provision also precludes the judge from raising community interests *sua sponte*. This is in response to the concern that if a community does not care sufficiently about the reorganization to participate, then its stake should not be considered sufficiently important to protect. Moreover, community protection will involve ongoing community participation, and if that participation is not evidenced, then the likelihood of success is small. But if the proposed changes are to be meaningful, community groups will need to be educated about their rights. In the environmental context, such groups as the Sierra Club have dedicated themselves to learning about and speaking out on issues affecting the environment. Communities touched by bankruptcy are not so organized. Some people may worry that if community leaders become educated about bankruptcy, they will seek to participate, which would further complicate an already complex bankruptcy system. But preserving efficient administration of the bankruptcy system is not a justification for denying parties access to the system.

These proposed amendments apply only in the context of reorganization cases. As such, unless the issue specifically involves confirmation in Chapters 11, 12, and 13, courts will still be unable to address community interests through Section 105. Therefore, a further amendment is needed to cover the nonconfirmation issues in which community interests are implicated (such as whether to permit joint filings or pay priority claims of workers before the end of a case). The lead-in to Section 105(d) reads, "The court, on its own motion or at the request of a party-in-interest, may . . ." A new subsection (3) could add: "*consider the interests of community.*" This amendment would settle the argument about freewheeling equity. Insertion of the suggested language is not a guarantee that reluctant judges will use this provision, but it gives those who want to do so the power.

All the suggested amendments operate by making community concerns explicit. That in and of itself is important. In a certain sense, overtly recognizing community is like explicitly recognizing the commitment of marriage. One argument against marriage is that it is not needed if two people are already acting as if they were married. The only thing they lack is the legal formality. But the legal formality is not insignificant. A variety of legal rights and obligations arise only in or because of marriage. Marriage also involves increased hurdles if the relationship is dissolved. Moreover, notwithstanding protests to the contrary, people who are married experience a different kind of commitment from those who are unmarried. Some of that difference has to do with societal perception; other aspects of it have to do with the internalized meaning of marriage to the participants. This does not mean that marriage is right for everyone or that people who are unmarried are not deeply committed to each other. It does not mean that the societal perceptions of marriage are correct or optimal. But it does suggest that explicitness makes a difference, in the eyes of the participants and to outsiders (friends, parents, co-workers, employers, or the government). By analogy, if consideration of community is made explicit, people will pay more attention to community concerns, and these concerns will carry increased significance.

The suggested Code amendments are not perfect. Such questions as how to interpret *substantial* and *redressable* will remain. Moreover, the balancing test will remain open to judicial interpretation. But as case law develops, binding precedent will determine how this balancing should take place. Although the cases will no doubt be extremely fact sensitive, a similar precedential evolution has happened in the context of Section 1113.[26] With respect to Section 105, courts would be likely to proceed cautiously, fearful of overstepping their bounds or creating reversible error. Practical questions would also need to be resolved. Who would represent communities, and how would those professionals be paid? When would communities need to speak before their rights eclipsed, and how, if at all, would relevant communities be notified of a bankruptcy filing in the first instance?

With appropriate statutory amendments, each of the three interests that a workable bankruptcy system needs to take into account—those of debtors, creditors, and community—will have a place at the bankruptcy table. These interests, however, will need to be balanced.

PART V

Creating the Balance

CHAPTER FOURTEEN

How to Balance

If the bankruptcy law were amended in the manner I suggested in the previous chapter, courts could encounter community interests in a variety of contexts—in confirmation of reorganization plans and in other situations where the court chooses to address community interests on its own motion. Balancing the interests of debtors, creditors, and community would be an implicit or explicit aspect of most bankruptcy cases.

A mechanism is needed for determining how that balancing takes place. Although balancing may appear ad hoc, it can actually be systematized at some level. This balancing requires not mandating an outcome, which is impossible given the vast number of possibilities, but establishing an approach, or a methodological orientation. The approach could be termed a contextual model. If each new case is viewed as a piece of clothing, then the contextual model operates like a master tailor. Nips, tucks, elastic, waistbands, hemming, and a touch of creativity are employed to fashion something that fits.

The model identifies the three interests to be balanced in each case: those of the debtor, creditors, and community. In an ideal world, all three interests would be perfectly balanced. The debtor would have a fresh start, creditors would be paid in an economically efficient manner, and community interests would be preserved.

But it is impossible to give each of the identified parties what it wants and still satisfy the other interests. Further, each of the identified strands is heterogeneous. The differences and similarities among the debtors, creditors, and communities require the recognition of a constantly shifting balance point. The job is to find where that balance exists in each new case.

The skills necessary to see what is happening in each bankruptcy case are similar to those employed by artists when they draw or paint. The contextual model should incorporate a perception of edges, space, relationships, shadows and light, and gestalt.[1] The perception of edges means seeing where bankruptcy law begins and ends and where other laws come into play. Because bankruptcy law is affected by a significant body of other law, the greater the extent of federal bankruptcy law, the fewer the inconsistencies in achieving shared national goals. Next, the perception of space means seeing that an object not only occupies its own space but creates other space, and both spaces are visible. This is like seeing both the doughnut and the doughnut hole. If we can see the spaces the bankruptcy participants both occupy and create, we can formulate a truer picture of both what bankruptcy is for those within the system and what it does to those outside the system. Third, we need to see the interrelationships among the three interests in bankruptcy. Sometimes the impact of one of the interests on the others is positive and at other times negative. Fourth, the perception of light and shadows enables us to see the differences, both marked and nuanced, within each of the three recognized groups. Finally, we must have an overall sense, the gestalt, of the bankruptcy system, encapsulated by the concept of equity. Once we have looked at all the parts, they need to be viewed as a whole, which can be greater than the sum of its parts. Applying gestalt to bankruptcy requires consideration of the overall outcome in any given bankruptcy case. We move from the separate perspectives of the debtor, its creditors, and the community to the combination of the three; we look at the duckrabbitpond.

The contextual model does not mean that the interests of community always trump other interests. Indeed, one of the strengths of the model is that the determination of which interests prevail cannot be made ex ante. Ex ante decision making occurs all the time in formalized business transactions and in everyday situations. Agreeing in a contract about how much the damages will be if the contract is breached prospectively is one such example. Another example is a parent's telling a child's caregiver that if a medical emergency occurs, the child should be taken to Moore Hospital. One scholar has taken this approach to heart and suggested that corporate entities should chose at their inception how they want to be treated if they encounter financial distress.[2]

Ex ante choices are problematic if they cannot be changed. A parent who, subsequent to the initial choice, heard bad things about Moore Hospital's emergency room could tell the caregiver to take the child to another hospital. A company that initially opted to liquidate might decide to reorganize in light of market trends. In more formalized situations, unilateral change is not so easy, even if facts and circumstances change; people who relied on the earlier scenario might now be disadvantaged.

My approach is different in that it recognizes that many decisions cannot and should not be made a priori. No matter how careful people are in making their original decisions, they change their minds when circumstances change, and that is not a bad thing. The desire and capacity to change are at once the beauty and the risk of living in an exquisitely complex society. Within a set of parameters, the basic contours of a problem can be understood and results predetermined. But precise outcomes cannot be forecast. Immutable decision making does not work in the real world unless we assume away an essential part of life—change.

The suggested model may strike people as immensely complex and fraught with ambiguities. As one commentator noted, it may seem less like a good solution than like good fiction.[3] This concern is worth considering. How will judges apply the contextual model? Will the Bankruptcy Code need to be completely rewritten to implement the contextual model? In the effort to balance, how will judges determine what interest is most important? Why create new interests when existing interests may already be voicing the positions of others? Won't idiosyncratic beliefs become the order of the day? Wouldn't decisions become politicized? Wouldn't we suddenly be bereft of any objective, predictable standards?

These reactions seem, on first impression, to present sizable challenges to the contextual model. But on one level, the questions reveal a faulty premise, namely, that decisions under current law are predictable, certain, objective, and nonpoliticized. Indeed, much of the criticism of current bankruptcy law centers on the absence of these very factors. More profoundly, it is erroneous to assume that decisions by any judge are neutral.[4] The real fiction is not the contextual model but that idea that there is some unbiased truth just waiting to be discovered. Nothing is purely objective except in an artificial world. It is accurate, though, that truth is more likely to be achieved in certain situations. If more facts are known, if decision makers are sensitive to their own biases, if reasoned debate takes place so multiple views can be heard and evaluated, and if feelings are given credence, then there is a greater likelihood that truth will be found.

The contextual model does not require that the Bankruptcy Code be revamped from start to finish. It does free up judges to use their equitable powers. But judges do not have complete discretion and flexibility within an existing body of statutory law. As the contextual model is applied, decisions—particularly those on the appellate level—will provide guidelines for implementation and will circumscribe the judge's freedom.

Of course, some judges may abuse the equitable power given them and seek to stamp their decisions with their own brand of bankruptcy philosophy. But most decision makers will be guided by the felt sense of what the three identified interests seek to achieve within the bankruptcy system.[5] Guided by the statute and the case law that will develop, judges will not quickly decide that creditors are entitled to nothing and that equity holders get to run away with all the cash. Judges will not decide that community interests are so critical that all the creditors should forgo recovery.

Three aspects of the contextual model are troubling. First, it assumes that all parties with a stake in the bankruptcy process will participate. Regrettably, this may not be so. Debtors will almost always participate. Perhaps communities will as well, once they are educated about their powers.[6] Secured lenders and unsecured creditors with a big economic stake in a case will participate. But creditors owed small amounts in small cases may not be active.[7] Currently, creditors owed small amounts generally do not participate, even on creditors' committees, because of the time and money that participation requires. Society needs to develop ways to remedy this problem, because the balancing system underlying the contextual model presumes there is something to balance. Educating creditors is one possible solution, as is added use of teleconferencing and other nondisruptive means of communicating. Another approach to consider is to compensate committee members at a fixed daily rate for their time, just as jurors are paid to serve. Although the rate would be well below the true value of the committee members' time, it would be a symbolic gesture. The gesture would, however, cost other unsecured creditors by depleting an already small asset pool.

Second, the contextual model does not provide answers. That makes largely irrelevant any decisions by creditors regarding what should happen if they are not paid. Stated differently, the contextual model nullifies or at least underplays ex ante choices a debtor and its creditors made. But living without answers is what happens in everyday life. We cannot tell whether what we do will always work. We cannot control how others will react to us. We cannot control subway delays or traffic jams. We cannot tell whether a big product order will come in. We cannot predict whether we will become ill or whether our expenses will suddenly increase because of a flash flood. If we try to control too much of our lives, we become constrained. So we learn to live with an acceptable level of uncertainty. And those who are the most comfortable with uncertainty are those most able to withstand what happens in everyday life. This uncertainty is difficult for creditors. If risks are known ahead of time, they can factor them into their pricing. If outcomes cannot be predicted, then the commercial marketplace becomes unstable, and that result benefits no one. Once the contextual model is operating, the uncertainties should diminish, and the cries of market uncertainty are sometimes more fabricated than real. But some disruption may accompany the proposed solution.

Third, the costs inherent in the conceptual model are in question. If the balancing favors community, who pays for preserving the community interest? As the model is structured, the loss would not fall on secured lenders, except perhaps for mortgagors extending the length of payments in a Chapter 13 case. Instead, it would fall on unsecured creditors. The loss would be somewhat dissipated by the bad debt deduction and by the prospects of continued business with the debtor. Still, unsecured creditors would pay.

One possible ameliorating factor would be for communities to help pay for their own salvation. Communities may not be able to bring money to the table in the traditional sense. But perhaps communities could offer the harmed creditors a tax benefit or business opportunities. Or perhaps a community could contribute to the estate through other means that would cut back on the creditors' loss. Suppose, for example, that the local community gave the debtor decreased property taxes for a two-year period in exchange for remaining in business. That economic benefit (which would cost the community members something due to a decreased tax base) would shift a loss from unsecured creditors onto community members.

Testing the Contextual Model

The examples that follow reveal that the contextual model is more than good fiction and can function at more than the theoretical level. Suppose, first, that a judge is considering two competing bids for a corporate debtor's assets. One bid is from a company that plans to keep the debtor's business largely intact. That bid is somewhat lower than the bid of a company that plans to break up the assets and sell them piecemeal, leaving no surviving business. Assume that the creditors will receive twenty-five cents on the dollar from the first bid as opposed to thirty-five cents on the dollar from the second bid. Depending on the particular facts, a judge, using the contextual model, could decide that the lower bid was better because the community where the debtor was located would retain an important employer. This decision would mean that the ten-cent decrease would come out of the pockets of the unsecured creditors, unless the local community was willing and able to contribute to the Chapter 11 plan. If the local community was willing to give the debtor a two-year moratorium on local property taxes, then the debtor could increase payments to its creditors by several cents, thereby diminishing their financial loss. Even with added incentives, however, balancing could foist some of the costs of reorganization onto unsecured creditors. If this occurs, any creditor who would be severely harmed by the proposed payout would have a safety valve: it could overturn the rebuttable presumption of pro rata distribution.

Suppose Smythe, a married, recently rehired car mechanic with two children, seeks relief under Chapter 13. His youngest child, who is emotionally disturbed, lives at home but needs constant therapeutic intervention. Smythe had planned to repay his unsecured creditors twenty cents on the dollar over three years. He has a thirty-year mortgage on his home (his payments equal four hundred dollars per month), and he is two months behind in payments. Under current law, Smythe cannot adjust the amount of the mortgage payments, although he can cure the arrearages. Suppose that if Smythe could extend his mortgage for an additional five years, thereby decreasing the monthly payments to the bank, he could manage. The community implicated here is the debtor's family, in particular his ill child. Without sacrificing collateral, the bank could assist the family by increasing the term of the loan, which it is unlikely to do voluntarily and which, absent the proposed amendment to Section 105(d), could not be accomplished under the Code. Moving the ill child to a medical facility would have real costs— both emotionally to the family and the child and monetarily to society, which would need to pay for the out-of-home care. One option would be for unsecured creditors to receive less; another possibility, as is done in Chapter 11, would be to require the bank to stretch out payments for five additional years. The second solution does not seem to be too high a price to pay in these exigent circumstances.

It is comforting to know that when harm occurs, the injured party will have an opportunity to be heard. There are those who could object to creating this special role for community when community interests can be voiced by other already recognized participants in the bankruptcy process. Debtors can, in appropriate circumstances, express the need for community continuity. In other cases, employees can speak for community. In still other situations, creditors can voice community concerns. But instances will exist in which the community perspective is not shared by others or, at a minimum, would not be articulated in the same way by others. So it is important that community have its own voice, even if it overlaps with other voices at times.

Everyone believes that their tale of woe, should they ever have one, will convince a court they are worthy of the requested relief. Because we all harbor fears of failure, we are willing to pay for a system that we do not now need to use. We are willing to pay attention to others because, when we need it, we want people to pay attention to us. We may complain that this benefit is costing us, but we would rather pay than be in the shoes of the person experiencing difficulty. We are thus buying solace.

Suppose a parent has two children, one of whom is sick and the other of whom is healthy. Assume the sick child has a curable disease, with a long recuperation period. The sick child receives all sorts of added attention from the parents and others. Certainly, the healthy child notices what is happening. The attention has largely been diverted away from her to the sick child. At some level, this produces anger. At a deeper level, the healthy child understands, or can be helped to understand and accept, her parents' behavior. She reaches this position not because she likes what is happening but because she recognizes that one day she, too, could be ill, and if she were, she would get the needed attention from parents and friends. The child is able to distinguish, at least at the subconscious level, the difference between short-term needs and long-term prospects.

Every bankruptcy case has parties like the healthy child. Perhaps they are the creditors who can withstand the loss but who nonetheless are not too keen on losing money. Perhaps they are the customers of creditors who may end up paying more for goods because of someone else's (the debtor's) failure. These parties have to sacrifice. But given a choice between being healthy or sick, they would chose health. And they are comforted by the realization that should they get sick, the balance will shift in their favor.

If a federal bankruptcy law were not in existence, the implementation of the contextual model by those states willing to adopt it would be problematic. The approach to and treatment of debtors, creditors, and communities could be vastly different, yielding different outcomes depending on where one lived. Moreover, many bankruptcies have issues crossing state lines, which means that different approaches would be pitted against each other, and forum shopping (selecting where a filing should take place depending on whether the forum uses the contextual model) would be used. Indeed, if the contextual model accomplishes nothing else, it provides a philosophical statement about our societal position on indebtedness and its treatment. That effort alone is affirmation of why the United States should have a federal bankruptcy law. Bankruptcy can and should further predetermined national social policy issues, and without a federal law, this goal cannot be accomplished with any degree of uniformity. Clearly, as is the case today, some variation in application of the federal law will exist. But Americans would do well by enabling debtors, creditors, and communities around the country to sit at a table and find that the meal being served is similar regardless of where they are located.

CHAPTER FIFTEEN

Conclusions and Recommendations

In this book, I set out to describe what the U.S. bankruptcy law is and what it ought to be. In the process, I have determined how important federal bankruptcy law is in a credit-based society. I have examined why some of the bankruptcy law's current provisions appear unfair when in fact they are not, and why some provisions that appear fair are, conversely, unfair. I have explored how debtors like Seat Co. and Smythe, their creditors, and their communities are and should be treated under the federal bankruptcy law.

What has emerged is a sense of the bankruptcy system's complexity. For debtors, the ideal system provides a fresh start, premised on a recognition that mistakes happen but debtors can be rehabilitated through forgiveness. For creditors, this system needs to incorporate the opportunity to achieve equality of outcome rather than equality of treatment, even if some creditors must then be treated differently from others. Finally, this system recognizes the need to take the interests of community into account.

The contextual model that I propose relies on particulars and treats each case as presenting its own distinct set of facts and circumstances. It relies heavily on faith in a thoughtful judiciary. It also assumes a judiciary with sufficient time to consider the issues. Within the contextual model, none of the three pillars—debtors, creditors, and community—will dominate over the others. Instead, each new bankruptcy case presents a question of how all three pillars can be accommodated, not in a vacuum but within the parameters established by the bankruptcy laws, existing precedent, and the specific facts of a given situation.

The contextual model is a clarion call for change that rests on two underlying assumptions. First, Americans have and will continue to live in a credit-based economy. Second, people are inherently altruistic. An omnipresent theme of this book is that nothing in life is free. What price Americans are willing to pay for failure is a question for which readers will have to reach their own conclusions. But, for me, it is clear that if society is to function productively and humanely, the bankruptcy system needs to mirror how society wants people to feel about themselves.

In this book, I propose a wide variety of changes. Change in how people think about issues is by far the most significant theme. But I also address change in nonbankruptcy laws that affect the bankruptcy system. I suggest different mechanisms for hearing disputes and resolving problems. I contemplate various demands on the judiciary. And I include specific changes to the existing bankruptcy laws.

Although changes in the approach to thinking about the bankruptcy system will be discussed for years to come, efforts to change specific Code provisions will not always wait for a later day. Congress considers at least some change to the Bankruptcy Code on an annual basis. With that reality in mind, it is useful to parse out the specific major changes to the Bankruptcy Code that I propose.

The first changes listed here are primarily addressed to debtors:

- Both individual and corporate debtors need an opportunity to choose whether to liquidate or reorganize rather than have that choice made for them by creditors, the court, or a trustee. For individual debtors with consumer debts, this means the elimination of Section 707(b).
- The eligibility requirements for Chapter 13 relief should be simplified. Rather than segregate secured and unsecured debts, an aggregate ceiling should be created. This involves revising Section 109(e).
- Joint filings should be extended beyond married couples to include those individuals who share joint financial relation-

ships, including parents and their adult children, friends, and lovers. This requires amending Section 302.

- All needy debtors should be eligible for relief in bankruptcy on an in forma pauperis basis. This requires amending various provisions of Title 28, including Section 1930.

- The new value exception to the absolute priority rule should be recognized, and contributions of human capital as well as new monies should be deemed to constitute new value. The adoption of a new definition of "new value exception" within Section 101 and an amendment of Section 1129 are needed.

- Federal rather than state exemption laws should be employed to create uniformity and predictability. Amendment to Section 522(b) is required.

- Efforts should be made to improve the likelihood of success in small Chapter 11 cases through the appointment of a business manager whose presence would not lift debtor exclusivity. Code sections 1104 and 1121 are implicated.

- Use of shared professionals or panels of experts should be instituted as a way of curbing costs and saving time. This would require change to both the conflicts and reimbursement provisions within the Code, including Sections 327–330. Amendment to the state's rules of professional responsibility would be needed as well.

- Limited liability should be curtailed and select limitations on discharge made applicable to corporate debtors to eliminate the markedly disparate treatment of individual and corporate debtors. This entails amending Sections 523, 727, and 1141.

- The nature and number of nondischargeable debts should be reevaluated, particularly the growing list in Chapter 13. This implicates Sections 523 and 1328.

- A requirement should be added stipulating that all debtors (individuals and businesses) be offered financial counseling prior to obtaining their discharge. Such counseling could take a wide range of forms, both private and public. This would require amendments to Sections 726, 1141, 1228, and 1328.

The following changes are primarily addressed to creditors:

- Selected disputes among creditors should be resolved outside the adversarial system, which would curtail the use of already scarce judicial time. Mediation is a possible avenue to pursue.
- The duties of the officials within the Office of the United States Trustee should be reformulated to provide greater monitoring of cases that go unmonitored owing to lack of creditors' involvement. This could be accomplished by amending Title 28, Section 586.
- Although equality of treatment would remain the norm, self-selecting creditors could rebut the presumption of pro rata distribution and seek better treatment because of irreparable injury. This better treatment could be a greater distribution, a speedier distribution, or some other payment arrangement. This could be accomplished by adding an entirely new section to the Code and amending Sections 507, 726, 1122, 1123, 1129, 1222, 1225, 1322, and 1325.
- Selection of creditors' committee members needs to be changed to include a more diverse constituency instead of only the largest creditors of the debtor. Some incentive to improve involvement of creditors is needed, perhaps per diem compensation. This requires amendment to Section 1102.
- The government's status as a priority creditor should be reconsidered, as should the first priority of bankruptcy professionals. These changes could be accomplished by amending Sections 503 and 507.
- Tort claimants and other involuntary creditors, except the government, should be able to rebut the presumption of pro rata distribution upon a showing of substantive unconscionability. This would require amendment to Sections 506, 507, 726, 1122, 1123, 1129, 1222, 1225, 1322, and 1325, among others.

- Separate classification of various unsecured claims should be permitted if necessary to balance the rights of unsecured creditors and to prevent one creditor from controlling the reorganization process. Home mortgagors should receive fewer protections. Amendments to Sections 1122, 1124, 1222, 1322, and 1325 would be needed.
- Entities acquiring claims or interests of creditors or equity holders post-petition should be denied compensation for fees, and the disclosure requirements should be curtailed to save costs to the estate. Additionally, acquired claims should count as claims of one creditor for voting purposes. Sections 327, 503, 1125, and 1126 would require amendment.
- The definitions of *debt, claims,* and *creditors* should be expanded to include future claimants. This would encompass amending Section 101.
- Greater consensus should be reached on how valuation of collateral is made, to provide greater predictability and uniformity. This might require a new Code section.

Finally, the following changes are primarily addressed to communities:

- The term *community* should be defined in Section 101 of the Bankruptcy Code. The definition should indicate that relevant communities are those with a nexus to the debtor and substantial and redressable injury.
- The Code's confirmation standards should specifically reference the need to consider the interests of community. A balancing test, akin to that created by Section 1113, would be created. A burden-of-proof section should be included. This would necessitate amending Sections 1129, 1225, and 1325.
- The court's equitable powers should explicitly reference the ability of courts to consider the interests of community. This would involve an amendment to Section 105.

Although all these suggestions can be read and considered separately, they are clearly part of a larger whole. In this book I treat bankruptcy as a vehicle for social change, and people are under-standably reluctant about this expansion. But using bankruptcy law to improve the lives of debtors, creditors, and communities should not be so frightening. Social change usually happens at a slow pace. Bankruptcy provides an opportunity to deal with a social problem immediately, not in the sense of creating a global solution but in terms of resolving an actual situation.

A hue and cry will no doubt be heard from judges and lawyers: "That is not my job; my job is to implement the law, not to make or argue social policy. There will be too much uncertainty, too few standards, and too much flexibility." But the dividing lines between enforcing law and making policy, between too many and too few standards, are never as clear as they may appear. By not acting, judges and lawyers are also making social policy. By viewing the world of bankruptcy in isolation, they are making a statement about bankruptcy's role and function in contemporary society.

The word *bankruptcy* is derived from the Italian root words *banca rotta*, which literally mean "bench broken," in reference to the benches where medieval merchants did business in village squares. Whether the practice of breaking the benches belonging to debtors was justifiable is not my question here. Instead, I am con-cerned with how to treat contemporary debtors, their creditors, and their community. Debtors' benches should be fixed, not broken. Creditors should be treated fairly, recognizing their diversity. Com-munities should be protected and, if possible, enhanced. We cannot change the etymology of the word *bankruptcy*, but perhaps we can begin to see the bench differently.

Currently, the word *bankrupt* is often used to mean "morally bereft." One book called *The Bankruptcy of America* has noth-ing to do with federal bankruptcy laws and everything to do with the unsatisfactory economic state of the country.[1] The dictionary defines a bankrupt as someone who is depleted and in a ruined state.[2] That cannot be the definition of the American bankruptcy system. Indeed, it has to be defined in the converse. Bankruptcy is all about responsibility and forgiveness. It is about health, not ruin.

It is about moral strength, not moral destituteness. It is about the future and not the past. It is about people's potential to grow and become.

A legal system designed to deal with failure says a lot about the United States as a nation. It speaks to people's deepest and most secret fears. Americans need a bankruptcy system that assuages those fears, that lets people live responsibly and productively in a world of failure. That is no small task. But it is achievable if Americans remember what is most important to its citizens: to take risks, make mistakes and be forgiven, to be treated fairly and equally—not in terms of treatment but in terms of outcome—and to act responsibly in helping the world become a better place for those of us here and those yet to come.

Introduction

1. Charles Warren, Bankruptcy in United States History 1 (1935).
2. *See, e.g.,* Barry E. Adler, "A World Without Debt," 72 Wash. U. L.Q. 811 (1994); Robert A. Rasmussen, "An Essay on Optimal Bankruptcy Rules and Social Justice," 1994 U. Ill. L. Rev. 1; Barry E. Adler, "Financial and Political Theories of American Corporate Bankruptcy," 45 Stan. L. Rev. 311 (1993); Lynn M. LoPucki, "The Trouble with Chapter 11," 1993 Wis. L. Rev. 729; Michael Bradley & Michael Rosenzweig, "The Untenable Case for Chapter 11," 101 Yale L.J. 1043 (1992); Edith H. Jones, "Chapter 11: A Death Penalty for Debtor and Creditor Interests," 77 Cornell L.J. 1043 (1992); Lucian A. Bebchuk, "A New Approach to Corporate Reorganizations," 101 Harv. L. Rev. 775 (1988); Douglas G. Baird, "The Uneasy Case for Corporate Reorganization," 15 J. Legal Stud. 127 (1986). For a summary of some of the recent debate, *see* David A. Skeel, "Markets, Courts, and the Brave New World of Bankruptcy Theory," 1993 Wis. L. Rev. 465.
3. *See, e.g.,* Bradley & Rosenzweig, *supra* note 2; James W. Bowers, "The Fantastic Wisconsylvania Zero-Bureaucratic-Cost School of Bankruptcy Theory: A Comment," 91 Mich. L. Rev. 1773 (1993); David Gray Carlson, "Philosophy in Bankruptcy," 85 Mich. L. Rev. 1341 (1987); Doug Henwood, "Failures in the System: Behind the Bankruptcy Boom," Nation, Oct. 5, 1992; "Bankruptcy News Reform," N.Y. Times, April 14, 1993, at A14. It is also useful to peruse the recent symposium issue of the *Washington University Law Quarterly,* which contains many articles fitting this description. *See* 72 Wash. U. L.Q. 797–1486.
4. *See, e.g.,* Philippe Aghion et al., "Improving Bankruptcy Procedure," 72 Wash. U. L.Q. 849 (1994); Michelle J. White, "Does Chapter 11 Save Economically Inefficient Firms?" 72 Wash. U. L.Q. 1319 (1994); Carlson, *supra*

note 3; Bradley & Rosenzweig, *supra* note 2; Philippe Aghion et al., "The Economics of Bankruptcy Reform," 8 J. L. ECON & ORG. 523 (1992); Thomas A. Jackson & Robert E. Scott, "On the Nature of Bankruptcy: An Essay on Bankruptcy Sharing and the Creditors' Bargain," 75 VA. L. REV. 155 (1989); Douglas G. Baird, "A World Without Bankruptcy," 50 L. & CONTEMP. PROBS. 173 (1987); Michelle J. White, "Personal Bankruptcy under the 1978 Bankruptcy Code: An Economic Analysis," 63 IND. L.J. 2 (1987).

    5. THOMAS A. JACKSON, THE LOGIC AND LIMITS OF BANKRUPTCY LAW (1986); Linda J. Rusch, "Bankruptcy Reorganization Jurisprudence: Matters of Belief, Faith, and Hope—Stepping into the Fourth Dimension," 55 MONT. L. REV. 9 (1994); Lawrence Ponoroff, "Enlarging the Bargaining Table: Some Implications of the Corporate Stakeholder Model for Federal Bankruptcy Proceedings," 23 CAP. U. L. REV. 441 (1994); Donald R. Korobkin, "Contractarianism and the Normative Foundations of Bankruptcy Law," 71 TEX. L. REV. 541 (1993); James W. Bowers, "Whither What Hits the Fan? Murphy's Law, Bankruptcy Theory, and the Elementary Economics of Loss Distribution," 26 GA. L. REV. 27 (1991); Mark J. Roe, "Commentary on 'The Nature of Bankruptcy,'" 75 VA. L. REV. 219 (1989); Elizabeth Warren, "Bankruptcy Policy," 54 U. CHI. L. REV. 775 (1987).

    6. For a discussion of the role of individualism in American thought, *see* JOHN LOCKE, THE SECOND TREATISE ON CIVIL GOVERNMENT (Prometheus Books 1986) (1690); THOMAS HOBBES, THE LEVIATHAN (Prometheus Books 1988) (1651); ROBERT BELLAH ET AL., HABITS OF THE HEART: INDIVIDUALISM AND COMMITMENT TO AMERICAN LIFE (1985); YEHOSHUA ARIEL, INDIVIDUALISM AND NATURALISM IN AMERICAN IDEOLOGY (1964); Martin S. Flaherty, "History 'Lite' in Modern American Constitutionalism," 95 COLUM. L. REV. 523 (1995); Jennifer Nedelsky, "Reconceiving Autonomy: Sources, Thought and Possibilities," 1 YALE J. L. & FEM. 7 (1989). For current approaches away from strict adherence to individualism, *see* AMATAI ETZIONI, THE SPIRIT OF COMMUNITY: RIGHTS, RESPONSIBILITIES, AND THE COMMUNITARIAN AGENDA (1993); ELIZABETH FOX-GENOVESE, FEMINISM WITHOUT ILLUSIONS: A CRITIQUE OF INDIVIDUALISM (1991); MARTHA MINOW, MAKING ALL THE DIFFERENCE: INCLUSION, EXCLUSION, AND AMERICAN LAW (1990); MARK Kelman, A GUIDE TO CRITICAL LEGAL STUDIES (1987); Thomas Lee Hazen, "The Corporate Persona, Contract and Market Failure, and Moral Values," 69 N.C. L. REV. 273 (1991); Linda C. McClain, " 'Atomistic Man' Revisited: Liberalism, Connection, and Feminist Jurisprudence," 65 CAL. L. REV. 1171 (1992); Robin West, "Jurisprudence and Gender," 55 U. CHI. L. REV. 1 (1988).

7. This statement was made by Robert Crandall, chief executive officer of American Airlines. *See* BNA's Bankruptcy Law Reporter, July 15, 1993, at 784–85.

8. *See, e.g.,* David M. Topol, "Hazardous Waste and Bankruptcy: Confronting the Unasked Questions," 13 Va. Envtl. L.J. 185 (1994); Thomas A. Smith, "A Capital Markets Approach to Mass Tort Bankruptcy," 104 Yale L. J. 367 (1994); Kathryn R. Heidt, "The Automatic Stay in Environmental Bankruptcies," 67 Am. Bankr. L.J. 69 (1993); Gary A. Saunders, "Post-Foreclosure Statutory Right of Redemption under Chapter 13 of the Bankruptcy Code: A Balance of State and Federal Interests," 37 N.Y.L. Sch. L. Rev. 635 (1992); Richard A. Marshack, "The Toxic Claim: Using Bankruptcy to Limit Environmental Liabilities," 19 Cal. Bankr. J. 193 (1991); Mark J. Roe, "Corporate Strategic Reaction to Mass Tort," 72 Va. L. Rev. 1 (1986).

9. *See, e.g.,* Leif M. Clark et al., "What Constitutes Success in Chapter 11? A Roundtable Discussion," 2 Am. Bankr. Inst. L. Rev. 229 (1994); Susan Jensen-Conklin, "Do Confirmed Chapter 11 Plans Consummate? The Results of a Study and Analysis of the Law," 97 Com. L.J. 297 (1992); Bradley & Rosenzweig, *supra* note 2; Lynn M. LoPucki, "The Debtor in Full Control— Systems Failure under Chapter 11 of the Bankruptcy Code," 57 Am. Bankr. L.J. 99 (1983).

10. For a sample of writings on the emergence of bankruptcy laws in formerly nonmarket economies, *see* Scott Horton, "Death of Communism and Bankruptcy Reorganization," 1994 ABI Jnl. LEXIS 2645; Jonathan L. Flaxer, "Bankruptcy in China," 1994 ABI Jnl. LEXIS 2707; Steve Campbell, "Brother, Can You Spare a Ruble? The Development of Bankruptcy Legislation in New Russia," 19 Bank. Dev. J. 343 (1994); Winston Harmer, "How an Australian Insolvency Guru Helped the Vietnamese Craft Their Insolvency Law, 25 Bankr. Ct. Dec. 34 (1994); Julia M. Metzger & Samuel L. Bufford, "Exporting United States Bankruptcy Law: The Hungarian Experience," 21 Cal. Bankr. J. 153 (1993).

11. *See, e.g.,* Joseph H. Boyett, Beyond Workplace 2000: Essential Strategies for the New American Corporation (1995); Paul R. Krugman, The Age of Diminished Expectations: U.S. Economic Policy in the 1990s (1990); Robert L. Heilbroner et al., In the Name of Profit (1972).

12. *See, e.g.,* Robert Wright, The Moral Animal: Evolutionary Psychology and Everyday Life (1994); James Lincoln Collier, The Rise of Selfishness in America (1991); Desmond Morris, The Naked Ape: A

ZOOLOGIST'S STUDY OF THE HUMAN ANIMAL (1967). For a literary rendition, *see* WILLIAM GOLDING, LORD OF THE FLIES (1954).

13. Barry S. Schermer, "Response to Professor Gross: Taking the Interests of Community into Account in Bankruptcy—A Modern-Day Tale of Belling the Cat," 72 WASH. U. L.Q. 1049 (1994); John D. Ayer, "So Far from God: An Essay on the Ethnography of Bankruptcy," 61 U. CIN. L. REV. 407 (1992).

14. For a discussion of corporate philanthropy, *see* JAMES W. MCKIE, SOCIAL RESPONSIBILITY AND THE BUSINESS PREDICAMENT (1975); JOHN G. SIMON ET AL., THE ETHICAL INVESTOR: UNIVERSITY AND CORPORATE RESPONSIBILITY (1972).

15. *See, e.g.,* Lawrence E. Mitchell, "Cooperation and Constraint in the Modern Corporation: An Inquiry into the Causes of Corporate Immorality," 73 TEX. L. REV. 477 (1995); E.C. Lashbrooke, Jr., "The Divergence of Corporate Finance and Law in Corporate Governance," 46 S.C. L. REV. 449 (1995); Gary Von Stange, "Corporate Social Responsibility Through Constituency Statutes: Legend or Lie?" 71 HOFSTRA LAB. L.J. 461 (1994); Nancy J. Knauer, "The Paradox of Corporate Giving: Tax Expenditures, the Nature of the Corporation, and the Social Construction of Charity," 44 DEPAUL L. REV. 1 (1994). *See also* ROBERT B. REICH, GOOD FOR BUSINESS: MAKING FULL USE OF THE NATION'S HUMAN CAPITAL (1995).

16. *See generally* Daniel B. Bogart, "Liability of Directors of Chapter 11 Debtors-in-Possession: 'Don't Look Back—Something May Be Gaining on You,'" 68 AM. BANKR. L.J. 155 (1994); Laura Lin, "Shift of Fiduciary Duty upon Corporate Insolvency: Proper Scope of Directors' Duty to Creditors," 46 VAND. L. REV. 1485 (1993); Mike Roberts, "The Conundrum of Directors' Duties in Nearly Insolvent Corporations," 23 MEMPHIS ST. U. L. REV. 273 (1993).

Chapter 1: How to Think about Bankruptcy

1. *See generally* E. A. FARNSWORTH, A TREATISE ON THE LAW OF CONTRACTS (1990); George M. Cohen, "The Fault Lines in Contract Damages," 80 VA. L. REV. 1225 (1994); Peter Linzer, "On the Amorality of Contract Remedies—Efficiency, Equity, and the Second Restatement," 81 COLUM. L. REV. 111 (1981). For a discussion of state collection remedies, *see generally* ELIZABETH WARREN & JAY LAWRENCE WESTBROOK, THE LAW OF DEBTORS AND CREDITORS: TEXT, CASES, AND PROBLEMS (2d ed. 1991).

2. *See generally* W. PAGE KEETON ET AL., PROSSER AND KEETON ON THE LAW OF TORTS (5th ed. 1984).

3. Under the Consumer Credit Protection Act, the amount of money that can be garnished from individuals is limited by federal law. 15 U.S.C. § 1673 (1982). In addition, various states limit the amount of income that can be garnished. *See generally* Cecelia M. Martaus, "Garnishment of Employee Wages in Ohio: Whose Money Is It Anyway?" 18 OHIO N.U. L. REV. 197 (1991).

4. The bankruptcy laws are housed in Title 11 of the United States Code. The Code has been amended on numerous occasions since its enactment. Although amended in 1996, the most recent group of major amendments is the Bankruptcy Reform Act of 1994, Pub. L. No. 103–395.

5. Regarding possible repeal of Chapter 11, *see* Michael Bradley & Michael Rosenzweig, "The Untenable Case for Chapter 11," 101 YALE L.J. 1043 (1992). For a discussion of the possibility of abandoning *all* federal bankruptcy law, *see* Barry E. Adler, "A World Without Debt," 72 WASH. U. L.Q. 811 (1994); Douglas G. Baird, "A World Without Bankruptcy," 50 LAW & CONTEMP. PROBS. 173 (1987). For a discussion of the repeal of Chapter 7, *see* John D. Ayer, "Abolish Chapter 7," NORTON BANKR. L. ADVISER 4–5 (Jan. 1996, issue 1).

6. *See generally* Pamela Bickford Sak & Henry N. Schiffman, "Bankruptcy Reform in Eastern Europe," 28 INT'L LAW. 927 (1994); Steve Campbell, "Brother, Can You Spare a Ruble? The Development of Bankruptcy Legislation in the New Russia," 10 BANKR. DEV. J. 343 (1994); Irvin Jay Robinson, "New Vietnam Law on the Bankruptcy of Enterprises," BCD, March 10, 1994, at A5; Jeffrey Hoberman, "Argentina's Proposed New Bankruptcy Law," BCD, June 16, 1994, at A5. The *New York Law School Journal of International Law* is dedicating an entire issue to comparing bankruptcy laws in the emerging nations with the extant law in the United States. *See* 17 N.Y.L. SCH. J. INT'L L. 1 (1996).

7. This approach is described (and rejected) by Ronald Dworkin in his book LIFE'S DOMINION at 28–29 (1993).

8. *See generally* DWORKIN, *supra* note 7; RUTH COLKER, PREGNANT MEN (1994). A similar view was expressed by John Dewey in ART AS EXPERIENCE (1993), a collection of his essays, wherein he states, "Order is not imposed from without but is made out of the relations of harmonious interactions that energies bear to one another." *Id.* at 14–15.

9. *See* Karen Gross, "Re-Vision of the Bankruptcy System: New Images of Individual Debtors," 88 MICH. L. REV. 1506 (1990) [hereinafter Gross, "Re-Vision"]; Karen Gross et al., "Ladies in Red: Learning from America's First Female Bankrupts," 40 AM. J. LEG. HIST. 1 (1996) [hereinafter Gross, "Ladies in Red"]. *See also* FEMINIST RESEARCH METHODS: EXEMPLARY READINGS IN THE SOCIAL SCIENCES (Joyce McCarl Nielson ed., 1990), in particular, the article by Kathryn Anderson titled "Beginning Where We Are: Feminist Methodology in Oral History," at 94–112. As Anderson says, we must start with "real, concrete people and their actual lives if [we are] to do more than reaffirm the dominant ideologies about women and their place in the world." *Id.* at 97.

10. *See* Gross, "Ladies in Red," *supra* note 9; TOWARDS A NEW PAST: DISSENTING ESSAYS IN AMERICAN HISTORY (Barton J. Bernstein ed., 1968) containing Jesse Lemisch, "The American Revolution Seen from the Bottom Up," at 3–46.

11. This drawing was used in 1900 by psychologist Joseph Jastrow (1863–1926). *See* BETTY EDWARDS, DRAWING ON THE ARTIST WITHIN 173 (1986). Apparently, the drawing was seen in a humorous publication called *Die Fliegenden*. *See* E. H. GOMBRICH, ART AND ILLUSION: A STUDY IN THE PSYCHOLOGY OF PICTORIAL REPRESENTATION 5–6 (1956). For a fuller discussion of rival form ambiguity more generally, *see* Edwards at 171–76; Gombrich at 5–9, 239–49.

12. Rival-form ambiguity (alternative perceptions) describes the brain's ability to perceive two interpretations of an image. The technique of creating alternate perceptions in art dates back to medieval manuscripts. *See* BETTY EDWARDS, DRAWING ON THE RIGHT SIDE OF THE BRAIN 49–59 (1989); BERNARD CHAET, THE ART OF DRAWING 56–58 (1978); GRAHAM COLLIER, FORM, SPACE AND VISION: UNDERSTANDING ART 36–38 (1972).

13. *See* AMATAI ETZIONI, THE SPIRIT OF COMMUNITY: RIGHTS, RESPONSIBILITIES, AND THE COMMUNITARIAN AGENDA 10–11 (1993); JOHN RAWLS, POLITICAL LIBERALISM (1993); Heather Fisher Lindsay, "Balancing Community Needs Against Individual Debtors," 10 J. LAND USE & ENVTL. L. 371 (1995); Anthony D. Taibi, "Banking, Finance, and Community Economic Empowerment: Structural Economic Theory, Procedural Civil Rights and Substantive Racial Justice," 107 HARV. L. REV. 1463 (1994); Rosa Eckstein, "Towards a Communitarian Theory of Responsibility: Bearing the Burden for the Unintended," 45 U. MIAMI L. REV. 843 (1991); Stephen L. Pepper, "Autonomy, Community, and Lawyers' Ethics," 19 CAP. U. L. REV. 939 (1990).

14. The seemingly infinite number of circles is demonstrated in art as well. *See* GOMBRICH, *supra* note 11, at 220; COLLIER, *supra* note 12, at 76–79; HENRY RANKIN POORE, COMPOSITION IN ART 43–47 (1969).

15. For a general discussion of the complex interrelationship between bankruptcy and environmental law, *see* KATHRYN HEIDT, ENVIRONMENTAL OBLIGATION IN BANKRUPTCY (1994); Michael A. Bloom, "Bankruptcy's Fresh Start vs. Environmental Cleanup: Statutory Schizophrenia," 6 VILL. ENVTL. L.J. 107 (1995); Kathryn Heidt, "Environmental Obligations in Bankruptcy: A Fundamental Framework," 44 FLA. L. REV. 153 (1992).

16. Context plays a central role in art. Indeed, artists use space to create context. More particularly, artists look at both objects themselves (positive space) and the shapes the objects create (negative space). That is, objects do not exist acontextually in space. They are within space and create new and different space. *See* GOMBRICH, *supra* note 11, at 222–31; COLLIER, *supra* note 12, at 85–97; EDWARDS, *supra* note 11, at 152–65; EDWARDS, *supra* note 12, at 98–107.

17. Lawyers are commonly confronted with a seeming conflict between their "personal" ethics and their "professional" ethics. *See generally* RAND JACK & DANA JACK, MORAL VISION AND PROFESSIONAL DECISIONS: THE CHANGING VALUES OF MEN AND WOMEN LAWYERS (1989); Stephen L. Pepper, "Counseling at the Limits of the Law: An Exercise in the Jurisprudence and Ethics of Lawyering," 104 YALE L.J. 1545 (1995); Deborah L. Rhode, "Institutionalizing Ethics," 44 CASE W. RES. L. REV. 665 (1995); Reed Elizabeth Lodge, "Out of Uncertainty: A Model of the Lawyer-Client Relationship," 2 CAL. INTERDISC. L.J. 89 (1993).

18. Quoted in ANTHONY D'AMATO & ARTHUR J. JACOBSON, JUSTICE AND THE LEGAL SYSTEM at xxi (1992).

19. Supreme Court Justice William H. Rehnquist has remarked, "It is . . . understandable that there is a dearth of recent bankruptcy cases . . . as compared with constitutional cases, labor cases, and other more *alluring* subjects." Quoted in Karen Gross, "Thurgood Marshall's Bankruptcy Jurisprudence: A Tribute," 67 AM. BANKR. L.J. 447, 455 (1993). Judith Resnik reports that Justice Antonin Scalia did not believe that Article III courts should have to deal with such a mundane matter as bankruptcy, as the court's time should be spent on important issues (that is, questions of constitutional law). Quoted in Gross, "Re-Vision," *supra* note 9, at 1535 n. 195 (1990).

Chapter 2: *Understanding the Bankruptcy Code*

1. *See generally* Kenneth N. Klee, "The Concept of 'Impairment' in Business Reorganizations," c946 ALI-ABA 499 (1994); Karen Gross, "Re-Vision of the Bankruptcy System: New Images of Individual Debtors," 88 MICH. L. REV. 1506 (1990); Stefan A. Riesenfeld, "Foreword," 38 VAND. L. REV. 665 (1985).

2. *See, e.g.,* H.R. 318, 104th Cong., 1st Sess. (1995) (introduced in January 1995 to create a priority for retiree health care benefits); S. 648, 104th Cong., 1st Sess. (1995) (introduced in March 1995 to clarify claims against banks in receivership); S. 769, 104th Cong., 1st Sess. (1995) (introduced in May 1995 to limit the value of exemptions).

3. FOUNDATIONS OF CORPORATE Law 63–79 (Roberta Romano ed., 1993); Frank H. Easterbrook & Daniel R. Fischel, "Limited Liability and the Corporation," 52 U. CHI. L. REV. 89 (1985); Paul Halpern et al., "An Economic Analysis of Limited Liability in Corporation Law," 30 U. TORONTO L.J. 117 (1980).

4. For example, corporate officers and directors can be implicated as "responsible persons" under the Comprehensive Environmental Response, Compensation, and Liability Act (CERCLA). 42 U.S.C. §§ 9601–9675 (1988). Corporate officers and directors can become personally liable for breach of their duties in respect to a retirement plan under the Employee Retirement Income Security Act (ERISA). 29 U.S.C. § 1109(a) (1988); 29 C.F.R. § 2509.75-4 (1994). Officers and directors can become personally liable for unpaid withholding taxes. 26 U.S.C. § 6672 (1994).

5. *See supra* note 3. A growing literature also suggests that, in the corporate context, limited liability has outlived its usefulness. *See* Henry Hansmann & Reiner Kraakman, "Do Capital Markets Compel Limited Liability? A Response to Professor Grundfest," 102 YALE L.J. 427 (1992); Joseph A. Grundfest, "The Limited Future of Limited Liability," 102 YALE L.J. 387 (1992); Henry Hansmann & Reiner Kraakman, "Toward Unlimited Shareholder Liability for Corporate Torts," 100 YALE L.J. 1879 (1991). The amount of bankruptcy literature on this topic is also growing.

6. *See generally* ROBERT E. GINSBERG & ROBERT D. MARTIN, BANKRUPTCY: TEXT, STATUTES, RULES Vol. 2 at § 15.06 (5th ed. 1995).

7. *Id.* at § 15.04(d).

8. *Toibb v. Radloff*, 501 U.S. 157 (1991).

9. Lynn M. LoPucki, "Strange Visions in a Strange World: A Reply to Professors Bradley and Rosenzweig," 91 MICH. L. REV. 79 (1992). This article takes issue with the proposition that managers always stand to benefit in Chapter 11.

10. *See generally* PATRICK A. MURPHY, CREDITORS' RIGHTS IN BANKRUPTCY §§ 1.16, 3.03, 16.02, 16.10 (2nd ed. 1993).

11. *See* DOUGLAS G. BAIRD, THE ELEMENTS OF BANKRUPTCY 259–66 (1993); Anthony L. Miscioscia, Jr., "The Bankruptcy Code and the New Value Doctrine: An Examination into History, Illusions, and the Need for Competitive Bidding," 79 VA. L. REV. 917 (1993); Bruce A. Markell, "Owners, Auctions, and Absolute Priority in Bankruptcy Reorganizations," 44 STAN. L. REV. 69 (1991); Richard L. Epling, "The New Value Exception: Is There a Practical Workable Solution?" 8 BANKR. DEV. J. 335 (1991); Douglas G. Baird & Thomas H. Jackson, "Bargaining After the Fall and the Contours of the Absolute Priority Rule," 55 U. CHI. L. REV. 738 (1988); *Norwest Bank Worthington v. Ahlers,* 485 U.S. 197 (1988).

12. *Norwest Bank Worthington v. Ahlers,* at 197. *See* Stewart Sterk, "Restraints on Alienation of Human Capital," 79 VA. L. REV. 383 (1993).

13. *See, e.g.,* Leslie Wayne, "Orange County, California, Pays a Price for a Step toward Recovery," N.Y. TIMES, June 14, 1995, at C10; Sallie Hofmeister, "Orange County, Calif., Makes Bankruptcy Filing," N.Y. TIMES, Dec. 7, 1994, at A1.

14. *In re City of Bridgeport,* 132 B.R. 85 (1991). *See* Dorothy A. Brown, "Fiscal Distress and Politics: The Bankruptcy Filing of Bridgeport as a Case Study in Reclaiming Local Sovereignty," 11 BANKR. DEV. J. 625 (1995); Michael W. McConnell & Randal C. Picker, "When Cities Go Broke: A Conceptual Introduction to Municipal Bankruptcy," 60 U. CHI. L. REV. 425 (1993); Rachel E. Schwartz, "This Way to the Egress: Should Bridgeport's Chapter 9 Filing Have Been Dismissed?" 66 AM. BANKR. L.J. 103 (1992).

15. For a general discussion of why individual debtors seek bankruptcy relief, *see* TERESA SULLIVAN ET AL., AS WE FORGIVE OUR DEBTORS: BANKRUPTCY AND CONSUMER CREDIT IN AMERICA (1989); Karen Gross, "The Debtor as Modern Day Peon: A Problem of Unconstitutional Conditions," 65 NOTRE DAME L. REV. 165 (1990).

16. *See generally* William C. Whitford, "The Ideal of Individualized Justice: Consumer Bankruptcy as Consumer Protection and Consumer Protection in Consumer Bankruptcy," 68 AM. BANKR. L.J. 397 (1994); Jean

Braucher, "Lawyers and Consumer Bankruptcy: One Code, Many Cultures," 67 Am. Bankr. L.J. 501 (1993); Lynn M. LoPucki & William C. Whitford, "Venue Choice and Forum Shopping in the Bankruptcy Reorganization of Large, Publicly Held Companies," 1991 Wis. L. Rev. 11 (1991); Gary Neustadler, "When Lawyer and Client Meet: Observation of the Interviewing and Counselling Behavior in the Consumer Bankruptcy Law Office," 35 Buff. L. Rev. 177 (1986).

17. *See* 11 U.S.C. § 109(b)(2). For a discussion of this topic, *see* Joseph A. Guzinski, "Other People's Money: Government, Bankruptcy and the Insolvency of Fiduciary Institutions," 1994 ABI Jnl. LEXIS 2774; Peter P. Swire, "Bank Insolvency Law Now That It Matters Again," 42 Duke L.J. 469 (1992).

18. The unavailability of in forma pauperis relief in bankruptcy was set forth in *United States v. Kras,* 409 U.S. 434 (1973). For a discussion of this case and the pilot program, *see* Henry J. Sommer, "In Forma Pauperis in Bankruptcy: The Time Has Long Since Come," 2 Am. Bank. Inst. L. Rev. 93 (1994); Karen Gross, "In Forma Pauperis in Bankruptcy: Reflecting on and Beyond *United States v. Kras,"* 2 Am. Bankr. Inst. L. Rev. 57 (1994) (with Shari Rosenberg).

19. For an article criticizing *United States v. Kras, see* Karen Gross, "Justice Thurgood Marshall's Bankruptcy Jurisprudence: A Tribute," 67 Am. Bankr. L.J. 447 (1993).

20. *Kras,* 409 U.S. at 458.

21. Susan Block-Lieb, "Why Creditors File So Few Involuntary Petitions and Why the Number Is Not Too Small," 57 Brook. L. Rev. 803 (1991).

22. Gross, *supra* note 15.

Chapter 3: Getting Down to Basics

1. The automatic stay is housed in Section 362 of the Bankruptcy Code. 11 U.S.C. § 362. Section 362(a) addresses the scope of the stay, Section 362(b) enumerates the exceptions to the stay, Section 362(c) focuses on the duration of the stay, and Section 362(d) identifies the standards for lifting the stay. For a general discussion of the stay, *see* Douglas G. Baird, The Elements of Bankruptcy 193–213 (1993).

2. In bankruptcy parlance, this is known as seeking "adequate protection," and the concept is housed in Section 361 of the Bankruptcy Code. The meaning of adequate protection was probed by the United States Supreme

Court in *United Savings Association v. Timbers of Inwood Forest Associates, Ltd.,* 484 U.S. 365 (1988).

3. Basic priorities appear in Section 507 of the Bankruptcy Code. Section 507(b) specifically deals with the priority accorded to claims if adequate protection fails. 11 U.S.C. § 507(b). For a general discussion of priorities, *see* MICHAEL J. HERBERT, UNDERSTANDING BANKRUPTCY 159–61, 170–73 (1995).

4. Section 541 is the overarching section governing what is (and is not) property of the estate. 11 U.S.C. § 541.

5. This topic was addressed by the United States Supreme Court in *United States v. Whiting Pools, Inc.,* 462 U.S. 198 (1983).

6. The treatment of the future income of individual debtors appears in several Bankruptcy Code provisions, namely, 11 U.S.C. §§ 541(a)(6), 1207(a)(2), and 1306(a)(2). There is some doubt over whether future income in a Chapter 11 case is property of the estate notwithstanding the plain language of Section 541(a)(6). *Compare In re Harp,* 166 B.R. 740 (Bankr. N.D. Ala. 1993) *and In re Herberman,* 122 B.R. 273 (Bankr. W.D. Tex. 1990) (both of which hold that future income is property of the estate) *with In re Fitzsimmons,* 725 F.2d 1208 (9th Cir. 1984) *and Larson v. Cameron,* 147 B.R. 39 (Bankr. D. N.D. 1992) (both of which hold that a portion of, or all, future income is excluded from the estate).

7. 11 U.S.C. §§ 541(a), 550.

8. Section 522 of the Bankruptcy Code deals with exemptions. Separate bodies of state and other federal laws also address exempt property. For a general discussion of exemptions, *see* HERBERT, *supra* note 3, at 185–202.

9. FLA. CONST. art. X, § 4; NEW YORK CPLR §§ 5205–5206 and NEW YORK DEBTOR & CREDITOR §§ 282, 283.

10. MICH. STAT. § 600.6023.

11. *See, e.g.,* Larry Rohrer, "Rich Debtors Finding Shelter under a Populist Florida Law," N.Y. TIMES, July 25, 1993, § 1, at 1; Martha Brannigan, "Florida Is Gaining Reputation as Haven for Debtors Who Seek to Shelter Wealth," WALL ST. J., Aug. 3, 1990, at B1.

12. *See* Lynn M. LoPucki & William C. Whitford, "Venue Choice and Forum Shopping in Bankruptcy Reorganization of Large, Publicly Held Companies," 1991 WIS. L. REV. 11.

13. Teresa Sullivan et al., "Laws, Models, and Real People: Choice of Chapter in Personal Bankruptcy," 13 LAW & SOC. INQ. 661 (1988); Michael J. Herbert & Domenic E. Pacitti, "Down and Out in Richmond, Virginia: The Distribution of Assets in Chapter 7 Bankruptcy Proceedings Closed

During 1984–87," 22 U. RICH. L. REV. 303, 316–17 (1988); William J. Woodward & Richard S. Woodward, "Exemptions as an Incentive to Voluntary
Bankruptcy: An Empirical Study," 88 COM. L.J. 309 (1983).

14. The avoiding powers are housed in Bankruptcy Code Sections 544,
547, and 548. For a general discussion of these sections, *see* DOUGLAS G.
BAIRD, *supra* note 1, at 100–104, 142–92.

15. The contours of Chapter 7 appear in 11 U.S.C. §§ 701–766. Other
chapters of the Code, namely, Chapters 3 and 5, affect the implementation
of the Chapter 7 provisions. In particular, the priority provisions, contained
in 11 U.S.C. § 507, affect the distribution of proceeds.

16. The key provisions related to discharge and antidiscrimination are
housed at 11 U.S.C. §§ 524 and 525. Within Chapters 11, 12, and 13, discharge provisions appear in 11 U.S.C. §§ 1141, 1228, and 1328.

17. The standards of confirmation appear within each reorganization
chapter. 11 U.S.C. §§ 1129, 1225, and 1325. For a general discussion of plans
of reorganization in Chapters 11, 12, and 13, *see* HERBERT, *supra* note 3, at
303–85.

18. *See* James Steven Rogers, "The Impairment of Secured Creditors'
Rights in Reorganization: A Study of the Relationship Between the Fifth
Amendment and the Bankruptcy Clause," 96 HARV. L. REV. 973 (1983).

19. This would be governed by Article 9 of the Uniform Commercial
Code, in particular Article 9-501 et seq. For a general discussion of the rights
of secured creditors outside of bankruptcy, *see* JAMES J. WHITE & ROBERT S.
SUMMERS, UNIFORM COMMERCIAL CODE 755–823, 901–932 (4th ed. 1995).

20. The Bankruptcy Code sections dealing with these issues appear in 11
U.S.C. §§ 506(b) AND (d), 362(a)(3),(4), and (5).

21. For a general discussion of how a secured claim can be treated in a
Chapter 11 plan, *see* HERBERT, *supra* note 3, at 332–34; Jack Friedman,
"What Courts Do to Secured Creditors in Chapter 11 Cram Down," 14
CARDOZO L. REV. 1495 (1993).

Chapter 4: Empiricism and Bankruptcy

1. Teresa A. Sullivan et al., "The Use of Empirical Data in Formulating
Bankruptcy Policy," 50 LAW & CONTEMP. PROBS. 195 (1987); Karen Gross,
"Re-Vision of the Bankruptcy System: New Images of Individual Debtors,"
88 MICH. L. REV. 1505 (1990).

2. *See, e.g.,* Karen Gross & Patricia Redmond, "In Defense of Debtor Exclusivity: An Assessment of Four Amendments to the Code," 69 AM. BANKR. L.J. 287 (1995); Robert Lawless et al., "A Glimpse at Professional Fees and Other Direct Costs in Small Firm Bankruptcies," 1994 U. ILL. L. REV. 847; Teresa Sullivan et al., "Local Legal Culture: Twenty Years of Experience from the Federal Bankruptcy Courts," 17 HARV. J.L. & PUB. POL'Y 801 (1994); Jean Braucher, "Lawyers and Consumer Bankruptcy: One Code, Many Cultures," 67 AM. BANKR. L.J. 501 (1993); Paul B. Lackey, "An Empirical Study and Proposed Bankruptcy Code Section Concerning the Propriety of Bidding Incentives in a Bankruptcy Sale of Assets," 93 COLUM. L. REV. 720 (1993); Susan Jensen-Conklin, "Do Confirmed Chapter 11 Plans Consummate? The Results of a Study and Analysis of the Law," 97 COM. L.J. 297 (1992); Lynn M. LoPucki & William C. Whitford, "Patterns in the Bankruptcy Reorganization of Large, Publicly Held Companies," 78 CORNELL L. REV. 597 (1993).

3. Lynn M. LoPucki, "The Demographics of Bankruptcy Law Practice," 63 AM. BANKR. L.J. 289 (1989); Anne M. Russell et al., "25 Hottest Careers," WORKING WOMAN, July 1, 1989, at 67.

4. John D. Ayer, "So Near to Cleveland, So Far from God: An Essay on the Ethnography of Bankruptcy," 61 U. CIN. L. REV. 407 (1992).

5. *See, e.g.,* Peter H. Schuck, "Why Don't Law Professors Do More Empirical Research?" 39 J. LEGAL EDUC. 323 (1989); Zipporah Bathsaw Wiseman, "Women in Bankruptcy and Beyond," 65 IND. L.J. 107 (1989).

6. For information related to the PACER (Public Access to Court Electronic Records) system and other electronic filing systems, *see, e.g.,* Margaret J. Evans, "Electronic Research in Federal Court Houses: Many Tools Available," NEW YORK L.J., July 10, 1995, at S3; John Flynn Rooney, "Court Automates Access to Bankruptcy Case Data," CHI. DAILY L. BULL., May 4, 1995, at 3; Nazareth A. M. Pantalon, "Legal Databases, Legal Epistemology, and the Legal Order," 86 LAW LIB. J. 679 (1994); Bruce Cummings Miller, "Electronic Bulletin Boards for Law Libraries," 82 LAW LIB. J. 737 (1990).

7. For a discussion of valuation issues in bankruptcy, *see* Robert M. Lawless & Stephen P. Ferris, "Economics and the Rhetoric of Valuation," 5 J. BANKR. L. & PRAC. 3 (1995); Mark X. Mullin & Robin E. Phelan, "How Much Is That Doggie in the Window: Valuation Issues in Bankruptcy Cases," 709 PL I/COMM 405 (1995); Chaim J. Fortgang & Thomas Moers Mayer, "Valuation in Bankruptcy," 32 UCLA L. REV. 1061 (1985).

8. Michael Bradley & Michael Rosenzweig, "The Untenable Case for Chapter 11," 101 YALE L.J. 1043 (1992).

9. Jensen-Conklin, *supra* note 2.

10. TERESA SULLIVAN et al., AS WE FORGIVE OUR DEBTORS: BANKRUPTCY AND CONSUMER CREDIT IN AMERICA (1989).

11. KEVIN J. DELANEY, STRATEGIC BANKRUPTCY: HOW CORPORATIONS AND CREDITORS USE CHAPTER 11 TO THEIR ADVANTAGE (1992).

12. Steven N. Kaplan, "Federated's Acquisition and Bankruptcy: Lessons and Implications," 72 WASH. U. L.Q. 1103 (1994).

13. Lawless et al., *supra* note 2.

14. For a general discussion of the lack of objective reality, *see* FEMINIST RESEARCH METHODS 69–93 (Joyce McCarl Nielsen ed., 1990); CATHERINE T. MCKINNON, TOWARD A FEMINIST THEORY OF STATE (1989); Margaret G. Farrell, "*Daubert v. Merrell Dow Pharmaceuticals, Inc.*: Epistemology and Legal Process," 15 CARDOZO L. REV. 2183 (1994); Jeanne L. Schroeder, "Subject: Object," 47 U. MIAMI L. REV. 1 (1992).

15. Judith Schenck Koffler, "The Bankruptcy Clause and Exemption Laws: A Reexamination of the Doctrine of Geographic Uniformity," 58 N.Y.U. L. REV. 22 (1983).

16. For a general discussion of the problems giving rise to the new amendment, *see* Bruce Grohsgal, "Hotel Revenues under the Bankruptcy Reform Act," 14 AM. BANKR. INST. J. 20 (1995); Ned W. Waxman, "The Bankruptcy Reform Act of 1994," 11 BANKR. DEV. J. 311 (1994–95). For a discussion of the problems of the amendment to Section 552, *see* Kathryn R. Heidt, "The Effect of the Bankruptcy Reform Act of 1994 on Commercial Secured Creditors," 69 AM. BANKR. L.J. 395 (1995).

17. This nonbankruptcy example is a variation on an actual study publicized in the popular press. Nancy Shute, "Life for the Lefties: From Annoying to Downright Risky," 25 SMITHSONIAN 130 (1994); Diane F. Halpern & Stanley Coren, "Handedness and Life Span," NEW ENG. J. MED., April 4, 1991, at 998.

18. For a general discussion of the events surrounding the passage of Section 707(b), *see* Karen Gross, "Preserving a Fresh Start for the Individual Debtor: The Case for Narrow Construction of the Consumer Credit Amendments," 135 U. PA. L. REV. 59 (1986). For some studies' suggestion that Section 707(b) has been problematic in application, *see* PERCEPTION AND REALITY: AMERICAN BANKRUPTCY INSTITUTE SURVEY ON SELECTED PROVISIONS OF THE 1984 AMENDMENTS TO THE BANKRUPTCY CODE, reprinted in Hearings

on S. 1616, S. 1358, S. 1863, & S. 2279 (1987); Michael D. Bruckman, "The Thickening Fog of 'Substantial Abuse': Can Section 707(a) Help Clear the Air?" 2 AM. BANKR. INST. L. REV. 193 (1994); Wayne R. Wells et al., "The Implementation of Bankruptcy Code Section 707(b): The Law and the Reality," 39 CLEV. ST. L. REV. 15 (1991).

19. SULLIVAN et al., *supra* note 10 at 265.

20. For an example of the plethora of data in respect to fruit flies, *see* Boyce Rensberger, "Fruit Flies as Romantic Rivals," WASH. POST, Jan. 23, 1995, at A2; Natalie Angier, "Sex and the Fruit Fly: Price of Promiscuity Is Premature Death," N.Y. TIMES, Jan. 24, 1995, at C1; Sue Kiesewetter, "Fruit Fly Study Reveals Genetic Clues," CIN. ENQUIRER, Apr. 21, 1994, at 26.

21. Teresa Sullivan et al., "Consumer Debtors Ten Years Later: A Financial Comparison of Consumer Bankrupts, 1981–1991," 68 AM. BANKR. L.J. 121 (1994); Teresa Sullivan et al., "Local Legal Culture: Twenty Years of Experience from the Federal Bankruptcy Courts," 17 HARV. J.L. & PUB. POL'Y 801 (1994).

22. For a detailed discussion of this work, *see* Karen Gross et al., "Ladies in Red: Learning from America's First Female Bankrupts," 40 AM. J. LEG. HIST. 1 (1996).

23. The foregoing points and related issues are addressed in Karen Gross, "In Forma Pauperis in Bankruptcy: Reflecting On and Beyond *United States v. Kras*," 2 AM. BANKR. INST. L. REV. 57 (1994) (with Shari Rosenberg); Henry J. Sommer, "In Forma Pauperis in Bankruptcy: The Time Has Long Since Come," 2 AM. BANK. INST. L. REV. 93 (1994).

Chapter 5: What Is Transpiring in Bankruptcy?

1. The data discussed in this chapter come from four main sources: (1) I used THE BANKRUPTCY YEARBOOK AND ALMANAC, published by New Generation Research, especially for the period 1991–95; (2) I used data from the Administrative Office of the United States Courts and had conversations with individuals within this office, most particularly Ed Flynn; (3) I consulted data from the American Bankruptcy Institute, which publishes some of its material in its journals; and (4) I referred to the weekly newsletter "Bankruptcy Court Decisions" (LRP Publications), which details information about the bankruptcy system.

2. *See* Lynn M. LoPucki & William C. Whitford, "Venue Choice and Forum Shopping in the Bankruptcy Reorganization of Publicly Held Com-

panies," 1991 WIS. L. Rev. 11 (1991). Each volume of THE BANKRUPTCY YEARBOOK AND ALMANAC details the names and locations of large Chapter 11 filings, and these listings confirm that many filings occur in the Southern District of New York.

3. *See* Philip Shuchman & Thomas L. Rhorer, "Personal Bankruptcy Data for Opt-Out Hearings and Other Purposes," 56 AM. BANKR. L.J. 1 (1982).

4. These figures are taken from TERESA SULLIVAN ET AL., AS WE FORGIVE OUR DEBTORS: BANKRUPTCY AND CONSUMER CREDIT IN AMERICA 17, 20 (1989).

5. *See* Remarks of Chief Justice William Rehnquist at the Spring Meeting of the American Bankruptcy Institute, *reprinted in* vol. 3, no.3, ABI BULL. (May 20, 1992).

6. These data are based on conversations with Jeff Baker of Poorman-Douglas Corporation and data that the company supplied to me. Although these data have not been independently verified, Poorman-Douglas acts as an agent for the clerk's office of various bankruptcy courts across the country and regularly reports the data given to me to the government.

7. *See, e.g.,* KEVIN J. DELANEY, STRATEGIC BANKRUPTCY: HOW CORPORATIONS AND CREDITORS USE CHAPTER 11 TO THEIR ADVANTAGE 61, 72 (1992); RONALD J. BACIGAL, THE LIMITS OF LITIGATION: THE DALKON SHIELD CONTROVERSY 99–100 (1990). *See also Kane v. Johns-Manville Corp.,* 843 F.2d 636 (2d Cir. 1988).

8. *See* Donald R. Korobkin, "The Unwarranted Case Against Repeal of Corporate Reorganization: A Reply to Bradley and Rosenzweig," 78 IOWA L. REV. 669 (1993); Elizabeth Warren, "The Untenable Case for Repeal of Chapter 11," 102 YALE L.J. 437 (1992).

9. Having served as the special representative in the Integrated Resources Chapter 11 case, I can speak to the accuracy of this number. The number was also referred to in open court and can be confirmed by counsel to the debtor, Willkie, Farr and Gallagher in New York (Myron Trepper, Esq.).

10. That number fell to 1.8% in 1994.

11. Because of the decrease in Chapter 11 cases, that number fell to 23.9% in 1994.

Chapter 6: Rehabilitating Debtors

1. *See, e.g.,* Charles Jordan Tabb, "The Scope of the Fresh Start in Bankruptcy: Collateral Conversions and the Dischargeability Debate," 59 GEO.

WASH. L. REV. 56 (1990); Teresa Sullivan et al., "Limiting Access to Bankruptcy Discharge: An Analysis of the Creditors' Data," 1983 WIS. L. REV. 1091 (1983); Douglass Boshkoff, "Limited, Conditional, and Suspended Discharges in Anglo-American Bankruptcy Proceedings," 131 U. PA. L. REV. 69 (1982).

2. Some authors have attempted to explain why we have the discharge. *See* Lawrence Ponoroff & F. Stephen Knippenberg, "Debtors Who Convert Their Assets on the Eve of Bankruptcy: Villains or Victims of the Fresh Start?" 70 N.Y.U. L. REV. 235 (1995); Margaret Howard, "The Theory of Discharge in Consumer Bankruptcy," 48 OHIO ST. L.J. 1047 (1987); Charles G. Hallinan, "The 'Fresh Start' Policy in Consumer Bankruptcy: A Historical Inventory and an Interpretive Theory," 21 U. RICH. L. REV. 49 (1986); Thomas H. Jackson, "The Fresh-Start Policy in Bankruptcy Law," 98 HARV. L. REV. 1393 (1985); Anthony Kronman, "Paternalism and the Law of Contracts," 92 YALE L.J. 763, 785–86 (1983); Philip Shuchman, "Theory and Reality in Bankruptcy: The Spherical Chicken," 41 LAW & CONTEMP. PROBS. 66 (1977).

3. The word *bankruptcy* is said to derive from either the Italian or French words for "broken bench." THE OXFORD ENGLISH DICTIONARY 935 (2d ed. 1989). For a general discussion of the treatment of debtors over the past centuries, *see* Robert Weisberg, "Commercial Morality, Merchant Character, and the History of Voidable Preference," 39 STAN. L. REV. 3 (1986); Vern Countryman, "Bankruptcy and the Individual Debtor—and a Modest Proposal to Return to the Seventeenth Century," 32 CATH. U. L. REV. 809 (1983); Jay Cohen, "The History of Imprisonment for Debt and Its Relations to the Development of the Discharge in Bankruptcy," 3 J. LEG. HIST. 153 (1982); Louis Edward Levinthal, "The Early History of Bankruptcy Law," 66 U. PA. L. REV. 223 (1918).

4. *See, e.g.,* JORAM GRAF HABER, FORGIVENESS (1991); JEFFRIE G. MURPHY & JEAN HAMPTON, FORGIVENESS AND MERCY (1988); Norvin Richards, "Forgiveness," 99 ETHICS 77 (1988); Paul Lauritzen, "Forgiveness: Moral Prerogative or Religious Duty," 15 J. REL. ETHICS 141 (1987). *See also* ANCHOR BIBLE DICTIONARY, Vol. 2 at 831 (1964); ETHICS, Vol. 1 at 316 (John K. Roth ed., 1994).

5. Haber, *supra* note 4, at 32 et seq.

6. Haber, *supra* note 4, at 59; KATHLEEN DEAN MOORE, PARDONS, JUSTICE, MERCY AND THE PUBLIC INTEREST (1989); Murphy & Hampton, *supra* note 4, at 35–87; Herbert Morris, "Persons and Punishment," in PUNISHMENT AND REHABILITATION 475 (Jeffrie F. Murphy ed., 1985).

7. *See generally* Clark Power, "Piaget on the Moral Development of Forgiveness: Identity or Reciprocity?" 37 HUMAN DEV. J. 81 (1994); Michael E. McCullough & Everett L. Worthington, "Encouraging Clients to Forgive People Who Hurt Them: Review, Critique and Research Prospectus," 22 J. PSYCHOL. & THEOL. 3 (1994); Barry Schlenker & Bruce Darby, "The Use of Apologies in Social Predicaments," 44 SOC.-PSYCHOL. Q. 271 (1981).

8. 2 KINGS 4:1–7.

9. *See generally* LEONARD SHENGOLD, SOUL MURDER: THE EFFECTS OF CHILDHOOD ABUSE AND DEPRIVATION (1989); Shelley A. Wright, "Physical and Emotional Abuse and Neglect of Preschool Children: A Literature Review," 41 AUSTRALIAN OCCUP. THERAPY J. 55 (1994); Judith Kestenberg, "Children under the Nazi Yoke: From the International Investigation of Systematic Persecution of Children," 28 JAHRBUCH DER PSYCHO. 179 (1991).

10. For a discussion on mistakes and risk taking in education, *see* KEVIN LEMAN, BRINGING UP KIDS WITHOUT TEARING THEM DOWN 58–59, 176–77 (1995); ALFIE KOHN, PUNISHED BY REWARDS 62–67, 139–40, 212–13 (1993).

11. For a general discussion of the nature and meaning of punishment, *see* LAWRENCE M. FRIEDMAN, CRIME AND PUNISHMENT IN AMERICAN HISTORY (1993); FRANKLIN E. ZIMRING & GORDON HAWKINS, CAPITAL PUNISHMENT AND THE AMERICAN AGENDA (1986); MICHAEL L. PERLIN, MENTAL DISABILITY LAW: CIVIL AND CRIMINAL LAW (1989); KARL A. MENNINGER, THE CRIME OF PUNISHMENT (1968); Robert Blecker, "Haven or Hell? Inside Lorton Central Prison: Experiences of Punishment Justified," 42 STAN. L. REV. 1149 (1990).

12. There is a vast literature on rehabilitation. *See, e.g.,* MICHAEL L. PERLIN, LAW AND MENTAL DISABILITY (1994); LAWRENCE M. FRIEDMAN, CRIME AND PUNISHMENT IN AMERICAN HISTORY (1993); ANDREW VON HIRSCH, DOING JUSTICE: THE CHOICE OF PUNISHMENTS (1986); ANDREW VON HIRSCH, PAST OR FUTURE CRIMES: DESERVEDNESS AND DANGEROUSNESS IN THE SENTENCING OF CRIMINALS (1985).

13. *See, e.g.,* Michelle J. White, "Does Chapter 11 Save Economically Inefficient Firms?" 72 WASH. U. L.Q. 1319 (1994); Philippe Aghion et al., "Improving Bankruptcy Procedure," 72 WASH. U. L.Q. 849 (1994); Douglas G. Baird, "The Uneasy Case for Corporate Reorganization," 15 J. LEGAL STUD. 127 (1986).

14. Letter written by Robert Gilmore, president of the Chamber of Commerce, dated December 18, 1821, and communicated to the Senate on January 10, 1822. 17th Congress, 1st Sess., Doc. 509. (MISC. 509 [17-1] ASPO 38).

15. "Cruelty and Justice in Glen Ridge," Editorial Desk, N.Y. TIMES, March 18, 1993, at A22.

16. BEYOND ECONOMIC MAN: FEMINIST THEORY AND ECONOMICS (Marianne A. Ferber & Julie A. Nelson eds., 1993) [hereinafter Ferber & Nelson]; Karen Gross, "Taking Community Interests into Account in Bankruptcy: An Essay," 72 WASH. U. L. REV. 1031 (1994); Martin D. Beier, "Economics Awry: Using Access Fees for Caseload Diversion," 138 U. PA. L. REV. 1175 (1990); Margaret Radin, "Market Inalienability," 100 HARV. L. REV. 1849 (1987); Susan Rose-Ackerman, "Inalienability and the Theory of Property Rights," 85 COLUM. L. REV. 931 (1985).

17. FERBER & NELSON, *supra* note 16; FRANCINE D. BLAU, THE ECONOMICS OF WOMEN, MEN AND WORK (1992); TERESA L. AMOTT & JULIE A. MATTHAEI, RACE, GENDER, AND WORK: A MULTICULTURAL ECONOMIC HISTORY OF WOMEN IN THE UNITED STATES (1991); MARILYN WARING, IF WOMEN COUNTED (1988); TERRY ARENDELL, MOTHERS AND DIVORCE: LEGAL, ECONOMIC, AND SOCIAL DILEMMAS (1986).

Chapter 7: Finding the Outliers among Us

1. *See generally* THE DEVELOPMENT OF SPEECH PERCEPTION: THE TRANSITION FROM SPEECH SOUNDS TO SPOKEN WORDS (Judith Goodman & Howard Nusbaum eds., 1994); INPUT AND INTERACTION IN LANGUAGE ACQUISITION (Clare Gallaway & Brian Richards eds., 1994).

2. For a general discussion of strict liability crimes, *see* Richard Singer, "Strict Criminal Liability: Alabama State Courts Lead the Way into the Twenty-First Century," 46 ALA. L. REV. 47 (1994); Laurie Levenson, "Good Faith Defenses: Reshaping Strict Liability Crimes," 78 CORNELL L. REV. 401 (1993); Richard G. Singer, "The Resurgence of Mens Rea, III: The Rise and Fall of Strict Liability," 30 B.C. L. REV. 337 (1989).

3. LAWRENCE M. FRIEDMAN, CRIME AND PUNISHMENT IN AMERICAN HISTORY (1993); ELLEN FRANKEL PAUL, CRIME, CULPABILITY, AND REMEDY (1990); SANFORD K. KADISH, BLAME AND PUNISHMENT: ESSAYS IN THE CRIMINAL LAW (1987).

4. For a general discussion of the rehabilitation of criminal defendants, *see* J.D. MABBOTT et al., PUNISHMENT AND THE DEATH PENALTY (1995); RUTH MASTERS, COUNSELLING CRIMINAL JUSTICE OFFENDERS (1994); Robert Blecker, "Haven or Hell? Inside Lortin Central Prison: Experiences of Punishment Justified," 42 STAN. L. REV. 1149 (1990).

5. 11 U.S.C. § 547(b).

6. 11 U.S.C. § 362(a).

7. *See generally* Frank Vitaro et al., "Predictive Accuracy of Behavioral and Sociometric Assessments of High Risk Kindergarten Children," 23 J. CLINICAL CHILD PSYCHOL. 272 (1994); Morton Mendelson et al., "Personality Predictors of Friendship and Popularity in Kindergarten," 15 J. APPLIED DEV. PSYCHOL. 413 (1994); John E. Lochman & Kathleen K. Wayland, "Aggression, Social Acceptance, and Race as Predictors of Negative Adolescent Outcomes," 33 J. AMER. ACAD. CHILD & ADOLESCENT PSYCHIATRY 1026 (1994); Jennifer White et al., "Measuring Impulsivity and Examining Its Relationship to Delinquency," 103 J. ABNORMAL PSYCHOL. 1922 (1994); G.R. Patterson et al., "Predicting Risk for Early Police Arrest," 8 J. QUANTITATIVE CRIMINOLOGY 335 (1992).

8. The category of nondischargeable debts is enumerated in 11 U.S.C. § 523(a). Section 523, after some 1996 amendments, contains seventeen categories of nondischargeable debt. For a discussion of some of the underlying explanations of nondischargeability, *see* Seth J. Gerson, "Separate Classification of Student Loans in Chapter 13," 73 WASH. U. L.Q. 269 (1995); Peter C. Alexander, "Divorce and Dischargeability of Debts: Focusing on Women as Creditors in Bankruptcy," 43 CATH. U. L. REV. 351 (1994); Jana B. Singer, "Divorce Obligations and Bankruptcy Discharge: Rethinking the Support/Property Distinction," 30 HARV. J. LEG. 43 (1993); Steven H. Resnicoff, "Is It Morally Wrong to Depend on the Honesty of Your Partner or Spouse? Bankruptcy Dischargeability of Vicarious Debt," 42 CASE W. RES. L. REV. 147 (1992); Sheryl L. Scheible, "Bankruptcy and the Modification of Support: Fresh Start, Head Start, or False Start?" 69 N.C. L. REV. 577 (1991); Lawrence Kalevitch, "Educational Loans in Bankruptcy," 2 N. ILL. U. L. REV. 325 (1982).

9. For a sample of writings on learning styles and approaches, *see* ALFIE KOHN, PUNISHED BY REWARDS (1993); RITA DUNN & SHIRLEY GRIGGS, LEARNING STYLES: QUIET REVOLUTION IN AMERICAN SECONDARY SCHOOLS (1988); RITA STAFFORD DUNE, TEACHING STUDENTS THROUGH THEIR INDIVIDUAL LEARNING STYLES: A PRACTICAL APPROACH (1978); ARTHUR CHICKERING, EXPERIENCE AND LEARNING: AN INTRODUCTION TO EXPERIENTIAL LEARNING (1977).

10. For a discussion of the vast differences among debtors and the difficulties of generalization in terms of characteristics and filing decisions, *see* TERESA SULLIVAN ET AL., AS WE FORGIVE OUR DEBTORS: BANKRUPTCY AND

CONSUMER CREDIT IN AMERICA (1989); Karen Gross, "Re-Vision of the Bankruptcy System: New Images of Individual Debtors," 88 MICH. L. REV. 1506 (1990); Philip Shuchman, "New Jersey Debtors, 1982–1983: An Empirical Study," 15 SETON HALL L. REV. 541 (1985); Philip Shuchman, "The Average Bankrupt: A Description and Analysis of 753 Personal Bankruptcy Filings in Nine States," 88 COM. L.J. 288 (1983).

11. For scholarship that promotes the sense that mega cases are at the core of bankruptcy, *see* KEVIN J. DELANEY, STRATEGIC BANKRUPTCY: HOW CORPORATIONS AND CREDITORS USE CHAPTER 11 TO THEIR ADVANTAGE (1992); LAWRENCE H. KALLEN, CORPORATE WELFARE: THE MEGA BANKRUPTCIES OF THE 80'S AND 90'S (1991); Thomas Coleman & David Woodrull, "Looking Out for Shareholders: The Role of the Equity Committee in Chapter 11 Reorganization Cases of Large Publicly Held Companies," 68 AM. BANKR. L.J. 295 (1994); Michael Bradley & Michael Rosenzweig, "The Untenable Case for Chapter 11," 101 YALE L.J. 1043 (1991).

12. For a discussion of small cases and their place within the bankruptcy system, *see generally* Donald R. Korobkin, "Vulnerability, Survival, and the Problem of Small Business Bankruptcy," 23 CAP. U. L. REV. 413 (1995); Robert Lawless et al., "A Glimpse at Professional Fees and Other Direct Costs in Small Firm Bankruptcies," 1994 U. ILL. L. REV. 847 (1994); Samuel L. Bufford, "What Is Right about Bankruptcy Law and Wrong with Its Critics," 72 WASH. U. L.Q. 829 (1994); Douglas G. Baird, "The Reorganization of Closely Held Firms and the 'Opt-Out' Problem," 72 WASH. U. L.Q. 913 (1994); A. Thomas Small, "Small Business Bankruptcy Cases," 1 AM. BANKR. INST. L. REV. 305 (1993); Timothy Curtin et al., "Debtors-Out-Of-Control: A Look at Chapter 11's Check and Balance System," 1988 ANN. SURV. BANKR. L. 87; Lynn M. LoPucki, "Debtor's in Full Control—Systems Failure under Chapter 11 of the Bankruptcy Code, Parts I and II," 57 AM. BANKR. L.J. 99, 247 (1983).

Chapter 8: Effectuating the Fresh Start Policy

1. 11 U.S.C. § 707(b). For a general discussion of this section, *see* Robert M. Thompson, "Consumer Bankruptcy: Substantial Abuse and Section 707 of the Bankruptcy Code," 55 Mo. L. REV. 247 (1990); Karen Gross, "Preserving a Fresh Start for the Individual Debtor: The Case for Narrow Construction of the Consumer Credit Amendments," 135 U. PA. L. REV. 59

(1986); Paul M. Black & Michael J. Herbert, "Bankcard's Revenge: A Critique of the 1984 Consumer Credit Amendments to the Bankruptcy Code," 19 U. RICH. L. REV. 845 (1985).

2. *See In re Green,* 934 F.2d 568 (4th Cir. 1991); *Fonder v. United States,* 974 F.2d 996 (8th Cir. 1992); *In re Kelly,* 841 F.2d 908 (9th Cir. 1988); *In re Heller,* 160 B.R. 655 (D. Kan. 1993).

3. EDWIN J. PERKINS, THE ECONOMY OF COLONIAL AMERICA (1988); Karen Gross et al., "Ladies in Red: Learning from America's First Female Bankrupts," 40 AM. J. LEG. HIST. 1 (1996); Charles Jordan Tabb, "The Historical Evolution of the Bankruptcy Discharge," 65 AM. BANKR. L.J. 325 (1991); Robert Weisberg, "Commercial Morality, the Merchant Character, and the History of the Voidable Preference," 39 STAN. L. REV. 3 (1986).

4. For a discussion of the role of lobbying and politics, *see* Teresa Sullivan et al., "An Analysis of the Creditors' Data," 1983 WIS. L. REV. 1091 (1983); Karen Gross, "Preserving a Fresh Start for the Individual Debtor: The Case for Narrow Construction of the Consumer Credit Amendments," 135 U. PA. L. REV. 59 (1986).

5. *See generally* Lisa J. McIntyre, "A Sociological Perspective on Bankruptcy," 65 IND. L.J. 123 (1989); Teresa Sullivan et al., "Rejoinder: Limiting Access to Bankruptcy Discharge," 1984 WIS. L. REV. 1087; Luize E. Zubrow, "Creditors with Unclean Hands at the Bar of the Bankruptcy Court: A Proposal for Legislative Reform," 58 N.Y.U. L. REV. 1383 (1983); Vern Countryman, "Bankruptcy and the Individual Debtor—and a Modest Proposal to Return to the Seventeenth Century," 32 CATH. U. L. REV. 809 (1983). Clearly, the credit industry takes a different view. *See* A. Charlene Sullivan, "Reply: Limiting Access to Bankruptcy Discharge," 1984 WIS. L. REV. 1069.

6. TERESA SULLIVAN ET AL., AS WE FORGIVE OUR DEBTORS: BANKRUPTCY AND CONSUMER CREDIT IN AMERICA 273–327 (1989).

7. *See* Teresa Sullivan et al., "Local Legal Culture: Twenty Years of Experience from the Federal Bankruptcy Courts," 17 HARV. J. L. & PUB. POL'Y 801 (1994); William C. Whitford, "The Ideal of Individualized Justice: Consumer Bankruptcy as Consumer Protection, and Consumer Protection in Consumer Bankruptcy," 68 AM. BANKR. L.J. 397 (1994); Jean Braucher, "Lawyers and Consumer Bankruptcy: One Code, Many Cultures," 67 AM. BANKR. L.J. 501 (1993); Gary Neustadter, "When Law and Client Meet: Observations of Interviewing and Counselling Behavior in the Consumer Bankruptcy Law Office," 35 BUFF. L. REV. 177 (1968).

8. William C. Whitford, "The Ideal of Individualized Justice: Consumer Bankruptcy as Consumer Protection, and Consumer Protection in Consumer Bankruptcy," 68 AM. BANKR. L.J. 397 (1994); William C. Whitford, "Has the Time Come to Repeal Chapter 13?" 65 IND. L.J. 85 (1989) [hereinafter Whitford, "Has the Time Come?"].

9. *See, e.g.,* Jacobo W. Chodakiewitz, "Managing Chronic Intractable Pain," 162 WESTERN J. MED. 259 (1995); Karen McNally Bensing, "Team Approach to Handling Pain," PLAIN DEALER, March 26, 1995, 6I.

10. Edith A. Jones, "Chapter 11: A Death Penalty for Debtor and Creditor Interests," 77 CORNELL L. REV. 1088 (1992); Michael Bradley & Michael Rosenzweig, "The Untenable Case for Chapter 11," 101 YALE L.J. 1043 (1992); Barry E. Adler, "Bankruptcy and Risk Allocation," 77 CORNELL L. REV. 439 (1992); James W. Bowers, "Groping and Coping in the Shadow of Murphy's Law: Bankruptcy Theory and the Elementary Economics of Failure," 88 MICH. L. REV. 2097 (1990); Douglas G. Baird, "The Uneasy Case for Corporate Reorganizations," 15 J. LEGAL STUD. 127 (1986).

11. For a general discussion of the problems of Chapter 11, *see* Charles Jordan Tabb, "The Future of Chapter 11," 44 S.C. L. REV. 791 (1993); Lynn M. LoPucki, "The Trouble with Chapter 11," 1993 WIS. L. REV. 729 (1993); Lynn M. LoPucki & William C. Whitford, "Patterns in the Bankruptcy Reorganization of Large, Publicly Held Companies," 78 CORNELL L. REV. 597 (1993); Whitford, "Has the Time Come?" *supra* note 8; Susan Jensen-Conklin, "Do Confirmed Chapter 11 Plans Consummate? The Results of a Study and Analysis of the Law," 97 COM. L.J. 297 (1992).

12. There is no nationwide study on confirmation rates, although the size and venue of a case appear to affect confirmation. The Administrative Office of the United States Courts estimated that confirmation rates were approximately 17% from 1979 to 1986 and approximately 25–30% from 1987 to 1989. *See* Ed Flynn, Statistical Analysis of Chapter 11 (1989) (unpublished monograph); Robert K. Rasmussen, "The Efficiency of Chapter 11," 8 BANKR. DEV. J. 319 (1991) (reporting results of the AO study and suggesting that four out of five cases fail before confirmation). A study published in 1992 of cases in one geographic region found confirmation rates of approximately 17%. *See* Jensen-Conklin, *supra* note 11, at 297. Large mega cases, although less than 1% of all Chapter 11 cases, confirm at significantly higher rates (above 85%). *See* Lynn M. LoPucki & William C. Whitford, "Venue Choice and Forum Shopping in Bankruptcy Reorganizations of

Large Publicly Held Companies," 1991 WIS. L. REV. 11. Confirmation rates of Chapter 13 cases, while higher than the 20–25% estimate for all Chapter 11 cases, are still less than 40%. *See* William C. Whitford, "Has the Time Come?" *supra* note 8, at 85.

13. *See* Leif M. Clark et al., "What Constitutes Success in Chapter 11? A Roundtable Discussion," 2 AM. BANKR. INST. L. REV. 229 (1994); Richard V. Butler & Scott M. Gilpatric, "A Re-Examination of the Goals and Purposes of Bankruptcy," 2 AM. INST. BANKR. L. REV. 269 (1994). The entire issue of this journal is dedicated to probing the meaning of success in Chapter 11.

14. See Karen Gross & Patricia Redmond, "In Defense of Debtor Exclusivity: Assessing Four of the 1994 Amendments to the Bankruptcy Code," 69 AM. BANKR. L.J. 287 (1995).

15. The Federal Judicial Center has issued a report detailing the alternative dispute resolution systems in operation in bankruptcy courts across the United States. *See* FEDERAL JUDICIAL CENTER, WORKSHOP FOR BANKRUPTCY JUDGES III, Vol. 1 (1995).

16. For a discussion of costs in Chapter 11, *see* Alexander L. Paskay & Frances Pilaro Wolstenholme, "Chapter 11: A Growing Cash Cow: Some Thoughts on How to Rein in the System," 1 ABI L. REV. 331 (1993); Martin J. Whitman & David M. Barse, "Professionals Paid by Debtors Ought to Represent the Debtors' Interests," 1 ABI L. REV. 367 (1993); "Cost of Bankruptcy: Roundtable Discussion," 1 ABI L. REV. 237 (1993).

17. Edward A. Adams, "Bankruptcy Fees Here Are Highest in the Nation," N.Y.L.J., June 25, 1993, at 1.

18. 11 U.S.C. § 330.

19. Learned Hand, "Historical and Practical Considerations Regarding Expert Testimony," 15 HARV. L. REV. 40, 56 (1901–2).

20. Limited liability is discussed at some length in chapter 2 of this book.

21. 11 U.S.C. § 523(a)(11), (12). Section 523(e) is also relevant because it defines who is to be considered a fiduciary.

22. For a general discussion of the absolute priority rule, *see* chapter 2 of this book. *See also* MICHAEL J. HERBERT, UNDERSTANDING BANKRUPTCY 343–47 (1995); DOUGLAS G. BAIRD, THE ELEMENTS OF BANKRUPTCY 71–82, 259–66 (1993); Bruce A. Markell, "Owners, Auctions, and Absolute Priority in Bankruptcy Reorganizations," 44 STAN. L. REV. 69 (1991); Douglas G. Baird & Thomas H. Jackson, "Bargaining after the Fall and the Contours of the Absolute Priority Rule," 55 U. CHI. L. REV. 738 (1988).

23. For a discussion of the problems of valuation, *see* Robert M. Lawless & Stephen P. Ferris, "Economics and the Rhetoric of Valuation," 5 J. BANKR. L. & PRAC. 3 (1995); David Gray Carlson, "Secured Creditors and the Eely Character of Bankruptcy Valuations," 41 AM. U. L. REV. 63 (1991); Chaim J. Fortgang & Thomas Moers Mayer, "Valuation in Bankruptcy," 32 UCLA L. REV. 1061 (1985).

24. *Norwest Bank Worthington v. Ahlers,* 485 U.S. 197 (1988).

25. *See* MARILYN WARING, IF WOMEN COUNTED: A NEW FEMINIST ECONOMICS (1990); Margaret Radin, "Market Inalienability," 100 HARV. L. REV. 1849 (1987).

26. *See* Douglass G. Boshkoff, "Fresh Start, False Start, or Head Start?" 70 IND. L.J. 549 (1995).

27. TERESA SULLIVAN ET AL., *supra* note 6, at 32, 319 (1989).

28. Lecture delivered by Professor Derrick Bell at New York Law School (videotape available from the New York Law School's Department of Public Affairs).

29. Whether this is the proper role for the judiciary is a matter of considerable debate. *See, e.g.,* GERALD N. ROSENBERG, THE HOLLOW HOPE: CAN COURTS BRING ABOUT SOCIAL CHANGE? (1991); Lino A. Graglia, "Do Judges Have a Policy-Making Role in the American System of Government?" 17 HARV. J.L. & PUB. POL'Y 119 (1994).

30. The value of storytelling has been recognized outside the bankruptcy arena. *See generally* Daniel A. Farber & Suzanna Sherry, "Telling Stories Out of School: An Essay on Legal Narrative," 45 STAN. L. REV. 807 (1993); Carol M. Rose, "Property as Storytelling: Perspectives from Game Theory, Narrative Theory, Feminist Theory," 2 YALE J.L. & HUMAN. 37 (1990); Richard Delgado, "Storytelling for Oppositionists and Others: A Plea for Narrative," 87 MICH. L. REV. 2411 (1989); Mari J. Matsuda, "Legal Storytelling: Public Response to Racist Speech: Considering the Victim's Story," 87 MICH. L. REV. 2320 (1989).

31. The addition of subsection (d) to Section 105 of the Code does move bankruptcy courts back into the administrative aspects of bankruptcy cases. 11 U.S.C. § 105(d). See Gross & Redmond, *supra* note 14.

32. Gordan Bermant et al., "A Day in the Life: The Federal Judicial Center's 1988–1989 Bankruptcy Time Court Study," 65 AM. BANKR. L.J. 491 (1989). *See also* Stephen A. Stripp, "An Analysis of the Role of the Bankruptcy Judge and the Use of Judicial Time," 23 SETON HALL L. REV. 1329 (1993).

33. For a discussion of pro bono programs generally, *see* James Podgers, "Chasing the Ideal," 80 ABA J. 56 (1994); Sophia M. Deseran, "The Pro Bono Debate and Suggestions for a Workable Program," 38 Clev. St. L. Rev. 617 (1990); Chesterfield H. Smith, "Mandatory Pro Bono Service Standard—Its Time Has Come," 35 U. Miami L. Rev. 727 (1981). For a discussion of pro bono programs in bankruptcy, *see generally* Henry J. Sommer, "In Forma Pauperis in Bankruptcy: The Time Has Long Since Come," 2 Am. Bank. Inst. L. Rev. 93 (1994); Susan Block-Lieb, "A Comparison of Pro Bono Representation Programs for Consumer Debtors," 2 Am. Bankr. Inst. L. Rev. 36 (1994); James L. Baillie, "Bankruptcy Lawyers, Bankruptcy Judges and Public Service," 67th Ann. Meeting Nat. Conf. Bankr. Judges, Oct. 1993, at 7–27; David T. Stanley & Marjorie Girth, Bankruptcy: Problem, Process, Reform 55 (1971). *See also* How to Begin a Pro Bono Program in Your Bankruptcy Court: A Starter Kit for Lawyers and Judges (ABA Section of Litigation, David C. Weiner, Chair) (1994).

Chapter 9: Thinking about Creditors

1. For a general discussion of the law and economics perspective, *see* Thomas A. Jackson, The Logic and Limits of Bankruptcy Law (1986); Mary Josephine Newborn, "The New Rawlsian Theory of Bankruptcy Ethics," 16 Cardozo L. Rev. 111 (1994); Susan Block-Lieb, "Fishing in Muddy Waters: Clarifying the Common Pool Analogy as Applied to the Standard for Commencement of a Bankruptcy Case," 42 Am. U. L. Rev. 337 (1993); John D. Ayer, "So Near to Cleveland, So Far from God: An Essay on the Ethnography of Bankruptcy," 61 U. Cin. L. Rev. 407 (1992).

2. This reference is contained in the teacher's edition to Douglas G. Baird & Thomas H. Jackson, Cases, Problems and Materials on Bankruptcy 18 (1990).

3. *See, e.g.,* Christopher W. Frost, "Bankruptcy Redistributive Policies and the Limits of the Judicial Process," 74 N.C. L. Rev. 75 (1995); Donald R. Korobkin, "Value and Rationality in Bankruptcy Decisionmaking," 33 Wm. & Mary L. Rev. 333 (1992); Lawrence Ponoroff & F. Stephen Knippenberg, "The Implied Good Faith Filing Requirement: Sentinel of an Evolving Bankruptcy Policy," 85 NW U. L. Rev. 919 (1991); Elizabeth Warren, "Bankruptcy Policy," 54 U. Chi. L. Rev. 775 (1987).

4. For the suggestion that economic efficiency and social goals are consistent, *see* Robert K. Rasmussen, "An Essay on Optimal Bankruptcy Rules

and Social Justice," 1994 U. ILL. L. REV. 1. An effort has been made to expand the traditional economic model to take account of normative considerations. *See, e.g.,* Robin Paul Malloy, "Toward a New Discourse of Law and Economics," 42 SYRACUSE L. REV. 27 (1991); Kenneth G. Dau-Schmidt, "Relaxing Traditional Economic Assumptions and Values: Toward a New Multidisciplinary Discourse on Law," 42 SYRACUSE L. REV. 181 (1991).

5. MICHAEL J. HERBERT, UNDERSTANDING BANKRUPTCY 174 (1995); DOUGLAS G. BAIRD, THE ELEMENTS OF BANKRUPTCY 85–86 (1993); ELIZABETH WARREN & JAY LAWRENCE WESTBROOK, THE LAW OF DEBTORS AND CREDITORS: TEXT, CASES, AND PROBLEMS 226 (2d ed. 1991).

6. The nonbankruptcy literature on equality enriches the discussion considerably. *See, e.g.,* William E. Nelson, "The Changing Meaning of Equality in Twentieth Century Constitutional Law," 52 WASH. & LEE L. REV. 3 (1995); Patricia A. Cain, "Feminism and the Limits of Equality," 24 GA. L. REV. 803 (1990); Michel Rosenfeld, "Decoding Richmond: Affirmative Action and the Elusive Meaning of Constitutional Equality," 87 MICH. L. REV. 1729 (1989).

7. For a general discussion of involuntary creditors, *see* TERESA SULLIVAN ET AL., AS WE FORGIVE OUR DEBTORS: BANKRUPTCY AND CONSUMER CREDIT IN AMERICA 293–301 (1989); Lynn M. LoPucki, "The Unsecured Creditor's Bargain," 80 VA. L. REV. 1887 (1994); Kathryn R. Heidt, "Products Liability, Mass Torts and Environmental Obligations in Bankruptcy: Suggestions for Reform, 3 ABI L. REV. 117 (1995); Kathryn R. Heidt, "Undermining Bankruptcy Law and Policy: Torwico Electronics, Inc. v. New Jersey Dept. of Environmental Protection," 56 U. PITT. L. REV. 627 (1995).

8. This example is drawn from the work of Linda Krieger and Patricia Cooney. *See* Linda J. Krieger & Patricia N. Cooney, "The Miller-Wohl Controversy: Equal Treatment, Positive Action and the Meaning of Women's Equality," 13 GOLDEN GATE U. L. REV. 513, 553 (1983).

9. *See, e.g.,* David L. Kirp, "Fetal Hazards, Gender Justice, and the Justices: The Limits of Equality," 34 WM. & MARY L. REV. 101 (1992); Michel Rosenfeld, "Substantive Equality and Equal Opportunity: A Jurisprudential Appraisal," 74 CALIF. L. REV. 1687 (1986); Sylvia A. Law, "Rethinking Sex and the Constitution," 132 U. PA. L. REV. 955 (1984).

10. FEMINIST JURISPRUDENCE: THE DIFFERENCE DEBATE (Leslie Friedman Goldstein ed., 1995); Mary Becker, "Strength in Diversity: Feminist Theoretical Approaches to Child Custody and Same-Sex Relationships," 23 STETSON L. REV. 701 (1994); Drucilla Cornell, "Sexual Difference, the Feminine,

and Equivalency: A Critique of MacKinnon's *Toward a Feminist Theory of the State*," 100 YALE L.J. 1147 (1991).

11. For a general discussion of the debate regarding affirmative action, *see* LANI GUINIER, THE TYRANNY OF THE MAJORITY: FUNDAMENTAL FAIRNESS AND REPRESENTATIVE DEMOCRACY (1994); STEPHEN L. CARTER, REFLECTIONS OF AN AFFIRMATIVE ACTION BABY (1991).

12. 11 U.S.C. § 506.

13. *See, e.g.*, Steve H. Nickles & Edward S. Adams, "Tracing Proceeds to Attorneys' Pockets (and the Dilemma of Paying for Bankruptcy)," 78 MINN. L. REV. 1079 (1994); Edward A. Adams, "Bankruptcy Fees Here Are Highest in the Nation," N.Y.L.J., June 25, 1993, at 1; Lyn Bixby, "Loss and Profit: Cashing in on Bankruptcy," HARTFORD COURANT, Sept. 5, 1993, at A1; Phyllis Furman & Peter Grant, "A Bankruptcy Court; Judges in N.Y. Extend a Flawed Law, Enriching Lawyers and Executives at the Expense of Creditors," CRAIN'S N.Y. BUS., April 5, 1993, at 1.

14. *See, e.g.*, Henry J. Sommer, "In Forma Pauperis in Bankruptcy: The Time Has Long Since Come," 2 AM. BANKR. INST. L. REV. 93 (1994); "Consumer Bankruptcy: A Roundtable Discussion," 2 AM. BANKR. INST. L. REV. 31 (1994) (comments by Hon. Geraldine Mund and Gary Klein, Esq.).

15. *See, e.g.*, Lynn M. LoPucki, "The Demographics of Bankruptcy Practice," 63 AM. BANKR. L.J. 289 (1989); "Bankruptcy Lawyers Gain Status, Wider Role in Corporate Strategy," WALL ST. J., July 9, 1987, at 31. *See also* THE DEVELOPMENT OF BANKRUPTCY AND REORGANIZATION LAW IN THE COURTS OF THE SECOND CIRCUIT OF THE UNITED STATES (1995).

16. For a general discussion of the import of protecting employees in bankruptcy, *see* Donald R. Korobkin, "Contractarianism and the Normative Foundations of Bankruptcy Law," 71 TEX. L. REV. 541 (1993); Donald R. Korobkin, "Rehabilitating Values: A Jurisprudence of Bankruptcy," 91 COLUM. L. REV. 717 (1991). *See also* Daniel Keating, "The Fruits of Labor: Worker Priorities in Bankruptcy," 35 ARIZ. L. REV. 905 (1993).

17. 11 U.S.C. §§ 507 (a)(4), 1114. *See* Karen E. Wagner, "Employee Benefit Claims in Bankruptcy," C887 ALI-ABA 255 (1994); Daniel Keating, "Bankruptcy Code § 1114: Congress' Empty Response to the Retiree Plight," 67 AM. BANKR. L.J. 17 (1993).

18. *See* Marguerite T. Smith & Elizabeth M. McDonald, "Who Cheats on Their Income Taxes?" MONEY, April 1991, at 101 (cover story); "Who Pays Taxes?" WASH. POST, April 6, 1982, at A18. *See also* Walter J. Henderson, Jr., "Criminal Liability under the Internal Revenue Code: A Proposal

to Make the 'Voluntary' Compliance System a Little Less 'Voluntary,'" 140 U. PA. L. REV. 1429 (1992).

19. Chrysler Corporation Loan Guarantee Act, 15 U.S.C. §§ 1871 et seq. (Supp. III 1979). For a more in-depth analysis of government bailouts, *see* Robert B. Reich, "Bailout: A Comparative Study in Law and Industrial Structure," 2 YALE J. on REG. 163 (1985).

20. For a discussion of the use of taxation as a method of achieving certain social ends and for a limited discussion of its potential within the bankruptcy arena, *see* Christopher W. Frost, "Bankruptcy Redistributive Policies and the Limits of the Judicial Process," 74 N.C. L. REV. 75, 135–38 (1995); Louis Kaplow & Steven Shavell, "Why the Legal System Is Less Efficient Than the Income Tax in Redistributing Income," 23 J. LEGAL STUD. 667 (1995); Jack F. Williams, "Rethinking Bankruptcy and Tax Policy," 3 ABI L. REV. 153 (1995).

21. For a discussion of this literature generally, *see* David Gray Carlson, "On the Efficiency of Secured Lending," 80 VA. L. REV. 2179 (1994); Paul M. Shupack, Solving the Puzzle of Secured Transactions," 41 RUTGERS L. REV. 1067 (1989); Alan Schwartz, "Security Interests and Bankruptcy Priorities: A Review of Current Theories," 10 J. LEGAL STUD. 1 (1981).

22. *See, e.g.,* David Gray Carlson, "The Classification Veto in Single Asset Cases under Bankruptcy Code Section 1129(a)(10)," 44 S.C. L. REV. 565 (1993).

23. *See* Philip Shuchman, "Data on the Durrett Controversy," 9 CARDOZO L. REV. 605 (1987). The Durrett controversy grew out of *Durrett v. Washington Nat'l Ins. Co.,* 621 F.2d 201 (5th Cir. 1980). In that case, the court determined that the bank's bid-in price at a noncollusive foreclosure sale was not adequate. From this case and others emerged the general principle that if a mortgage lender did not pay at foreclosure at least 70% of a home's fair market value, the sale was not reasonable and could be avoided as a fraudulent transfer. The result in *Durrett* led some commentators to believe that home lending would be curtailed, a consequence that did not come to pass. The *Durrett* issue was subsequently dealt with by statute.

24. For a discussion of this type of shift in perspective, *see* Aleta G. Estreicher, "Beyond Agency Costs: Managing the Corporation for the Long Term," 45 RUTGERS L. REV. 513 (1993); William W. Bratton, Jr., "Corporate Debt Relationships: Legal Theory in Time of Restructuring," 1989 DUKE L.J. 92 (1989).

Chapter 10: Rethinking Equality of Distribution

1. 11 U.S.C. § 1102.

2. *See, e.g.,* Edward S. Adams, "Governance in Chapter 11 Reorganizations: Reducing Costs, Improving Results," 73 B.U. L. Rev. 581 (1993).

3. 11 U.S.C. § 1122(b).

4. *See* Bruce A. Markell, "Clueless on Classification: Toward Removing Artificial Limits in Chapter 11 Claim Classification," 11 Bankr. Dev. J. 1 (1994–95).

5. Douglas G. Baird, "The Reorganization of Closely Held Firms and the 'Opt-Out' Problem," 72 Wash. U. L.Q. 913 (1994).

6. *See, e.g.,* Paul R. Glassman, "Third Party Injunctions in Partnership Bankruptcy Cases," 49 Bus. Law. 1081 (1994); Douglas Laycock, "The Death of the Irreparable Injury Rule," 103 Harv. L. Rev. 687 (1990).

7. For literature on Rule 11 generally, *see* Lawrence M. Grosberg, "Illusion and Reality in Regulating Lawyer Performance: Rethinking Rule 11," 32 Vill. L. Rev. 575 (1987). For literature on Rule 9011 within the bankruptcy system, *see* Nancy B. Rapoport, "Seeing the Forest and the Trees: The Proper Role of the Bankruptcy Attorney," 70 Ind. L.J. 783 (1995); Scott J. Hyman, "Sanctions in Bankruptcy Court: The Bite of Rule 9011," 3 Leg. Mal. Rep. 9 (1992).

8. *See* the discussion in chapter 9 of this book, *supra* chapter 9, note 7.

9. *See, e.g.,* Andrew Price, "Tort Creditor Superpriority and Other Proposed Solutions to Corporate Limited Liability and the Problem of Externalities," 2 Geo. Mason L. Rev. 439 (1995); Kathryn R. Heidt, "Products Liability, Mass Torts and Environmental Obligations in Bankruptcy: Suggestions for Reform," 3 Am. Bankr. Inst. L. Rev. 117 (1995); Lynn M. LoPucki, "The Unsecured Creditors' Bargain," 80 Va. L. Rev. 1887 (1994); Christopher M.E. Painter, "Tort Creditor Priority in the Secured Credit System: Asbestos Times, the Worst of Times," 36 Stan. L. Rev. 1045 (1984).

10. For a general discussion of the whole area of mass torts, including in bankruptcy, *see* Thomas A. Smith, "A Capital Markets Approach to Mass Tort Bankruptcy," 104 Yale L.J. 367 (1994); Leslie Bender, "Feminist Re(Torts): Thoughts on the Liability Crisis, Mass Torts, Power and Responsibilities," 1990 Duke L.J. 848; Richard A. Epstein, "The Unintended Revolution in Product Liability Law," 10 Cardozo L. Rev. 2193 (1989).

11. *See* Kevin J. Delaney, Strategic Bankruptcy: How Corporations and Creditors Use Chapter 11 to Their Advantage (1992); Ronald J.

BACIGAL, THE LIMITS OF LITIGATION: THE DALKON SHIELD CONTROVERSY (1990); LAURENCE H. KALLEN, CORPORATE WELFARE: THE MEGABANKRUPTCIES OF THE 80'S AND 90'S (1991).

12. See Bender, *supra* note 10; Theresa A. Gabaldon, "The Lemonade Stand: Feminist and Other Reflections on the Limited Liability of Corporate Shareholders," 45 VAND. L. REV. 1387 (1992).

13. *See, e.g.,* Anthony T. Kronman, "Paternalism and the Law of Contracts," 92 YALE L.J. 763 (1983); Richard A. Epstein, "Unconscionability: A Critical Reappraisal," 18 J. L. & ECON. 293 (1973); Arthur A. Leff, "Unconscionability and the Code—The Emperor's New Clause, 115 U. PA. L. REV. 485 (1967).

14. For a general discussion of the costs of regulation, *see* RICHARD EPSTEIN, SIMPLE RULES FOR A COMPLEX SOCIETY (1995); DAVID SCHOENBROD, DELEGATION AND ITS DISCONTENTS: POWER WITHOUT RESPONSIBILITY (1993); STEPHEN G. BREYER, REGULATION AND ITS REFORM (1982).

Chapter 11: Two Thorny Issues Concerning Creditors

1. For a general discussion of alternative dispute resolution in the bankruptcy context, *see, e.g.,* FEDERAL JUDICIAL CENTER, WORKSHOP FOR BANKRUPTCY JUDGES III, Vol. 1 (1995); Lisa A. Lomax, "Alternative Dispute Resolution in Bankruptcy: Rule 9019 and Bankruptcy Mediation Programs," 63 AM. BANKR. L.J. 55 (1994); Kim Dayton, "The Myth of Alternative Dispute Resolution in the Federal Courts," 76 IOWA L. REV. 889 (1991); Edward A. Morse, "Mediation in Debtor/Creditor Relationships," 20 U. MICH. J.L. REF. 587 (1987). The Southern District of New York is presently studying its mediation project, and the results of the data will appear in a report. (Preliminary data is available from the author.)

2. *See generally* DONOVAN, LEISURE, NEWTON AND IRVINE: ADR PRACTICE HANDBOOK (John Wilkinson ed., 1990); AMERICAN ARBITRATION ASSOCIATION, GEN. REPT., ARBITRATION AND THE LAW (1992–93); CHARLES B. CRAVEN, EFFECTIVE NEGOTIATION AND SETTLEMENT (1993); SUSAN M. LEESON & BRYAN M. JOHNSTON, ENDING IT: DISPUTE RESOLUTION IN AMERICA (1988).

3. 11 U.S.C. § 502.

4. 11 U.S.C. § 502(c)(1).

5. For a discussion and definition of future claimants, *see generally* Kathryn R. Heidt, "Products Liability, Mass Torts and Environmental Obligations in Bankruptcy: Suggestions for Reform," 3 AM. BANKR. INST. L.

Rev. 117 (1995); John W. Ames et. al., "Toxins-Are-Us: Future Claimants in Mass Tort Bankruptcy Cases—Good News and Bad News for Debtors and Reorganization Cases from the Southern District of Florida," 1994 ABI Jnl. LEXIS 2747 (1994); Harvey J. Kesner, "Future Asbestos Related Litigants as Holders of Statutory Claims under Chapter 11 of the Bankruptcy Code and Their Place in the Johns-Manville Reorganization," 62 Am. Bankr. L.J. 159 (1988).

6. See *In re Johns-Manville Corp.*, 7 F.3d 32 (2d Cir. 1993); *In re Brooklyn Navy Yard Asbestos Lit.*, 971 F.2d 831 (2d Cir. 1992); *In re A.H. Robins*, 972 F.2d 709 (4th Cir. 1989).

7. *See* Linda S. Mullenix, "Class Actions, Personal Jurisdiction, and Plaintiffs' Due Process: Implications for Mass Tort Litigation," 28 U.C. Davis L. Rev. 871 (1995); Stacy L. Rahl, "Modification of a Chapter 11 Plan in the Mass Tort Context," 92 Colum. L. Rev. 192 (1992); Russell A. Eisenberg & Frances Gecker, "Due Process and Bankruptcy: A Contradiction in Terms?" 10 Bankr. Dev. J. 47 (1993–94).

8. For a general discussion of trading claims, *see* Robert K. Rasmussen & David Skeel, Jr., "An Economic Analysis of Corporate Bankruptcy Law, 3 Am. Bankr. Inst. L. Rev. 85, 101–4 (1995); Chaim J. Fortgang & Thomas Moers Mayer, "Developments in Trading Claims: Participation and Disputed Claims," 15 Cardozo L. Rev. 733 (1993); Joy F. Conti et al., "Claims Trafficking in Chapter 11—Has the Pendulum Swung Too Far?" 9 Bankr. Dev. J. 281 (1992); Andrew Africk, "Trading Claims in Chapter 11: How Much Influence Can Be Purchased in Good Faith under Section 1126?" 139 U. Pa. L. Rev. 1393 (1991); Chaim J. Fortgang & Thomas Moers Mayer, "Developments in Trading Claims and Taking Control of a Corporation in Chapter 11," 13 Cardozo L. Rev. 1 (1991).

9. *See* W. Andrew P. Logan, III, "Claims Trading: The Need for Further Amending Federal Rule of Bankruptcy Procedure 3001(e)(2)," 2 Am. Bankr. Inst. L. Rev. 495 (1994); *In re Pleasant Hill Partners, L.P.*, 163 B.R. 388 (Bankr. N.D. Ga. 1994); *In re Papercraft Corp.*, 165 B.R. 980, 991–993 (Bankr. W.D. Pa. 1994); *In re Allegheny Int'l, Inc.*, 100 B.R. 241 (Bankr. W.D. Pa. 1988); *In re Revere Copper & Brass, Inc.*, 58 B.R. 1 (Bankr. S.D. N.Y. 1985).

10. *See* 11 U.S.C. § 1126.

11. *See* Chaim J. Fortgang & Thomas Moers Mayer, "Trading Claims and Taking Control of Corporations in Chapter 11," 12 Cardozo L. Rev. 1,

88–89 (1990); *In re Gilbert,* 104 B.R. 206 (Bankr. W.D. Mo. 1989); *In re Columbia Iron Works,* 142 F. 234 (E.D. Mich. 1904).

12. For a general discussion of such defense tactics as poison pills, *see* ROBERT C. CLARK, CORPORATE LAW 571–92 (1986); Roberta Romano, "A Guide to Takeovers: Theory, Evidence and Regulation," 9 YALE J. on REG. 119 (1992); Larry E. Ribstein, "Takeover Defenses and the Corporate Contract," 78 GEO. L.J. 71 (1989); Gregg A. Jarrell et al., "The Market for Corporate Control: The Empirical Evidence Since 1980," 2 J. ECON. PERSP. 49 (1988).

Chapter 12: The Interests of Community

1. For a general discussion of this controversy, *see* Christopher W. Fox, "Bankruptcy Redistributive Policies and the Limits of the Judicial Process," 74 N.C. L. REV. 75 (1995).

2. *See* Michael Bradley & Michael Rosenzweig, "The Untenable Case for Chapter 11," 101 YALE L.J. 1043, 1056 n. 44, 1088 n.108; James W. Bowers, "Rehabilitation, Redistribution or Dissipation: The Evidence for Choosing among Bankruptcy Hypotheses," 72 WASH. U. L.Q. 955 (1994); Philippe Aghion et al., "Improving Bankruptcy Procedure," 72 WASH. U. L.Q. 849 (1994); Hugh M. Ray & Nancy Clarkson, "Bankruptcy Law Reform: A Need for Change? A Creditor's Perspective," 48 CONSUMER FIN. L.Q. REP. 476 (1994).

3. *See* Christopher W. Frost, "Bankruptcy Redistributive Policies and the Limits of the Judicial Process," 74 N.C. L. REV. 75 (1995); Barry S. Schermer, "Response to Professor Gross: Taking the Interest of Community into Account in Bankruptcy—A Modern-Day Tale of Belling the Cat," 72 WASH. U. L.Q. 1049 (1994).

4. Carol Sanger, "The Reasonable Woman and the Ordinary Man," 65 S. CAL. L. REV. 1141 (1992); Susan Deller Ross, "Proving Sexual Harassment," 65 S. CAL. L. REV. 1451 (1992); L.F. Fitzgerald & A.M. Ormerod, "Perceptions of Sexual Harassment: The Influence of Gender and Context," 15 PSYCHOL. OF WOMEN Q. 281 (1991); Regina Austin, "Employer Abuse, Worker Resistance, and the Tort of Intentional Infliction of Emotional Distress," 41 STAN. L. REV. 1 (1988); Jill Laurie Goodman, "Sexual Harassment: Some Observations on the Distance Travelled and the Distance Yet to Go," 10 CAP. U. L. REV. 445 (1981); *Ellison v. Brady,* 924 F.2d 872 (9th Cir. 1991).

5. 140 Cong. Rec. S12834 (daily ed. Sept. 14, 1994); 140 Cong. Rec. S12979 (daily ed. Sept. 20, 1994); Tom Marganthau et al., "The Military Fights Gender Wars," Newsweek, Nov. 14, 1994, at 35; Eric Schmitt, "Retired Admiral Assails Senator over Sex Harassment Complaint," N.Y. Times, Nov. 4, 1994, at A23; "Drum Out Sexual Harassment," Patriot Ledger, March 11, 1994, at 14.

6. Within the fields of law and economics, there has been a movement to expand the traditional neoclassical approach. *See generally* Robin Paul Malloy, Law and Economics: A Comparative Approach to Theory and Practice (1990); Robin Paul Malloy, "Is Law and Economics Moral?—Humanistic Economics and a Classical Liberal Critique of Posner's Economic Analysis," 24 Val. U. L. Rev. 147 (1990); Jean Braucher, "Toward a Broader Perspective on the Role of Economics in Legal Policy Analysis: A Retrospective and an Agenda from Albert O. Hirshman," 13 Law & Soc. Inquiry 741 (1988).

7. Linda Rusch, "Bankruptcy Reorganization Jurisprudence: Matters of Belief, Faith, and Hope—Stepping into the Fourth Dimension," 55 Mont. L. Rev. 9 (1994); Donald R. Korobkin, "Contractarianism and the Normative Foundations of Bankruptcy Law," 71 Tex. L. Rev. 541 (1993); David Gray Carlson, "Bankruptcy Theory and the Creditors' Bargain," 61 U. Cin. L. Rev. 453 (1992); Donald R. Korobkin, "Rehabilitating Values: A Jurisprudence of Bankruptcy," 91 Colum. L. Rev. 717 (1991); Karen Gross, "The Debtor as Modern Day Peon: A Problem of Unconstitutional Conditions," 65 Notre Dame L. Rev. 165, 200 (1990).

8. For a discussion of the problems confronting women professionals, *see* Mona Harrington, Women Lawyers: Rewriting the Rules (1994); T. E. Apter, Working Women Don't Have Wives: Professional Success in the 1990's (1995); Joan C. Williams, "Sameness Feminism and the Work/Family Conflict," 35 N.Y.L. Sch. L. Rev. 347 (1990); Mary Joe Frug, "Securing Job Equality for Women: Labor Market Hostility to Working Mothers," 59 B.U. L. Rev. 55 (1979).

9. For a discussion of the intersecting nature of categories, *see* Judy Scales-Trent, Notes of a White Black Woman: Race, Color, Community (1995); Judy Scales-Trent, "Women in the Lawyering Process: The Complications of Categories," 35 N.Y.L. Sch. L. Rev. 337 (1990).

10. *See, e.g.,* Michel Rosenfeld, "Metro Broadcasting, Inc. v. FCC: Affirmative Action at the Crossroads of Constitutional Liberty and Equality," 38 UCLA L. Rev. 583 (1991); Michel Rosenfeld, "Affirmative Action, Justice

and Equalities: A Philosophical and Constitutional Appraisal," 46 OHIO ST. L.J. 845 (1985); Drucilla Cornell, "Dialogic Reciprocity and the Critique of Employment at Law," 10 CARDOZO L. REV. 1575 (1989).

11. "Small Merchandisers Fade Away in Old Downtowns," ASBURY PARK PRESS, Oct. 29, 1995, at C2; Jim Okerblom, "Up against Wal-Mart; While Cities Covet Tax Revenues, Smaller Shops Fear for Survival," SAN DIEGO UNION-TRIB., Oct. 17, 1995, at C1; Charlie Le Duff, "Mom and Pop Hang Tough on Austin St.," N.Y. TIMES, June 25, 1995, § 13, at 10; Jacques Steinberg, "Fears and Fanfare for the New Store in Town: A Giant Retailer Opens Its Doors and Main Street Will Never Be the Same," N.Y. TIMES, March 31, 1994, at B1. For a discussion of the value of small-business survival in bankruptcy, *see* Donald R. Korobkin, "Vulnerability, Survival, and the Problem of Small Business Bankruptcy," 23 CAP. U. L. REV. 413 (1995).

12. Jerome Kassirer, "Managed Care and the Morality of the Marketplace," 333 NEW ENG. J. MED. 50 (1995).

13. *See generally* Steven J. Heyman, "Foundation of the Duty to Rescue," 47 VAND. L. REV. 673 (1994); Thomas C. Galligan, Jr., "Aiding and Altruism: A Mythopsycholegal Analysis," 27 MICH. J.L. REF. 439 (1994); Jules L. Coleman, "Tort Law and the Demands for Corrective Justice," 67 IND. L.J. 349 (1992); Mark K. Osbeck, "Bad Samaritan and the Duty to Render Aid: A Proposal," 19 U. MICH. L.J. REF. 315 (1985).

14. *See generally* Peter F. Lake, "Revisiting Tarasoff," 58 ALB. L. REV. 97 (1994); Leslie Bender, "An Overview of Feminist Torts Scholarship," 78 CORNELL L. REV. 575 (1993); John M. Adler, "Relying upon the Reasonableness of Strangers: Some Observations about the Current State of Common Law Affirmative Duties to Aid or Protect Others," 1991 WIS. L. REV. 867 (1991).

15. *See Godinez v. Moran*, 113 S. Ct. 2680 (1993) (Blackmun, J., dissenting).

16. Renee Tawa, "Test-Takers Who Helped Ill Man Denied Extra Time on Bar Exam," LOS ANGELES TIMES, February 27, 1993, at B3.

17. *See, e.g.,* Ronn S. Davids, "Constituency Statutes: An Appropriate Vehicle for Addressing Transition Costs," 28 COLUM. J.L & SOC. PROBS. 145 (1995); Terry A. O'Neill, "Employees' Duty of Loyalty and the Corporate Constituency Debate," 25 CONN. L. REV. 681 (1993); Michael E. DeBow & Dwight R. Lee, "Shareholders, Nonshareholders and Corporate Law: Communitarianism and Resource Allocation," 18 DEL. J. CORP. L. 393 (1993); Thomas Lee Hazan, "The Corporate Persona, Contract (and Market) Failure, and Moral Values," 69 N.C. L. REV. 273 (1991); Oliver Williamson, "Corporate Governance," 93 YALE L.J. 1197 (1984).

18. Norwood P. Beveridge, "Does a Corporation's Board of Directors Owe a Duty to Its Creditors?" 25 St. Mary's L.J. 586 (1994); Laura Lin, "Shift of Fiduciary Duty upon Corporate Insolvency: Proper Scope of Directors' Duty to Creditors," 46 Vand. L. Rev. 1485 (1993).

19. Karen Gross, "Taking Community into Account in Bankruptcy: An Essay," 74 Wash. U. L.Q. 1031 (1994).

20. Walter Goldschmidt, As You Sow: Three Studies in the Social Consequences of Agribusiness (1978); David Kline, "The Embattled Independent Farmer," N.Y. Times, Nov. 29, 1981, § 6 (magazine), at 138.

21. Nancy Shields, "City Held Hostage," Asbury Park Press, Nov. 11, 1993, at 1; *In re Carabetta Enterprises, Inc.,* 162 B.R. 399 (Bankr. D. Conn. 1993).

22. The basics of communitarianism are contained in Amitai Etzioni's book The Spirit of Community: Rights, Responsibilities, and the Communitarian Agenda (1993). The communitarian movement has created its own journal titled *The Responsive Community.* This publication provides numerous articles that describe and address the meaning of communitarianism. *See* Rosa Eckstein, "Towards a Communitarian Theory of Responsibility: Bearing the Burden for the Unintended," 45 U. Miami L. Rev. 843 (1991); Stephen L. C. Pepper, "Autonomy, Community, and Lawyers' Ethics," 19 Cap. U. L. Rev. 939 (1990).

23. Some of this material was inspired by an unpublished paper titled "Protecting Community Interests in Bankruptcy Proceedings," by Robert M. Lawless (a copy of the paper is available from the author). For a discussion of questions of standing in public interest cases, *see* Eric R. Claeys, "The Article III, Section 2 Games: A Game-Theoretic Account of Standing and Other Justiciability Doctrines," 67 S. Cal. L. Rev. 1321 (1994); Glenn D. Grant, "Standing on Shaky Ground," 57 Geo. Wash. L. Rev. 1408 (1989).

24. *See, e.g., In re El San Juan Hotel Corp.,* 149 B.R. 263 (D. P.R. 1992); *U.S. v. Grundhoefer,* 916 F.2d 788 (2d Cir. 1990); *Duke Power Co. v. Carolina Envt'l. Study Group,* 438 U.S. 59 (1978).

25. *See* Eric I. Abraham, "Justice Ginsburg and the Injury in Fact Element of Standing," 25 Seton Hall L. Rev. 267 (1994); Richard J. Pierce, Jr., "Lujan v. Defenders of Wildlife: Standing as a Judicially Imposed Limit on Legislative Power," 42 Duke L.J. 1170 (1993); Lawrence Gerschwer, "Informational Standing under NEPA; Justiciability and the Environment Decisionmaking Process," 93 Colum. L. Rev. 996 (1993).

Chapter 13: Which Communities Matter?

1. For a discussion of the meaning of revisionist history, *see* SARA M. EVANS, BORN FOR LIBERTY: A HISTORY OF WOMEN IN AMERICA 1–6 (1989).

2. *See, e.g., United States v. Ron Pair Enterprises, Inc.,* 489 U.S. 235 (1989); *Finney v. Smith,* 141 B.R. 94 (E.D. Va. 1992).

3. Charles Jordan Tabb & Robert M. Lawless, "Of Commas, Gerunds and Conjunctions: The Bankruptcy Jurisprudence of the Rehnquist Court," 42 SYRACUSE L. REV. 823 (1991). For other articles discussing the Supreme Court's approach to decision making in bankruptcy, *see* Thomas G. Kelsh, "An Apology for Plain-Meaning Interpretation of the Bankruptcy Code," 10 BANKR. DEV. J. 289 (1994); Robert K. Rasmussen, "A Study of the Costs and Benefits of Textualism: The Supreme Court's Bankruptcy Cases," 71 WASH. U. L.Q. 535 (1993); Karen Gross, "Justice Thurgood Marshall's Bankruptcy Jurisprudence: A Tribute," 67 AM. BANKR. L.J. 447 (1993); Adam J. Wiensch, "The Supreme Court, Textualism, and the Treatment of Pre-Bankruptcy Code Law," 79 GEO. L.J. 1831 (1991).

4. BENJAMIN N. CARDOZO, THE NATURE OF THE JUDICIAL PROCESS (1921).

5. *See, e.g.,* Joseph C. Hutcheson, "The Judgment Intuition: The Function of the 'Hunch' in Judicial Decision," 14 CORNELL L. REV. 274 (1929).

6. STANLEY FISH, DOING WHAT COMES NATURALLY: CHANGE, RHETORIC, AND THE PRACTICE OF THEORY IN LITERARY AND LEGAL STUDIES 10–13 (1989).

7. William C. Whitford, "The Idea of Individualized Justice: Consumer Bankruptcy as Consumer Protection and Consumer Protection in Consumer Bankruptcy," 68 AM. BANKR. L.J. 397 (1994).

8. *See In re Abacus Broadcasting Corp.,* 154 B.R. 682 (Bankr. W.D. Tex. 1993).

9. *See* FED. R. BANKR. P. 1014.

10. 11 U.S.C. § 1161–1174. The import of these provisions is also noted by Christopher W. Frost in "Bankruptcy Redistributive Policies and the Limits of the Judicial Process," 74 N.C. L. REV. 75 (1995).

11. *See* 11 U.S.C. §§ 1170(a)(2), 1173(a)(4).

12. *See, e.g., Palmer v. Mass.,* 308 U.S. 79 (1939); *In re Chicago, Milwaukee, St. Paul & Pacific Railway Company,* 830 F.2d 758 (7th Cir. 1987); *In re Boston & Maine Corp.,* 719 F.2d 493 (1st Cir. 1983); *Atlantic Coast Line RR Co. v. St. Joe Paper,* 216 F.2d 832 (5th Cir. 1954); *In re Delaware & Hudson Ry. Co.,* 124 B.R. 169 (D. Del. 1991). *See also In re Public Service Co.,* 108 B.R. 854 (Bankr. D. N.H. 1989).

13. See *In re Casco Bay Lines,* 25 B.R. 747 (Bankr. 1st Cir. 1982); *In re Casco Bay Lines,* 14 B.R. 18 (Bankr. 1st Cir. 1981). *See also* Robert M. Lawless, "Protecting Community Interests in Bankruptcy Proceedings" (a copy of this manuscript is on file with the author).

14. *See* RICHARD H. THALER, QUASI RATIONAL ECONOMICS (1991).

15. This example is drawn from an actual case in Florida, which is the subject of an unpublished decision.

16. *In re Continental Airlines, Inc.,* 148 B.R. 207 (D. Del. 1992); *In re Wheeling-Pittsburgh Corp.,* 113 B.R. 187 (Bankr. W.D. Pa. 1990). *See also* KEVIN J. DELANEY, STRATEGIC BANKRUPTCY: HOW CORPORATIONS AND CREDITORS USE CHAPTER 11 TO THEIR ADVANTAGE (1992).

17. *National Labor Relations Board v. Bildisco and Bildisco,* 465 U.S. 513 (1984).

18. *See* Christopher D. Cameron, "How 'Necessary' Became the Mother of Rejection: An Empirical Look at the Fate of Collective Bargaining Agreements on the Tenth Anniversary of Bankruptcy Code Section 1113," 34 SANTA CLARA L. REV. 841 (1994).

19. The stay is housed in Section 362(a). The government exception is housed in Section 362(b)(5).

20. See *In re Kuck,* 116 B.R. 821 (Bankr. S.D. Ala. 1990); *Penn Terra Ltd. v. Dept. of Environmental Resources,* 733 F.2d 267 (3rd Cir. 1984). *See also* Kathryn R. Heidt, "Products Liability, Mass Tort and Environmental Obligations in Bankruptcy," 3 AM. BANKR. INST. L. REV. 117, 140–42 (1995).

21. 11 U.S.C. § 1301(a). *See* ROBERT GINSBERG & ROBERT MARTIN, BANKRUPTCY TEXT, STATUTES, RULES, FORMS, Part 15, at 15–26.1.

22. 11 U.S.C. § 363(h).

23. Preliminary Report of the Bankruptcy Working Group of Second Circuit Gender Fairness Committee (1996) (a copy of the report is available from the author).

24. See, e.g., *Norwest v. Ahlers,* 485 U.S. 197, 206 (1988); *Bonded Financial Services v. European American Bank,* 838 F.2d 890 (7th Cir. 1988); *Finney v. Smith,* 141 B.R. 94, 98 (E.D. Va. 1992); *In re Public Service Co. of New Hampshire,* 108 B.R. 854 (Bankr. N.H. 1989).

25. *In re Favre,* 186 B.R. 769 (Bankr. N.D. Ga. 1995).

26. *See* MICHAEL J. HERBERT, UNDERSTANDING BANKRUPTCY 402–5 (1995); DOUGLAS G. BAIRD, THE ELEMENTS OF BANKRUPTCY 130–31 (1993).

Chapter 14: How to Balance

1. BETTY EDWARDS, DRAWING ON THE RIGHT SIDE OF THE BRAIN (1989); BETTY EDWARDS, DRAWING ON THE ARTIST WITHIN (1986).

2. *See* Robert K. Rasmussen & David A. Skeel, "The Economic Analysis of Corporate Bankruptcy Law," 3 AM. BANKR. INST. L. REV. 85 (1993); Robert K. Rasmussen, "Debtor's Choice: A Menu Approach to Corporate Bankruptcy," 71 TEX. L. REV. 51 (1992).

3. Barry S. Schermer, "Response to Professor Gross: Taking the Interests of Community into Account—A Modern-Day Tale of Belling the Cat," 72 WASH. U. L.Q. 1049 (1994).

4. *See* Judith Resnik, "On the Bias: Feminist Reconsiderations of the Aspirations of Our Judges," 61 S. CAL. L. REV. 1877; Dennis E. Curtis & Judith Resnik, "Images of Justice," 96 YALE L.J. 1727 (1987).

5. This is reminiscent of the approach suggested by Benjamin Cardozo in his book THE NATURE OF THE JUDICIAL PROCESS (1921). *See also* Joseph Hutcheson, Jr., "The Judgment Intuitive," 14 CORNELL L.Q. 274 (1929).

6. *See* Robert M. Lawless, "Protecting Community Interest in Bankruptcy Proceedings" (a copy of this manuscript is on file with the author).

7. Karen Gross & Patricia Redmond, "In Defense of Debtor Exclusivity: An Assessment of Four New Code Amendments," 69 AM. BANKR. L.J. 287 (1995); Timothy Curtin et al., "Debtor-Out-Of-Control: A Look at Chapter 11's Check and Balance System," 1988 ANN. SURV. BANKR. L. 87; Lynn M. LoPucki, "Debtor in Full Control—Systems Failure under Chapter 11 of the Bankruptcy Code? (Parts I and II)," 57 AM. BANKR. L.J. 99, 247 (1983).

Chapter 15: Conclusions and Recommendations

1. STEPHEN DELOS WILSON, THE BANKRUPTCY OF AMERICA: HOW THE BOOM OF THE 80'S BECAME THE BUST OF THE 90'S (1992).

2. WEBSTER'S NINTH NEW COLLEGIATE DICTIONARY 129 (1991).

GLOSSARY

Absolute Priority Rule: The mechanism by which no junior class of creditors is entitled to recover unless all senior classes are repaid in full or consent to a lesser repayment amount. 11 U.S.C. § 1129(b)(2)(B).

Administrative Expenses: Claims entitled to priority payment, ahead of virtually all other claims, particularly those of unsecured creditors. The common administrative expenses are professional fees and post-petition wages. 11 U.S.C. §§ 503(b), 507.

Automatic Stay: The mechanism that provides that most actions taken against the debtor must be stopped during the course of a bankruptcy case. 11 U.S.C. § 362(a). There are provisions for stay relief, and the stay is not permanent. It is terminated when a plan is confirmed or a case is closed. 11 U.S.C. § 362(b), (c).

Avoiding Powers: The ability of a trustee or the debtor-in-possession to avoid certain pre-petition transfers, the most common of which are preferences and fraudulent conveyances. 11 U.S.C. §§ 544, 545, 547, 548, 550.

Bankruptcy Act: The Bankruptcy Act of 1898, as amended; the precursor to the Bankruptcy Code.

Bankruptcy Code: The Bankruptcy Reform Act of 1978, as amended, which appears as Title 11 of the United States Code. The Bankruptcy Code is also known as the Code. 11 U.S.C. §§ 101–1330.

Chapter 7: The liquidation chapter of the Code, for which most individuals and businesses are eligible debtors. 11 U.S.C. §§ 701–766.

Chapter 11: The reorganization chapter of the Code primarily used by businesses. 11 U.S.C. §§ 1101–1174.

Chapter 13: The reorganization chapter of the Code used by individuals with regular income and debts within certain prescribed limits. 11 U.S.C. §§ 1301–1330.

Claim: The right to payment or, in some circumstances, to an equitable remedy. 11 U.S.C. § 101(5).

Confirmation: The process under which a plan of reorganization is approved by the Court. 11 U.S.C. §§ 1129, 1225, 1325.

Court: The court in which a bankruptcy case is pending; usually the United States Bankruptcy Court, although jurisdiction can rest in the United States District Court. 28 U.S.C. §§ 157, 1334.

Cramdown: The ability of the debtor to confirm a plan over the objections of creditors, particularly secured creditors. 11 U.S.C. §§ 1129, 1225, 1325.

Creditor: An entity that has a claim against the debtor. 11 U.S.C. § 101(10).

Debtor: The individual, corporation, partnership, trust, or other eligible entity that has sought relief under the Bankruptcy Code. Under the Bankruptcy Act, the debtor was referred to as a "bankrupt," a more pejorative term. 11 U.S.C. § 101(13).

Debtor-in-Possession: The name of the debtor during the course of a Chapter 11 case, because that debtor is entitled to continue to operate the business or affairs and carry out the duties of a trustee. The debtor-in-possession is commonly referred to as the DIP. 11 U.S.C. §§ 1101(1), 1107.

Discharge: The freedom from payment of obligations following completion of a bankruptcy. 11 U.S.C. §§ 523, 727, 1141, 1228, 1328.

Dismissal: The termination of a bankruptcy case, which can occur at the request of the debtor, a creditor, a party in interest, or the court. In some instances, a debtor whose case is dismissed is precluded from seeking access to the bankruptcy system for a designated period. 11 U.S.C. §§ 109(g), 707, 1112, 1208, 1307.

Entity: An all-inclusive term to encompass individuals, corporations, partnerships, governmental units, and the United States Trustee. 11 U.S.C. § 101(15).

Examiner: A person appointed by the court when a debtor has engaged in questionable conduct. This appointment, unlike that of a trustee, does not oust the debtor-in-possession from running the business. The appointment of an examiner is statutorily mandated in cases with unsecured claims in excess of $5 million if so requested by a party-in-interest, the U.S. Trustee, or the court. The judge has the authority to define the scope of the examiner's duties. 11 U.S.C. § 1104(c).

Executory Contracts: Loosely defined as contracts as to which there are obligations of the parties as yet unperformed or incomplete. Most executory contracts and leases can be assumed, assigned, or rejected in the course of a bankruptcy case, assuming certain prescribed conditions are satisfied. 11 U.S.C. §§ 365, 1113, 1114.

Exemptions: The property that a debtor is entitled to retain, free of the interests of creditors, under applicable state or federal law. 11 U.S.C. § 522.

Federal Law: The body of laws, including many aspects of the Bankruptcy Code, that are passed by Congress and, if the Supremacy Clause is applicable, take precedence over competing state law.

Fraudulent Transfers: Transactions in which a debtor transfers property either without equivalent value while insolvent or with intent to defraud creditors. Under both state and federal law, fraudulent transfers must be reversed. Unlike preferences, they are considered wrongful activity by a debtor. 11 U.S.C. §§ 544, 548.

Involuntary Filing: A case commenced by one or more creditors against a debtor. Filing creditors must be able to demonstrate that the debtor is not generally paying its bona fide debts as they become due. This is different from and less stringent than an insolvency requirement. If creditors file involuntary cases in bad faith, they can be subjected to damages, including punitive damages. Such filings constitute less than 1% of all cases. 11 U.S.C. § 303.

Joint Filings: A petition filed by a husband and a wife. Cases that are not filed jointly (because they do not involve a husband and a wife) can be consolidated, however, either substantively or for administrative convenience. 11 U.S.C. § 302.

Judge: The term used most frequently for United States Bankruptcy Judges, who are Article I appointees serving fourteen-year terms. United States District Judges, who are Article III appointees with life tenure, can serve as judges in bankruptcy cases, although that is the exception rather than the rule. 28 U.S.C. §§ 152–154, 1334.

Jurisdiction: The power of a particular court to hear the indicated matter. Jurisdiction is a topic of considerable controversy within the bankruptcy system. Most matters can be heard by the bankruptcy court but not necessarily finally determined by that court. Personal injury tort claims must be heard in the applicable United States District Court. Still other matters must be heard by state courts. 28 U.S.C. §§ 157, 1334.

Liquidation: The reduction of all of a debtor's nonexempt assets into cash for purposes of distribution to creditors. This is generally the most rapid type of bankruptcy procedure. 11 U.S.C. §§ 701–766.

Nondischargeable Debts: Those specific debts that the Code identifies as nondischargeable, the most common of which are obligations to pay alimony, maintenance, and child support; fraudulently incurred obligations; drunk driving obligations; selected student loans; and restitution orders. 11 U.S.C. § 523.

Petition: The formal document whose filing triggers the beginning of a bankruptcy case. 11 U.S.C. § 301.

Preferences: Payments made by the debtor to creditors on account of antecedent debts within ninety days before a bankruptcy filing. Subject to certain important exceptions, these payments must be returned to the estate. Insiders (those with what the law defines as close relationships with the debtor) have a preference period of one year. The ability to avoid preferential payments is one of the trustee's key avoiding powers. 11 U.S.C. § 547.

Priority Claims: Those claims that are entitled to be paid ahead of other claims. These include claims for administrative expenses, certain taxes, wages, severance pay, and consumer deposits. 11 U.S.C. § 507.

Property: A broadly defined term that brings into the estate all the interest of the debtor in property—legal and equitable, wheresoever and by whomever it is being held. 11 U.S.C. § 541.

Reorganization: The concept of permitting a debtor to repay creditors over time out of future income and assets rather than sell available assets to repay creditors.

Secured Creditor: A creditor that holds collateral as security for the debtor's obligations. That security can take a wide range of forms, including tangible personal property, real estate, and accounts receivable. 11 U.S.C. § 506; Article 9 of the Uniform Commercial Code.

State Law: Each state has its own laws that principally govern the rights of its citizens. These include state contract and tort laws and state laws governing ownership and transfer of property. There are also state exemption laws and state procedures for enforcing judgments. Wide variation can exist among state laws, which means that the citizens of different states can be treated in materially different ways.

Trustee: This term has multiple meanings under the Code. It can refer to a trustee specifically appointed in a Chapter 11 case, in which event the debtor ceases to continue in possession. 11 U.S.C. § 1104. This term can also mean the trustee automatically appointed in a Chapter 7 case or the standing trustee in a Chapter 12 or 13 case. 11 U.S.C. §§ 701–704, 1202, 1302. It can also refer to the United States Trustees, agents of the Justice Department who are appointed throughout the country and who oversee the administrative aspects of all bankruptcy cases, leaving the adjudicative functions to bankruptcy judges. 28 U.S.C. § 581.

Undersecured Creditor: A creditor for which the value of the collateral secured is less than the total debt owed. 11 U.S.C. § 506(a), (b), (d).

Unsecured Creditor: A creditor that does not have collateral to secure the obligation owed by the debtor and that must look solely to the debtor's unencumbered, nonexempt assets for recovery. 11 U.S.C. §§ 506(b), 726(a).

Voluntary Case: A bankruptcy case initiated by the debtor. This type of case stands in contrast to involuntary cases, which are initiated by creditors. More than 99% of all bankruptcy cases are voluntary. 11 U.S.C. §§ 301, 303.

INDEX